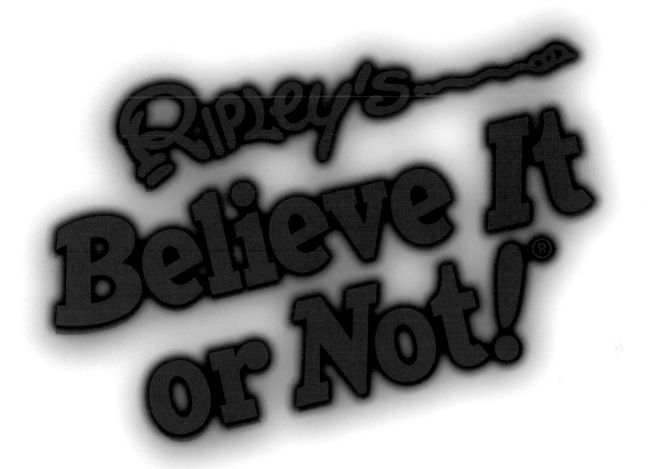

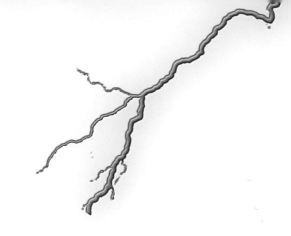

Executive VP Norm Deska
VP, Exhibits & Archives Edward Meyer

Publisher Anne Marshall

Editorial Director Rebecca Miles
Senior Researcher & Picture Manager James Proud
Editorial Assistant Dominic Lill
Additional Research Rosie Alexander
Text Geoff Tibballs
Additional Text James Proud, Dominic Lill
Editors Judy Barratt, Sally McFall
Factchecker Alex Bazlinton
Indexer Hilary Bird

Art Director Sam South
Design Dynamo Design
Reprographics Juice Creative

ISBN: 978-1-60991-109-6

For information regarding permission, write to
VP Intellectual Property
Ripley Entertainment Inc.
Suite 188, 7576 Kingspointe Parkway
Orlando, Florida 32819

Email: publishing@ripleys.com

Manufactured in China
in May/2014 by Leo Paper
1st printing

Library of Congress Control Number: 2014935555

PUBLISHER'S NOTE
While every effort has been made to verify the accuracy of the entries in this book, the Publishers cannot be held responsible for any errors contained in the work. They would be glad to receive any information from readers.

WARNING
Some of the stunts and activities in this book are undertaken by experts and should not be attempted by anyone without adequate training and supervision.

Ripley's
Believe It
or Not!®

REALITY SHOCK!

RIPLEY
PUBLISHING

a Jim Pattison Company

Check out this crazy, noodle-slurping dude— on page 129!

CONTENTS

The Talented
Robert Ripley

→ Once in a blue moon, someone appears with true star quality. You know the kind of person—a door opens, they walk in and the whole room turns to look and wonder. Marilyn Monroe had that rare, proper, X-factor, Nelson Mandela, too, and Jack Kennedy... and so did Robert Ripley.

Never anything but dapper in sharp suits and spats, Ripley was the guy to know, from 1918 when he started work at *The New York Globe*, penning his daily Believe It or Not! cartoon that reported on the world's wildest weird-ities, until the day he died in 1949 after a lifetime spent in pursuit of strange stories.

The big star in a giant solar system, Ripley had a multitude of dazzling achievements spinning around him. There were the museums— Odditoriums—that he built to house the bizarre artifacts he collected, a pioneering TV and radio career that saw him reporting from a shark tank and from behind Niagara Falls, and his worldwide exploration, which took him to Papua New Guinea, ice-bound Russia and central China— locations which, at the time, most people had barely even heard of. No wonder that Americans couldn't get enough of him. At one time, he was said to be more popular than the President!

Today, the Ripley's empire has gone galactic—with 31 Odditoriums, three aquariums, a warehouse stacked with thousands of exhibits, 30,000 photos and 100,000 cartoons, and a huge fan base that extends right around the world.

At the peak of his popularity, Ripley received 170,000 letters a week—more than Father Christmas—and fans across the U.S. mobbed him for autographs.

At home, Ripley mixed with the literati and glitterati of the U.S. In Port Moresby, in Papua New Guinea, it was more a case of headhunters (left), and in Fiji it was a human cannibal (right), both 1932.

NEHI NEWS

Volume 2, No. 2

MARCH, 1940

Columbus, Ga.

WARM DAYS AHEAD
MORE BUSINESS
GREATER PROFITS

STUDY YOUR SALES
MANUAL. IT MEANS
MONEY TO YOU.

RADIO PROGRAM HITS NEW POPULARITY PEAK

After a series of spectacular broadcasts, which moved at a fast clip, ROYAL CROWN'S CBS 88-station coast-to-coast radio program featuring "Believe-It-Or-Not" Bob Ripley has hit a new popularity peak. Following the opener in New York February 16th, Ripley and the cast sojourned to Florida, where two outstanding programs were broadcast. The listening audience has steadily increased and the program is now rated one of the top half-hour shows on the air.

Stimulated by scores of favorable program reviews, which include the prized Variety and Radio Daily columns, and innumerable letters and gratifying expressions from ROYAL CROWN Bottlers, the cast is determined to march the program to an even greater height.

The St. Augustine, Florida, "Marine Studio" program was heralded a broadcast triumph by many radio columnists, and proved an exciting venture for Bob Ripley and the listeners. The daring presentation won a number of hearty program endorsements and many letters stated that ROYAL CROWN was putting thrill into radio listening.

In pictorial form we review the highlights of the program broadcast from Marineland—located near St. Augustine, Florida.

CBS

TOO LATE NOW! Bob Ripley dons the diver's suit . . . willingly but not enthusiastically.

TO SHARK-INFESTED WATERS! Down in the deep he goes to tell the world how it feels to meet a man-eating shark face to face.

A HUNGRY PORPOISE FED BY HAND! Lurching forward at great speed, the mammal feeds from human hands.

CBS CBS

WE'RE ON THE AIR! Action and thrills are sent through these radio engineers to over a million listening radio fans.

In 1940, the *Nehi News* gave Robert Ripley's broadcasting aptitude the splash it deserved. In the same year, *Radio Guide* said Ripley's radio show was "consistently the most interesting and thrilling program on the air." Robert Ripley's unbelievable broadcasting achievements included being the first person to broadcast around the world simultaneously and, as featured in this *Nehi News* front cover, in 1940 he presented the world's first underwater radio broadcast—from the bottom of a shark-filled tank in Florida's Marineland. Ripley's continues its association with the aquatic world today with its three world-class aquariums, the largest of which opened in Toronto, Canada, in 2013.

Hawaii was one of Ripley's favorite destinations, and he would make five trips to the islands in his lifetime. On his last trip, in 1948, he rode a traditional outrigger canoe in the surf with some locals, something he had enjoyed on his first journey to the islands in 1922. These canoes have been raced in islands in the Pacific for centuries.

LOOK what we've been up to!

→ Here at Ripley's we pride ourselves that everything in this book is definitely true—no picture is doctored, no story exaggerated, and nothing is ever invented.

Such standards don't make life easy. Ripley's researchers, correspondents, writers and editors spend all year hunting for the special ingredients that make up each one of our books—trawling through files, combing social media, following up leads that could end up at home or abroad. The trail might wind up in a story that's bigger and bolder than any before... but if there's no proof of truth, it's not in!

We've collected thousands of stories for this new book, and have met some amazing people along the way—some of our favorites are featured here.

THE LENGTHS WE GO TO!

→ In 1933, Robert Ripley was photographed measuring the mustache of Desar Arjan Dangar, a policeman in Kathiawar, India (inset, right). Almost 80 years later, Ripley's Archivist, Edward Meyer, was traveling through Rajasthan, India, when he came across Ram Singh Chauhan, another man with an extra long mustache. Guess what? He turned out to be the grandson of the original long-mustached gentleman—and both of them had a mustache over 8½ ft (2.6 m) long!

COUNT US IN!

Ever wondered how someone with incredibly long nails goes about everyday life? We caught up with **Ayanna Williams** at home in Houston, Texas, to find out.

Page 124

Ripley's saw a picture of **Katzen Hobbes** and loved her tiger-style tattoos, so we decided to go and photograph them for ourselves.

Page 235

Ripley's bought this etching of Paul McCartney on a VW Beetle hood by U.S. artist Michael Stodola...

...and we acquired Dutch artist Max Zorn's portrait of Marilyn Monroe, made from packing tape.

RIPLEY'S WENT SHOPPING!

TIGER HAIRBALL!

This year, Ripley's took possession of a giant, smelly hairball that had been removed from the stomach of a tiger! Now, Ripley's have hairballs from cows in its collection already, but this one was trickier to remove. As Edward, our Archivist, pointed out. "If a cow wakes up during surgery, it only moos at you!" Check out the full story on page 91.

ART GOOD ENOUGH TO EAT!

When artist Carl Warner visits his local supermarket, he fills his shopping basket with food that he transforms into stunning landscape works of art. Smoked salmon becomes a sea at sunset, and broccoli forms coral around which radishes swim like tropical fish. Ripley's London Odditorium held an exhibition of his work, including this mouthwatering winter scene made from pastries.

WELL DONE! →

When master carvers Ray Villafane and Andy Bergholtz set about a 1000-lb (454-kg) pumpkin in Hong Kong and transformed it into a giant gremlin, we were so impressed that we awarded them our Ripley's Believe It or Not! certificates. We don't hand out awards often, but it was the biggest carved pumpkin we've ever seen! See pages 208–209.

1,000 lbs

We caught up with magician and sideshow performer **Jason Black, aka Black Scorpion,** in Austin, Texas, to find out what motivates him and to take some amazing pictures.

Page 116

When Ripley's found out about amazing Russian contortionist **Vittalli Illis,** we invited him to our Odditorium in London, England, for a body-bending photoshoot.

Page 18

Page 192

When Brooklyn-based artist **Ariana Page Russell** sent Ripley's photos of her unusual skin art, we flew her down to our Orlando HQ to take some more shots.

Ripley's Believe It or Not!®
www.ripleybooks.com

School Odditorium!

With Ripley's Believe It or Not! books being firm favorites in their classroom, ingenious fourth graders at Kelly Mill Elementary School in Forsyth County, Georgia, made their very own **Ripley's Odditorium** at their school. Packed with weird and wonderful exhibits handmade by the students, it attracted 1,500 visitors!

This papier–mache model shows the unbelievably long hair of Asha Mandela, featured in Ripley's *Strikingly True*.

A giant snowman (top) and a tall King Penguin (standing beside its creator, Matthew Arundale) were two of the larger exhibits.

RIPLEY TATTOO

→ Christopher Sudduth from Phoenix, Arizona, loves Ripley's so much he has a tattoo of Robert Ripley holding a shrunken head on his arm. He says it's "a tribute to the most interesting man ever."

The original photo on which Christopher based his tattoo.

Magical Mail

WINNER!

Ripley's ran a Ready, Set, Mail contest this year to find the weirdest piece of mail that could be sent to our Florida HQ, with just one rule—no envelope, box or wrapping of any kind could be used, and the address and postage had to be stuck directly to the item. Here are some of the items we received, including Michele Cassidy's winning entry— an entire McDonald's meal glued to a paper plate, with the address on the underside!

01

BELIEVE IT!

Skateboarding mouse

Shane Willmott has taught his pet mice to skateboard by building them a miniature skate park in the backyard of his home in Queensland, Australia, where they ride mouse-sized boards down vertical ramps and even through a ring of fire. Shane, who has also taught his mice to surf, said: "They love it. Mice are built to surf and skate because their center of gravity is so low. When they do fall off, they want to get straight back on board."

subway loot Using dental floss and mousetrap glue, Puerto Rican native Eliel Santos makes around $150 a day by retrieving cash, jewelry and iPhones that have fallen down New York City subway grates.

stinky town A pile of goat manure spontaneously caught fire at a farm in Windsor, Vermont, spreading a stink throughout the town and up to 5 mi (8 km) away.

fish smuggler A Vietnamese man tried to smuggle seven live tropical fish into New Zealand by hiding them in plastic bags in his pants pockets—but his plan floundered when Auckland Airport officials noticed water dripping from his bulging clothes.

chimney geese People in Victorian Britain who could not afford chimney sweeps dropped live geese down their chimneys instead.

$17,500 tip Aurora Kephart, a bartender at Conway's Restaurant and Lounge in Springfield, Oregon, is often tipped by a customer with tickets from the state lottery. In October 2013 one such ticket won her $17,500.

sting operation An attempted armed carjacking in Craighall, South Africa, was foiled when the suspects were chased down the street by an angry swarm of bees.

CREATIVE STOWAWAYS

SQUASHED IN A CAR DASHBOARD

Officials at the Mexico–U.S.border stopped a suspicious-looking car in 2001 and found a 135-lb (61-kg) woman squashed in the dashboard, peering out through the glove compartment.

STOWED AWAY IN A BUS WHEEL ARCH

A 21-year-old Tunisian man stowed away in the wheel arch of a bus for 30 hours in 2011, hanging on grimly as it traveled 500 mi (800 km) across Europe.

SEWED INTO THE SEAT OF A CHEVROLET

In 2001, Mexico's Enrique Aguilar Canchola sewed himself into the seat of a Chevrolet minivan in an attempt to sneak into California, but was discovered when border guards spotted his legs and arms sticking out from the base of the seat.

HID INSIDE THE LANDING GEAR OF A JUMBO JET

A 20-year-old Romanian man hid inside the landing gear of a jumbo jet on its 97-minute flight from Vienna, Austria, to London, England, in 2010 and survived despite enduring temperatures of –42°F (–41°C) and a severe lack of oxygen.

HID IN A PLANE'S OVERHEAD LOCKER

A man hid in a plane's overhead luggage compartment at Pearson Airport, Toronto, in 2012, but was discovered before the flight took off for Panama City.

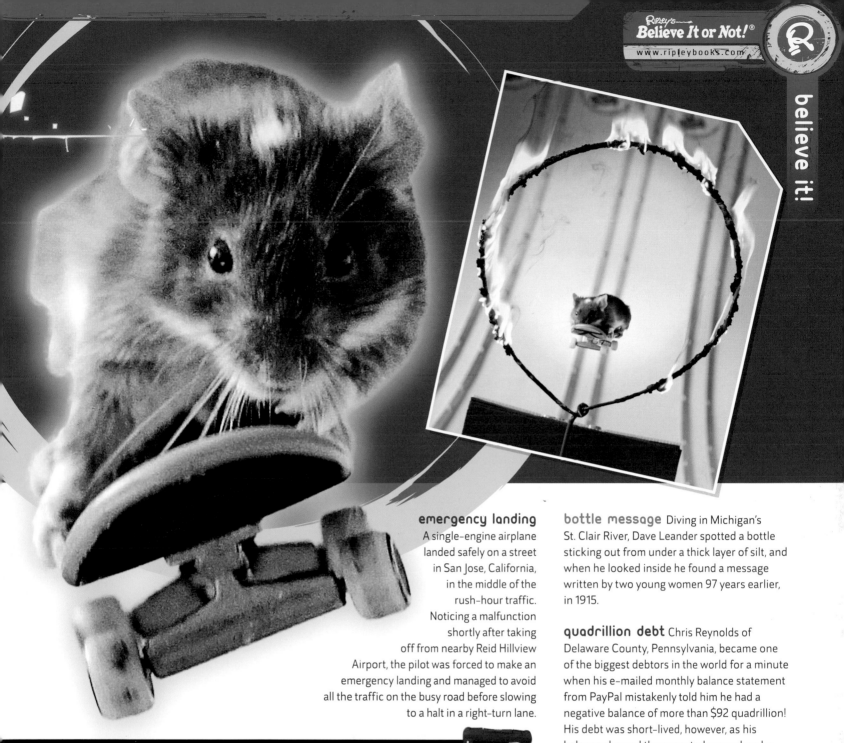

emergency landing

A single-engine airplane landed safely on a street in San Jose, California, in the middle of the rush-hour traffic. Noticing a malfunction shortly after taking off from nearby Reid Hillview Airport, the pilot was forced to make an emergency landing and managed to avoid all the traffic on the busy road before slowing to a halt in a right-turn lane.

bottle message

Diving in Michigan's St. Clair River, Dave Leander spotted a bottle sticking out from under a thick layer of silt, and when he looked inside he found a message written by two young women 97 years earlier, in 1915.

quadrillion debt

Chris Reynolds of Delaware County, Pennsylvania, became one of the biggest debtors in the world for a minute when his e-mailed monthly balance statement from PayPal mistakenly told him he had a negative balance of more than $92 quadrillion! His debt was short-lived, however, as his balance showed the expected zero when he logged into his PayPal account.

time traveler

Ed Grigor from Endicott, New York, lost a gold watch engraved with his name in 1959—but 53 years later it was found over 2,000 mi (3,200 km) away in Las Vegas, Nevada, and returned to him.

termite terror

An elderly lady in southern China lost over $10,000 of her savings after termites chewed through the bills. The termites actually nibbled more than $60,000 worth of cash that she had kept in a drawer, but luckily the bank managed to verify many of the damaged bills.

MAILED OUT OF A JAIL

Turkish prisoner Yasar Bayrak went on the run after he successfully mailed himself out of a jail in Willich, Germany, in 2008 in a giant FedEx box used for dirty laundry.

HIDING IN AN AIRLINE CARGO CONTAINER

Roberto Viza Egües fled Cuba for Paris, France, in 2000 after hiding in an Air France cargo container at Havana Airport. After a 14-hour flight in freezing temperatures, he arrived in France where his application for asylum was denied.

PACKED HIMSELF IN A SUITCASE

Mexican prisoner Juan Ramirez Tijerina tried to escape jail in Chetumal by packing himself into his girlfriend's suitcase. Guards spotted Maria del Mar Arjona looking nervous after visiting him when she left the prison pulling a bulky case. When they opened it, they found 19-year-old Ramirez, who was serving a 20-year sentence for illegal weapons possession, curled up inside.

garden treasure A 6-in-thick (15-cm), carved granite garden step at Bronwen Hickmott's home in Devon, England, turned out to be a Buddhist temple moonstone—an elaborately carved decorative stone artifact—that's at least a thousand years old. It was one of only seven of its type in the world and sold for over £550,000 ($875,000) at an auction!

wrong face A man who used counterfeit $100 bills to buy goods at a store in North Attleborough, Rhode Island, made the mistake of putting a picture of Abraham Lincoln on the notes instead of Benjamin Franklin.

Family photo on the Moon!

PHOTO ON MOON → When U.S. astronaut Charles Duke landed on the Moon as part of the Apollo 16 mission, he left a family photo on the lunar surface hoping that intelligent alien life forms might discover it. Before placing the picture showing himself, his wife and two sons in a plastic folder, he wrote on the back: "This is the family of Astronaut Duke from Planet Earth. Landed on the Moon, April 1972."

banker error A tired German bank clerk fell asleep with his finger on the number 2 key on his computer keyboard—and ended up turning a simple 62.40 euro transfer in to a customer's account into a withdrawal from the account of a whopping 222,222,222.22 euros ($293 million).

toddler mayor
Bobby Tufts was re-elected mayor of Dorset, Minnesota, in August 2013—even though he was not yet old enough to attend preschool! He was first chosen to be mayor of the small town (population about 25) in 2012 at age three, and his pro-ice-cream campaign proved such a vote-winner that he was elected again 12 months later.

same name Two weeks after moving into a house in Barnsley, England, in 2012, 40-year-old former soldier Richard Midgley found three 1937 gas masks in an old box in the attic, including one with his name on it!

lucky ticket After accidentally throwing a scratch-off lottery ticket in the trash, Joseph and Joanne Zagami of North Attleborough, Massachusetts, retrieved it to find they had won $1 million.

quarters back
Ordered to repay $500,000 in insurance money, a man from Harrisburg, Illinois, protested against the decision by paying off $150,000 of the amount in quarters. He had the 50-lb (23-kg) bags of coins—that's 160 bags weighing a total of almost four tons—delivered by truck.

CHECK THIS!

→ Although it was written and signed to the value of Australian $2,240, this giant billboard check looked worthless to most Australians until they realized it was actually legal tender. National Australia Bank put up four oversized checks—two in Sydney and two in Melbourne—to promote its mortgage rates, and once word spread that the checks could be cashed at a NAB branch, there was a mad rush to rip them down from the billboards. Luka Pendes was one of the four lucky winners fast enough to cash in on the offer.

Resin Layers

➔ **Keng Lye from Singapore creates incredible 3-D paintings—such as this lifelike octopus—by using multiple layers of resin.**

He pours resin into a container, then covers it with plastic wrap to protect it from dust and to allow it to harden. Once the resin is dry, he paints it in minute detail with acrylic paint. He adds layers of resin and acrylic paint, giving depth and realism to the composition, until the object is finished. The whole process is so laborious that even the simplest artwork can take him up to five days to complete, but the end result is worth all the effort.

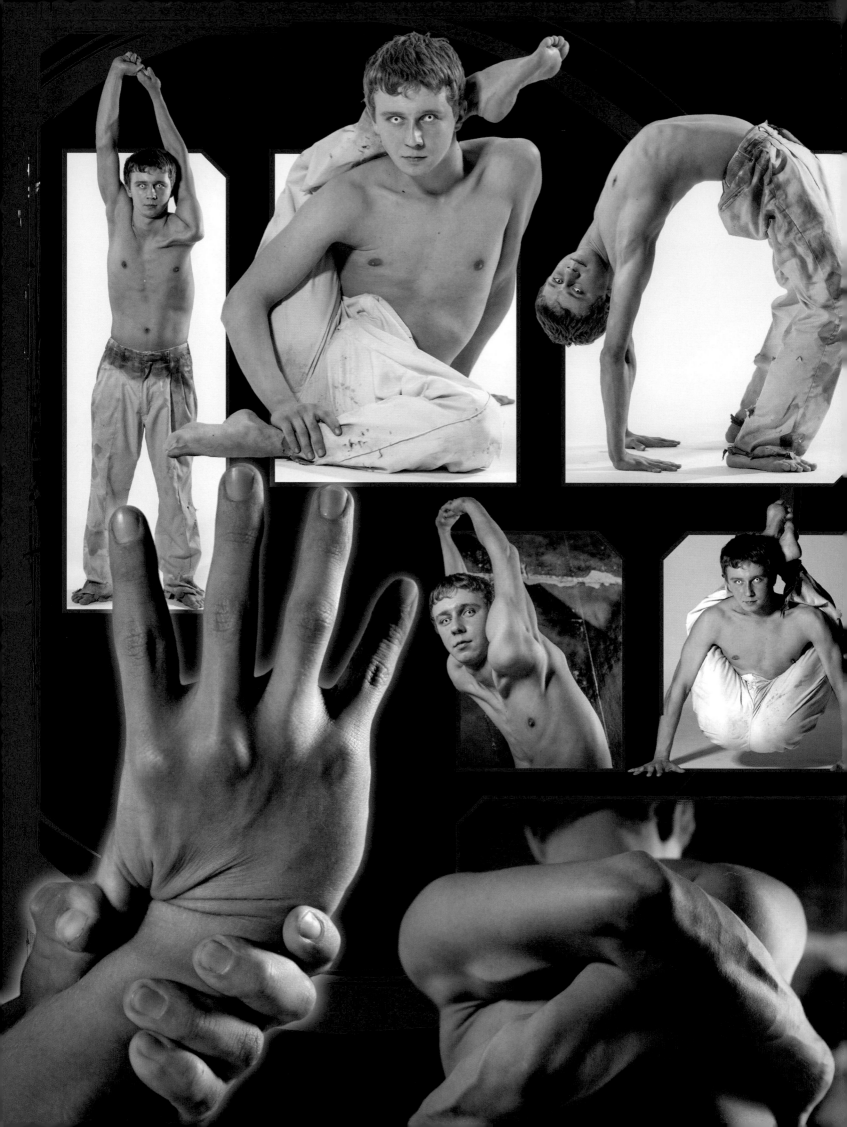

Twisted Mister→

➔ **Vittalii Illis, a slim 20-year-old Russian contortionist with the Circus of Horrors traveling theater show, can dislocate his shoulder blades both ways, popping them right out of their sockets and back again at will.**

He shocks audiences by dislocating his shoulders to rotate his arms back and around his body so that they meet at the front. He can also crawl around the stage on all fours in a creepy spider walk with his legs twisted in front of his body and his hands behind.

Vittalii, who also performs juggling, acrobatics and tightrope walking, was born with natural flexibility. He joined a circus in Russia when he was six as an acrobat, but his coach was so impressed with his ability to twist his body into seemingly impossible positions that he developed his act as a contortionist.

Now Vittalii does extensive stretching exercises every day to keep in whatever shape he chooses.

Ripley's ask

Do you train every day? *Yes, I do training every day, for about 1½ hours.*

Does your act hurt at all? *No, thanks to my natural flexibility, and because I train every day, it is easy for me.*

When you train, do you work on the same tricks? *Not every day. I like to discover something new or I see what other contortionists do and try to replicate it.*

Do you enjoy working in the Circus of Horrors? *Yes, the show is very unusual, not like an ordinary circus. I like the program very much, so I decided to come back and now it is my second year.*

Does anybody else in your family work in a circus? *No, I am the only one. My family is quite ordinary. None of my family members has ever worked in a circus or as a rubber man.*

What do you do in your time off? *I like soccer very much—I am a Chelsea fan. On weekends I like to watch films. I like comedies a lot—I like to have a laugh.*

TUTU MAN

➜ Since 2003, professional photographer Bob Carey has taken over 200 self-portraits dressed in a pink tutu all over the U.S.A., in places such as the Grand Canyon, the New York City subway, and even in the snow. His wife Linda was diagnosed with breast cancer and they both believed that laughter would be the best medicine. They wanted to share this idea with the world, so they self-published the pictures in a book, *Ballerina*, the proceeds from which are donated to their Carey Foundation, which supports families affected by breast cancer.

lost king A skeleton found beneath a city-center parking lot in Leicester, England, in 2012 was proved by DNA testing to be that of King Richard III of England who was killed at the nearby Battle of Bosworth in 1485. After the battle, his body was missing for more than 500 years.

honesty pays The honesty of homeless man Billy Ray Harris of Kansas City, Missouri, who returned a diamond ring that had been accidentally dropped into his collection cup, was rewarded when he received almost $192,000 in donations from 6,000 people around the world after the ring's owner, Sarah Darling, set up an online fund-raising page for him.

cheap wedding When Georgina Porteous and Sid Innes got married near Inverness, Scotland, in 2013, their wedding day cost them just £1 ($1.50)—the price Georgina paid for the vintage wedding gown that she bought on a website where people can swap unwanted items. The bride handcrafted the rings herself from deer antlers, the 70 guests brought their own food to the reception and everything else was either donated or sourced for free.

SLEEPING PARTNER ➜
Guy Whittall enjoyed a peaceful night's sleep in Humani Lodge, Zimbabwe, unaware that an 8-ft-long (2.4-m) Nile crocodile was lying under his bed the whole time. In the morning, Guy dangled his bare feet over the edge of the bed, inches from the 330-lb (150-kg) monster's teeth. Later, the housemaid's screams alerted him to his unwelcome guest.

Martin Kober from Buffalo, New York, found a **$300 million painting** by Michelangelo behind his couch.

Inocenta Hernandez discovered a 3-ft-wide (0.9-m), 40-ft-deep (12-m) **sinkhole** had opened up under her bed in Guatemala City, Guatemala, in 2011.

Linda DeForest and her family had to be evacuated from their new home in Indiana in 2010 when they found a **live mortar shell** in the basement. It was safely disarmed the next day.

A man in the U.K. found a **3,000-year-old Egyptian jar** in his garden.

An 18-in (45-cm) **venomous tiger snake** slithered into a patient's bed in a hospital in Melbourne, Australia, on Christmas Eve 2012, but had to be put down after injuring itself in the bed's mechanism.

In 2012, an elderly woman in Central Russia was surprised to find a **drunk burglar** snoring peacefully under her bed.

To escape the rain, an 8-ft-tall (2.4-m) **black bear** broke into a family home in Naples, Florida, in August 2013 and went to sleep in the pool house, where he was found by seven-year-old Mason MacDonough and his babysitter.

AMAZING DISCOVERIES

Ripley's Believe It or Not!®
www.ripleybooks.com
believe it!

message intact Lucy Elliott, 12, from Coventry, England, threw a message in a plastic bottle out to sea off the coast of Cornwall in 1994 and 19 years later it washed up on a beach in Norway 750 mi (1200 km) away. Incredibly, the handwritten message was still sufficiently legible for the finder to trace her.

tidy robot Researchers at the University of California, Berkeley, have taught a robot how to fold laundry. Faced with a pile of towels, the robot picks it up with its arms and uses a pair of high-resolution cameras to estimate its shape. Once it finds two adjacent corners, it starts folding, smoothing the towel after each fold to make a neat stack.

robot attendant Alex Cressman and Laura Wong had a 10-lb (4.5-kg) bomb disposal robot serve as ring bearer at their wedding in Annapolis, Maryland. The bride, a mechanical engineer, helped design the Dragon Runner robot, which was controlled during the ceremony and reception by one of her friends wearing a special backpack.

picture perfect Five years after losing her camera while scuba diving in Hawaii, Lindsay Scallan of Newnan, Georgia, learned that it had been found 6,000 mi (9,660 km) away in Taiwan. Although the camera was covered in seaweed and barnacles, her pictures were still intact on its memory card.

shock reunion When Christine Greenslade, 66, decided to trace the whereabouts of her old schoolfriends in Penzance, England, in 2013, they were stunned to find she was still alive after a local newspaper had erroneously printed her obituary in 1980.

riders' screams The Gold Striker roller coaster at the Great America theme park in Santa Clara, California, was shut down temporarily because riders were screaming too loudly. As the shrieks exceeded the decibel limit agreed with adjacent properties, Great America covered a portion of the track in a soundproof tunnel before reopening the ride.

walrus mystery When London's St. Pancras train station was being renovated in 2003, archeologists discovered a 19th-century burial site containing 1,500 human bodies and the remains of a 13-ft-long (4-m) Pacific walrus. The walrus bones were in a coffin with eight human skeletons.

diamond find Twelve-year-old Michael Dettlaff from Apex, North Carolina, made $11,996 profit in just ten minutes thanks to an Arkansas diamond park's policy of allowing visitors to keep what they find. The boy scout paid $4 admission to the Crater of Diamonds State Park on July 31, 2013, and quickly found a 5.16-carat diamond valued at $12,000.

spy trees During World War I, engineers along the Western Front would cut down trees during the night and replace them with prefabricated observation posts that had been hand-decorated as highly detailed replica trees.

NASAL POWER

→ Nie Yongbing took just 21 minutes to inflate four tires with his nose—while two adults stood on each tire.

For the stunt in Chengdu, China, Nie held a 131-ft-long (40-m) rubber hose to his right nostril and kept his left nostril and left ear covered to prevent pressure leaks. His doctor once told him that blowing up balloons with his nose would improve his health, but balloons did not prove challenging enough so he graduated to tires.

HEIGHT DIFFERENCE

It's no joke if Sultan treads on his bride's toes while dancing. For his enormous, record-breaking feet are each 14 in (36 cm) long.

→ Turkish farmer Sultan Kosen married a woman who is 2 ft 7 in (0.79 m) shorter than him and who barely comes up to his waist. Merve Dibo is 5 ft 8 in (1.73 m) tall, but is still dwarfed by her 8-ft-3-in (2.52 m) groom — the world's tallest man.

Sultan had to order a custom-made suit from nearly 20 ft (6 m) of fabric and size 28 shoes for the wedding, which took place in his home city of Mardin in October 2013 and was attended by dignitaries including Turkey's president and prime minister.

He is one of only ten people to have grown above 8 ft (2.44 m), his stature caused by a rare condition called pituitary gigantism, which causes the body to continually produce growth hormones. His height was normal until the age of ten, when he began a growth spurt that did not stop until 2011.

As a result of his height, the 30-year-old had despaired of ever finding a bride. After the wedding he said: "It was unfortunate that I could not find a suitable girl of my own size, but I've found the person for me."

The world's tallest man towers over his fiancée on their henna night, the ceremony held one day before the wedding.

Merve holds on to Sultan's huge 11-in (28-cm) hand. He has the biggest hands in the world.

police search Two four-year-old boys sparked a full-scale, five-hour search by police officers in Bremen, Germany, after pedaling more than 4 mi (6.4 km) from home on their toy tractors.

walmart wedding In February 2012, Susan and Wayne Brandenburg got married in the layaway section of the same Shallotte, North Carolina, Walmart store where they had first met seven years earlier.

yellow pages Plasterer Jimmy Newton from Devon, England, took up some flooring in a house and found a yellowing newspaper cutting containing a picture of himself on a soccer team in 1985, 28 years earlier.

freeway proposal More than 300 bikers blocked off part of the busy #10 Freeway in Los Angeles, California, so that Hector "Tank" Martinez could get down on one knee on the tarmac to propose to his beloved girlfriend Paige Hernandez.

coin toss A 2013 mayoral election in the Philippines was decided by the toss of a coin. Marvic Feraren and Boyet Py both received 3,236 votes to be mayor of San Teodoro, so under the country's election code the two men flipped a coin five times and Feraren won.

shoeshine tips Shoeshine man Albert Lexie has given the Children's Hospital of Pittsburgh, Pennsylvania, more than $200,000 from the tips that he has collected over the last 30 years.

memorable date Cheryl Bennett and Steven DeLong of Amesbury, Massachusetts, decided to get married on January 9, 2013, because it was the same date as the town's ZIP code—01913.

blind devotion Blind couple Claire Johnson and Mark Gaffey from Stoke-on-Trent, England, fell in love and got engaged after their seeing-eye dogs Venice and Rodd hit it off during training classes.

bonkers for conkers A company that runs parking lots in Manchester and Leeds, U.K., introduced a temporary scheme in the fall of 2013 whereby motorists could pay for parking time with conkers—the fruit of the horse chestnut tree. Each conker was worth 20p (32 cents) apiece.

leap babies Louise Estes of Provo, Utah, has given birth on three consecutive leap days—in 2004, 2008 and 2012—making her one of only two women in the world known to have had three leap-day babies. The Henriksen family of Norway also recorded February 29 births in 1960, 1964 and 1968.

snail mail Scott McMurry of Vienna, Virginia, received a postcard from his mother in April 2012—55 years after she put it in the mail.

Artist Tracie Koziura changed her name to **Rebel Wolf**—because she loves wolves and was a bit of a rebel.

American teenager Jennifer Thornburg changed her name to **CutoutDissection.com** to protest against animal dissection in schools. She likes to be called Cutout for short.

Daniel Westfallen from Essex, England, legally changed his name to **Happy Adjustable Spanners** as a bet after a night out.

To highlight his love of superheroes and sci-fi, Daniel Knox-Hewson (left) changed his name to **Emperor Spiderman Gandalf Wolverine Skywalker Optimus Prime Goku Sonic Xavier Ryu Cloud Superman HeMan Batman Thrash**. His friend, Kelvin Borbidge (right), became **Baron Venom Balrog Sabretooth Vader Megatron Vegeta Robotnik Magneto Bison Sephiroth Lex Luthor Skeletor Joker Grind.**

Beezow Doo-Doo Zopittybop-Bop-Bop, formerly known as Jeffery Drew Wilschke, hit the headlines with his bizarre name and then again when he was arrested on drug charges.

An Englishman changed his name to **Stormhammer Deathclaw Firebrand** because he thought his original name, Richard Smith, was too boring.

In 2005, Terri Iligan sold her name on ebay and for $15,199 she became known as **GoldenPalace.com.**

Ceejay Epton changed her name to **Ceejay A Apple B Boat C Cat D Dog E Elephant F Flower G Goat H House I Igloo J Jellyfish K Kite L Lion M Monkey N Nurse O Octopus P Penguin Q Queen R Robot S Sun T Tree U Umbrella V Violin W Whale X X-Ray Y Yo-Yo Z Zebra Terryn Feuji-Sharemi** because she thought it would help her son to learn the alphabet.

Australian actor and director Greg Pead changed his name to **Yahoo Serious** in 1980 and 20 years later unsuccessfully sued the search engine Yahoo! for trademark infringement.

[YOUR / UPLOADS]

AUTOGRAPH TATTOOS

Dennis Elliott, from Jackson, Michigan, tells Ripley's that he collects autographs of his favorite athletes and celebrities—and then goes straight to a tattoo parlor to have the exact autograph inked on his skin. More than 40 stars, including Mike Tyson, Coolio, Magic Johnson, Dennis Rodman and Hulk Hogan, have already indirectly signed his body.

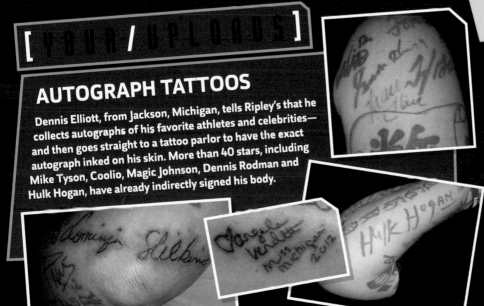

23

cow costume An 18-year-old man was accused of stealing 26 gal (98 l) of milk—worth $92—from a Walmart store in North Stafford, Virginia, while dressed as a cow. He made his escape on all fours and proceeded to hand out the stolen milk to passersby.

blank space When the dictator of Zaire, Joseph Mobutu, was overthrown in 1997, his face was cut out of thousands of banknotes to save printing new ones.

bungling burglar Police in Southington, Connecticut, caught a thief in March 2012 after he accidentally butt-dialed the 911 emergency services number while carrying out a robbery.

wooly haul In November 2013, thieves stole 160 sheep from a field near the aptly named village of Wool in Dorset, England.

queasy rider Car mechanic Guenter Schroeder from Germany drank so much beer one evening that he ended up falling asleep on top of a horse. Having missed his last bus home, he stumbled across some stables and curled up on the horse's warm blanket even though the animal was standing up!

lottery luck Three members of the Oksnes family, from the tiny Austevoll Islands off Norway's west coast, have won the lottery in six years, picking up a combined jackpot of more than $4 million.

naked protest Hundreds of cyclists rode through the streets of Lima, Peru, in March 2013 without any clothes on in the city's eighth annual naked bike ride to protest over poor traffic safety.

> **THIRTY CELLS IN SWISS PRISONS HAVE BEEN PAINTED PINK IN AN ATTEMPT TO CALM DOWN AGGRESSIVE INMATES.**

ear print A man was arrested for multiple burglaries in the French city of Lyon after leaving his ear print behind at 80 robberies. He would press his ear up to the front door to check that nobody was at home, but in doing so left behind incriminating evidence.

sleep driver Thought to be suffering from a type of sleepwalking disorder, a woman drove 185 mi (300 km) from Hamilton, New Zealand, to Tauranga, while asleep at the wheel. She drove for five hours—and even sent text messages from her cell phone along the way. She was eventually found slumped over the wheel in the driveway of her former home.

webbed wetsuit Inspired by BASE jumpers' wingsuits, French designer Guillaume Binard has invented a wetsuit with webbing between the legs and arms to enable divers to glide through the water like a manta ray.

chance discovery In 2013, Peter Dodds from Derbyshire, England, bought an old biography of Winston Churchill from a local charity shop and found it contained a postcard sent in 1988 by his own brother in the U.S.A. to their mother.

discount donuts A 48-year-old man was arrested in Pasco County, Florida, for impersonating a police officer in an attempt to get cheap donuts. The man regularly flashed a fake badge to workers at a Dunkin' Donuts stall and demanded a police discount before staff became suspicious and alerted the real cops.

aerial escape Dropped from an airplane at 14,000 ft (4,270 m), escape artist Anthony Martin from Sheboygan, Wisconsin, freed himself from shackles and a locked casket while plummeting toward the ground at 130 mph (209 km/h) before safely deploying his parachute. He had been handcuffed to a belt around his waist and chained to the inside of the wooden casket. A prison door lock for which no key existed was screwed into place to make the casket supposedly escape-proof, but, although the box rocked wildly from side to side on its rapid descent, Martin pushed his way to freedom at about 6,500 ft (1,980 m).

SQUIRREL KNOT →

→ In June 2013, six young squirrels were found in Regina, Saskatchewan, knotted together by their tails so that they could move in only one direction as a large furry mass. They were carefully untangled at an animal clinic and all released back into the wild with their tails intact.

➜ **Franz Reichelt was an Austrian-born French tailor who invented a revolutionary parachute suit in the early 20th century.**

The invention and popularization of airplanes and flight at this time had caused safety concerns about falling from a great height, and this led to a number of people trying to invent an effective parachute. One such man was Franz Reichelt, who designed a parachute suit to be worn like a coat, so that the wearer could blend in with the general public while wearing the safety device.

Franz refined his "flying coat," and after numerous failed tests with dummies dropped from various heights, he decided that the reason his invention did not work was because of the short drop distances. He applied to test his suit by jumping from the Eiffel Tower in Paris, France—then the tallest manmade structure in the world—but had to wait for more than a year before he was granted permission. On February 4, 1912, Franz stood on the first platform of the Eiffel Tower, some 200 ft (60 m) off the ground, wearing his parachute suit while his friends tried to convince him to abandon the test. With his attempt captured on film, he jumped, fell and hit the frozen ground without the parachute deploying, causing a dent in the French pavement, and, sadly, his own death.

Fell to his death from the Eiffel Tower!

THE FLYING TAILOR

no sweat! Swedish engineers have invented the Sweat Machine, a device that converts human sweat into drinking water. It works by extracting perspiration, which is 99 percent water, from people's clothes and purifying it.

slow thief After robbing a woman in the parking lot of a shopping mall near Melbourne, Australia, a 64-year-old man was arrested at the scene because he was too slow putting his walker into his getaway car.

upside down A 160-year-old, four-anna (less than half a cent) Indian postage stamp with the head of Queen Victoria accidentally printed upside down is now worth more than $100,000.

pen pals After exchanging approximately 3,000 letters over a period of a staggering 74 years, pen pals Norma Frati of Portland, Texas, and Audrey Sims of Perth, Australia, finally met for the first time in 2013 when 83-year-old Audrey flew to the U.S.A. The women had been pen pals since Norma was 13 years old and Audrey was only nine.

cloud nine Five couples from New Zealand got married at an altitude of 41,000 ft (12,500 m). The group wedding ceremony took place in the business cabin of a Fiji Airways plane en route from Auckland to Nadi, Fiji.

suspicious mind U.S. President Franklin D. Roosevelt would never travel on the 13th day of the month and would never host a White House dinner with 13 guests.

hair today Thieves stole $35,000 worth of hair—intended to be used in extensions and weaves—from a business in Macon, Georgia.

late delivery The R.M.S. *Titanic* sank in 1912 with more than seven million pieces of mail on board, all of which the U.S. would be required to help deliver if they could be recovered.

viking treasure When David Taylor from County Down, Northern Ireland, found a dirty piece of metal in a field, his wife Lynda told him to throw it away. He ignored her and it turned out to be a 1000-year-old, silver Viking arm ring.

CAR BURIAL ➜ Following her death in 1998, 84-year-old Rose Martin was lowered by crane into a grave at Tiverton, Rhode Island, inside her beloved 1962 Chevrolet Corvair. The burial hole was lined with concrete, and the steering wheel, seats, windows and engine were removed from the car to make room for Rose's coffin. Although it took up four burial plots, 6 in (15 cm) still had to be sawed off the rear of the car so that it would fit into the grave.

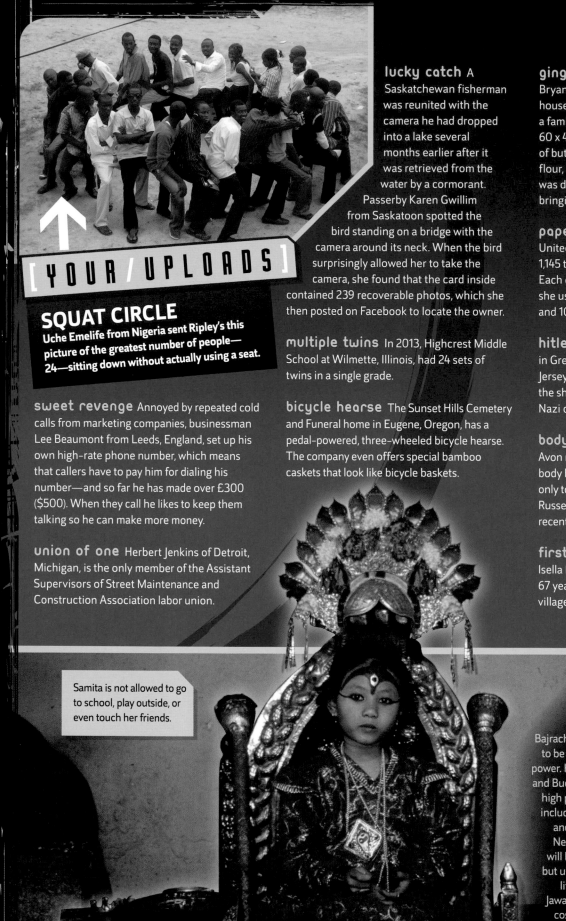

SQUAT CIRCLE

Uche Emelife from Nigeria sent Ripley's this picture of the greatest number of people—24—sitting down without actually using a seat.

lucky catch A Saskatchewan fisherman was reunited with the camera he had dropped into a lake several months earlier after it was retrieved from the water by a cormorant. Passerby Karen Gwillim from Saskatoon spotted the bird standing on a bridge with the camera around its neck. When the bird surprisingly allowed her to take the camera, she found that the card inside contained 239 recoverable photos, which she then posted on Facebook to locate the owner.

multiple twins In 2013, Highcrest Middle School at Wilmette, Illinois, had 24 sets of twins in a single grade.

bicycle hearse The Sunset Hills Cemetery and Funeral home in Eugene, Oregon, has a pedal-powered, three-wheeled bicycle hearse. The company even offers special bamboo caskets that look like bicycle baskets.

sweet revenge Annoyed by repeated cold calls from marketing companies, businessman Lee Beaumont from Leeds, England, set up his own high-rate phone number, which means that callers have to pay him for dialing his number—and so far he has made over £300 ($500). When they call he likes to keep them talking so he can make more money.

union of one Herbert Jenkins of Detroit, Michigan, is the only member of the Assistant Supervisors of Street Maintenance and Construction Association labor union.

gingerbread mansion Residents of Bryan, Texas, built a full-sized gingerbread house that was big enough to accommodate a family of five. The house, which measured 60 x 42 ft (18 x 13 m), used 1,800 lb (816 kg) of butter, 7,200 eggs, 7,200 lb (3,266 kg) of flour, 2,925 lb (1,327 kg) of brown sugar and was decorated with 22,304 pieces of candy, bringing its calorie count to 36 million!

paper dolls Amnah Al Fard from the United Arab Emirates spent two years making 1,145 three-dimensional, miniature paper dolls. Each doll took about three hours to make and she used a total of 2,500 ft (762 m) of paper and 10 lb (4.5 kg) of glue.

hitler's toilet Adolf Hitler's toilet has been in Greg Kohfeldt's autoshop in Florence, New Jersey, since 1952. The toilet was installed by the shop's previous owner and came from the Nazi dictator's favorite yacht, the *Aviso Grille*.

body blow Police divers searched the River Avon near Bath, England, after reports that a body had been seen floating on the surface, only to discover that it was a life-size dummy of Russell Crowe, which had been used during the recent filming of *Les Misérables* in the city.

first born In September 2013, Francesco Isella became the first baby to be born in 67 years in Lissa, Italy, and boosted the tiny village's population to six.

Samita is not allowed to go to school, play outside, or even touch her friends.

LIVING GODDESS

➜ A ten-year-old Nepalese girl, Samita Bajracharya, is a living goddess or Kumari, believed to be an incarnation of Kali, the Hindu goddess of power. Kumaris, who are worshiped by both Hindus and Buddhists, are selected as toddlers by Buddhist high priests and must meet more than 30 criteria, including good health, a golden, unscratched skin and no missing teeth. Kumari means "virgin" in Nepalese, so when Samita reaches puberty she will be considered unclean and will lose her title, but until then she leads a privileged but sheltered life. For her appearance at a chariot festival in Jawalakhel, Samita was dressed in the traditional costume that is passed down from one Kumari to the next. Before her arrival, workers hosed down her path and sniffer dogs were brought in to ensure her safety. Then, she was carried from her home by her family, making sure that her painted feet did not touch the ground, while devotees rushed forward to offer her flowers and money and to catch a glimpse of the child goddess.

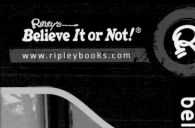

VILLAGE OF THE DOLLS

➜ **There are more life-sized straw dolls than humans in the remote village of Nagoro, Japan.**

There are only 51 people in the village but 150 dolls, each one representing a resident who has moved away or died. Created by local woman Mizuki Ayona, the dolls, dressed in rags and old clothes, appear all over the village—on fences, at the bus stop, and one in the abandoned school following the death of its last student.

treasure haul In 2013, treasure hunters Rick and Lisa Schmitt from Sanford, Florida, together with their grown-up children Hillary and Eric, found an estimated $300,000 worth of gold coins and chains from the wreckage of a fleet of 11 ships that sank in a 1715 hurricane while en route from Havana to Spain.

delayed twins Maria Jones-Elliott from Glenmore, Ireland, gave birth to twin girls 87 days apart. Baby Amy was born three months prematurely, but then the contractions stopped. The mother stayed in hospital for nearly three months until the other twin, Katie, was born.

lost car A man in Munich, Germany, was reunited with his car two years after forgetting where he had parked it. After a night of drinking in December 2010 and an unsuccessful search the following day, he reported the vehicle missing, but a traffic warden stumbled across it in October 2012—2½ mi (4 km) from where the owner thought he had parked it.

grave mistake Former New York City mayor Ed Koch meticulously planned his funeral down to the last detail, even going so far as to visit his own grave site and pen his own epitaph—but following his death in 2013 it was noticed that his tombstone mistakenly listed his year of birth as 1942 instead of 1924.

rare coin A rare 1913 Liberty Head nickel, which had first been discovered in a car wreck before being mistakenly branded a fake and left abandoned in a closet for decades, sold at an auction in Chicago, Illinois, for more than $3.1 million in 2013.

canned air In 2013, responding to his country's pollution problem, Chinese businessman Chen Guangbiao started selling cans of fresh air for $1.

family trio When Jayne Loughland of Wales collected an item from an auction in 2013, it was wrapped in a few pages of the local newspaper from September 9, 1982. Glancing at the paper, she saw her own name, on the next page she saw a picture of her husband and on another page a picture of her sister-in-law's husband. So three people from the same family appeared on three pages from the same paper that was printed years before they became related.

double parking Frank Pavlik and his daughter Hannah were both born in Illinois parking lots—33 years apart bar one day. Frank was born in the lot of a shopping mall in Joliet in 1980. One day before his 33rd birthday, Hannah arrived unscheduled in the parking lot of a gas station in Oswego.

MAN KNOCKED OUT IN MIDDLE OF SKYDIVE

■ Experienced skydiver James Lee from Gloucestershire, England, miraculously survived after being knocked unconscious by another jumper in a freak accident at 12,500 ft (3,800 m). After jumping from the plane over Wiltshire, 25-year-old Lee was hit on the back of the head by a fellow skydiver, the impact knocking him out. Seeing him in distress, two other parachutists bravely delayed activating their own cords and saved his life by diving towards him and pulling his cord to deploy his chute. Lee soon regained consciousness and floated down safely to the ground—but with no memory of the drama that had occurred.

wallet returned Burton Maugans of Acworth, Georgia, lost his wallet while waterskiing in North Carolina in 1989—and 24 years later it was returned to him after Jim Parker found it and searched the Internet for its owner. The wallet still contained Maugans' high school ID, a library card and an old bank card.

loving couple High school sweethearts Les and Helen Brown of Long Beach, California, were born on the same day in 1918, were married for 75 years, and died just one day apart in July 2013.

tables turned When his plan to break into a third-floor apartment in Valjevo, Serbia, went wrong, a thief was left hanging high above the ground on a TV antenna. He had to be rescued by the owner of the apartment he had intended to rob, who then handed him over to the police.

miles away Four-year-old Jasmine Hudson threw a message in a bottle off the pier at Bournemouth, England, hoping that it would reach her aunt in nearby Guernsey, but instead five months later she received a letter saying it had been found over 10,500 mi (17,000 km) away in Largs Bay, South Australia.

secret inscription Abraham Lincoln's pocket watch had a secret message engraved on the inside—and the President did not even know about it. The inscription describing the start of the American Civil War was engraved by jeweler Jonathan Dillon in 1861 but remained hidden until 2009 when Dillon's great-great-grandson contacted the Smithsonian's National Museum of American History, where the watch is kept, and told them about the rumored message. When an expert opened the historic watch, the secret was finally revealed.

shortened name A Hawaiian woman, Janice Keihanaikukauakahihuliheekahaunaele, has a surname so long that it will not fit on her driver's license. It has 35 letters plus a Hawaiian mark called an 'okina, but the state documents only have room for 35 letters, so Hawaii County had to issue her license and state ID without her first name and with the last letter of her surname chopped off.

baby vote Before the birth of their baby, Katie Reise and fiancé Chris Vollmershausen from Toronto, Ontario, prepared a short list of boys' and girls' names and sent out 100 ballots to friends and family to help them choose a name.

gopher bounty A mother and son from Minnesota were charged in 2013 with stealing nearly $5,000 worth of frozen gopher feet and then selling them to local townships that offer rewards to limit the rising gopher population.

card currency In 1685, soldiers in Quebec, Canada, were paid in playing cards, with promissory notes written on the back, after the French colonial government ran out of money.

flying ostrich Wacky Dutch inventor Bart Jansen has created the world's first flying ostrich—by fitting an engine and propellers to a stuffed bird. After procuring a dead ostrich from a farm, Jenson and technical engineer Arjen Beltman took it to a taxidermist to have it skinned and tanned before it was mechanized and taken for its maiden remote-controlled flight.

grave tour Since visiting the final resting place of President John F. Kennedy at Arlington National Cemetery, Virginia, in 1985, Mark Dabbs from West Midlands, England, has spent $75,000 visiting the graves of more than 200 famous people on six continents, including Bruce Lee in Seattle, Washington, Leon Trotsky in Mexico City and Mao Tse-tung in Beijing, China.

TECHNICOLOR CHEESECAKE

➔ Customer Angelina Carroll was knocked out by the tie-dye cheesecake she was served at the Summerville, South Carolina, branch of U.S. pizza chain Mellow Mushroom. The colorful sweet treat was chocolate and vanilla flavor with a drizzle of strawberry syrup.

FREAKY FUNGUS → Found high on the Tibetan plateau, a bizarre parasitic fungus known as "worm grass" infects the ghost moth caterpillar, and then consumes it from the inside, killing it and then sprouting from its head. The fungus, *Ophiocordyceps sinensis*, has been regarded as a miracle ingredient in Chinese traditional medicine for centuries, and is said to aid various ailments including cancer, and to act as a powerful stimulant and aphrodisiac. It is sold while still attached to the caterpillars and can fetch prices upwards of $3,500 per pound—ten times the price of silver.

Fungus sprouting from caterpillar's head

spoon escape A man used a regular spoon to break out of a maximum-security prison in Moscow, Russia. Oleg Topalov became only the fourth person in 20 years to escape from Matrosskaya Tishina when he dug a hole in his cell roof with a spoon, opened a ventilation shaft and then climbed onto the prison roof before scaling the perimeter fence.

brother's prank While Dutch teenager Jamiro Smajic was on holiday in Italy, his older brother, Tobias Mathijsen, played a prank on him by tilting his bedroom 90 degrees. Over the course of two days, Tobias fixed furniture to walls, attached posters to the ceiling and even installed a light at an angle of 90 degrees. A series of pranks between the brothers started when Jamiro altered his brother's Facebook profile and Tobias responded by painting Jamiro's entire bedroom pink while he was away.

double joy Twins Aimee and Ashlee Nelson gave birth to baby boys just two hours apart at the same hospital in Akron, Ohio. Aimee, who went into labor five days early, gave birth to son Donavyn at 12.11 p.m. on December 31, 2012, and Ashlee's son Aiden followed at 2.03 p.m.

barbie ticket Two young sisters from American Fork, Utah, left their 2-ft-high (60-cm), pink toy Barbie car on the road outside their house overnight and woke up in the morning to find police officers had given them a friendly "abandoned vehicle" ticket.

virtual assistant Brent Council in London, England, spent £12,000 ($19,000) replacing its front desk receptionist at the town hall with a hologram called Shanice.

glowing coin In 2012, the Royal Canadian Mint released a 25-cent coin that featured a dinosaur with a glow-in-the-dark skeleton.

SHEEP CABINET

→ If counting sheep is supposed to help you sleep, this bedside table made from a stuffed, dead sheep could be the perfect gift for wealthy insomniacs.

It's the work of Spanish artist Oscar Tusquets, who has turned the corpses of 21 sheep into items of furniture, complete with drawers. Each cabinet is priced at $82,000. His flock consists of 20 white sheep and one black sheep with white legs—a reference to the Catalan expression "a black sheep with white legs" to describe something that is impossible.

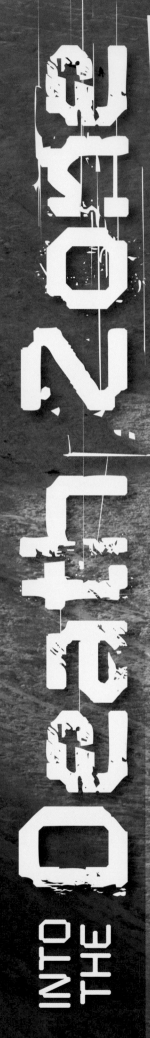

→ Towering 20 times the height of the Empire State Building, Mount Everest, the highest point on the planet, is home to one of the most unpredictable environments on Earth, experiencing temperatures plunging to –70°F (–57°C), and hurricane force winds.

More than 5,000 climbers are believed to have scaled the 29,029-ft (8,848-m) summit, yet despite modern techniques and hi-tech equipment, the mountain is still a lethal place for humans, posing terrible threats of avalanches, falling ice and frostbite. Since the first recorded attempt on the mountain in 1922, hundreds of climbers have lost their lives trying to climb Everest. A 2006 study found that for every ten climbers that reach the top, one dies.

Despite the risks, climbing Everest is more popular than ever, and when there is a window of good weather there can be hundreds of mountaineers making the climb at the same time. There are worries that the numbers are making the trip even more dangerous—causing bottlenecks, lines, tangled ropes, and even arguments between climbers. Any time wasted on the mountain uses up vital oxygen and energy, and increases the risk of being caught out by the weather—climbers are advised to turn around if they haven't reached the summit by 2 p.m. on their final day, as deadly storms can close in suddenly in the afternoon.

EARLY PIONEERS

When George Mallory was asked why he wanted to climb Mount Everest, the British mountaineer replied, "Because it's there." Mallory wanted to be the first to conquer Everest, and made three attempts. The first, in 1922, was without oxygen tanks; then, in 1924, he made his final ascent, with Andrew Irvine. They climbed in clothing that offered little protection against the cold, but this time they took oxygen. A member of their team spotted them less than 2,000 ft (610 m) from the summit, but Mallory and Irvine never returned to camp. In 1999, Mallory's frozen remains were discovered at 26,760 ft (8,157 m), leaving the question of whether or not he and Irvine reached the summit unanswered.

the death zone

→ When climbing Everest, any time wasted in the "death zone"—over 26,250 ft (8,000 m)—can be life-threatening. At this altitude the air contains only 30 percent as much oxygen as at sea level, and the lack of oxygen makes breathing hard and leads to lethargy, loss of appetite and mental confusion. Those suffering from this severe altitude sickness have been described as having no idea where they are or how they got there. In extreme cases, the brain can swell and induce a coma. If a climber encounters difficulties in the death zone and cannot continue, then it is extremely risky for others to attempt a rescue. Congestion in the death zone was blamed for the deaths of six climbers in one weekend in 2012.

lincoln hall

➔ In May 2006, the experienced Australian mountaineer Lincoln Hall was descending from the summit when he was struck down with altitude sickness. His brain began to swell and his climbing companions were forced to leave him for dead at 28,200 ft (8,600 m). He spent the night alone, hallucinating, but incredibly he survived until the morning, when a group of ascending climbers found him sitting in the snow, suffering from severe frostbite. They abandoned their ascent in order to save his life. Had he not been found, he would have been the 12th climber to die on Everest that year.

A traffic jam at 29,000 ft (8,839 m). Climbers wait to ascend the Hillary Step in 2012, just 30 feet (9 m) from the summit. Four climbers died on this day in 2012. Mountaineers have suggested fixing a ladder to the step to accommodate the increasing numbers of climbers.

A line of climbers makes it way up the Lhotse Face, 25,000 ft (7,620 m) up the mountain.

GRIM MARKER

Today's climbers must walk past gruesome reminders of the perils they face. Climbers rarely remove bodies from the mountain owing to the extreme conditions, and retrieval by helicopter is impossible as the thin air prevents flying above 23,000 ft (7,000 m). So, bodies can remain where they fell for decades, preserved by the cold. One such grisly landmark is the body of Indian climber Tsewang Paljor, which has lain at 28,000 ft (8,534 m) since 1996. Known as "Green Boots," he is visible on a well-used route on the North Col ascent.

▲ In 2001, Frenchman Marco Siffredi became the first man to snowboard from the top of Everest, riding 17,400 ft (5,300 m) down to base camp. He disappeared the following year while attempting a second Everest descent.

▲ Extreme temperatures on Everest can cause "Khumbu cough," when cold air freezes the lungs and results in a cough so violent it can break ribs.

▲ Everest climbers lose an average of 22 lb (10 kg) of bodyweight, as the ascent and descent consume huge amounts of energy, and the thin air at high altitudes makes it hard to process food.

▲ The Tibetans call the peak Chomolungma, and the Nepalese call it Sagarmatha. The name Everest comes from the British surveyor and geographer Sir George Everest.

▲ Climbing Everest is not cheap—a license to climb from the Nepalese authorities costs $25,000, and a fully guided expedition can be as much as $100,000.

FIRST TO THE TOP

At 11.30 a.m. on May 29, 1953, Edmund Hillary and the Sherpa Tenzing Norgay became the first men to step foot on the top of Mount Everest. Their ascent took seven weeks but, after spending 15 minutes at the summit, they returned to base camp in three days. Just over 50 years later, in 2004, Sherpa Pemba Dorje climbed the mountain in 8 hours and 10 minutes. Hillary's son Peter has climbed Everest five times.

33

A DYEING TRADITION

→ Ohaguro is an ancient Vietnamese and Japanse tradition in where married women, and some men, dye their teeth black for protection against evil spirits.

The tradition was widely practiced from prehistoric times up until the mid-19th century, and some women still perform Ohaguro today.

The lacquer used in teeth-blackening prevented tooth decay, much like a modern-day dental sealant and, by using it, women could keep a full set of teeth all their lives. Ancient human remains reveal skeletons with all their teeth—albeit dyed black—proving the practice to be more medically beneficial than you might expect.

Dyeing teeth black was a way not only to ward off evil spirits, but also to ensure you yourself were not mistaken for an evil spirit—who were said to have sharp, white teeth. This distinctive blackened look, which was seen as beautiful, became part of Vietnamese women's identity and a way for them to distinguish themselves from the Chinese, who kept their teeth white.

tooth currency Dolphin teeth have been used as currency in the Solomon Islands for centuries. They are preferred to paper notes and it is still common for a Solomon Islander to be able to purchase a bride using dolphin teeth.

algae power For six months, an apartment complex in Hamburg, Germany, was powered entirely by algae. Fed via a water circuit, the algae was grown in a series of panels mounted onto the sun-facing sides of the building. When ready to be harvested, it was turned into a pulp that was processed at a biogas plant to create renewable energy.

sticky structure Measuring a huge 490 x 230 ft (150 x 70 m) and standing 85 ft (26 m) tall, the Metropol Parasol in Seville, Spain, is the world's largest wooden building— and is held together entirely by glue.

no sweat! A customary farewell among the Kanum-Irebe people of New Guinea is to stick a finger in a person's armpit, sniff the finger and rub the scent on themselves.

school site There has been a public school on the site where Shishi High School in Chengdu, China, now stands—for more than 2,100 years.

deer goggles The Inuit people of the Arctic traditionally made snow goggles from carved caribou bones and sinew.

living cemetery Owing to a shortage of housing, more than 6,000 people live among the dead as squatters in the North Cemetery of the Philippines capital, Manila. Wooden and corrugated iron shacks are perched on top of hundreds of stacked tombs and the 133-acre (54-ha) site has sprouted fast-food stalls, karaoke parlors and Internet cafés, while still staging up to 80 funerals a day.

TRAMPOLINE ROAD

→ Visitors to the 2012 Archstoyanie Art Festival in Nikola-Lenivets, Russia, were able to bounce along a 170-ft-long (52-m) trampoline road built through the middle of a forest. Made from reinforced rubber, the road, called Fast Track, was designed by a team of Estonian architects who wanted to explore new and fun ways of getting from one place to another.

RIPLEY'S RESEARCH

To achieve the dyed black teeth of the Ohaguro tradition, the mouth first needs to be sanitized. This is done by brushing the teeth and picking them clean with a dried betel nut before scrubbing them with powdered coal mixed with salt. Next, the day before the dyeing, the person chews a lemon and holds it in his or her mouth before rinsing out the mouth with rice wine to erode the tooth enamel. The dyeing is then completed with a dark brown solution called *kanemizu*, which is made by dissolving iron filings in vinegar. To finish off, the person rinses out the mouth with fish sauce.

DANGEROUS WALKWAYS

DEADLY CROSSING

➜ A group of Indonesian schoolchildren risked their lives by tiptoeing their way across a collapsed suspension bridge over a swollen river to reach their school in the village of Sanghiang Tanjung until a new bridge could be built. The 530-ft-long (162-m) bridge collapsed in January 2012 as a result of flooding, but the children still decided to take the dangerous route on a daily basis as the alternative was a 3-mi (5-km) walk to school.

SOLITARY LIFE

➜ Maxime Qavtaradze, a 60-year-old monk, has lived in solitude at the top of the 131-ft-high (40-m) Katskhi Pillar in Georgia for more than 20 years—and has to have food winched up to him by his followers. He leaves the limestone pillar only twice a week to pray, a precarious ladder descent that takes him 20 minutes. Luckily, as a former crane driver, he has a head for heights. When he first moved in, the accommodation was so basic that he had to sleep in an old fridge.

SEE-THROUGH PATH

➜ You really need a head for heights to take on this new Chinese tourist attraction—a 200-ft-long (60-m), 3-ft-wide (0.9-m) glass path built high on the side of Tianmen Mountain. There is just 2½ in (6.4 cm) of glass between you and a sheer drop of 4,700 ft (1,433 m) to the ground below. Cleaners are obviously not keen to work on the path, so tourists are asked to put on shoe covers before setting off in order to help keep the walkway from getting dirty.

DON'T LOOK DOWN

➜ Daredevil tourists in Shaanxi Province, China, line up for the chance to walk along a treacherous 12-in-wide (30-cm) pathway built on the side of a vertical cliff and with a sheer drop of hundreds of feet into the valley below. They must wear a special safety harness to navigate this section of the 700-year-old Chang Kong Cliff Road, which is made of wooden boards just wide enough for a footstep.

STAIRWAY TO HEAVEN

➜ To give Chinese tourists the thrill of mountaineering without the danger, this 300-ft-high (90-m) spiral staircase has been installed on the wall of the Taihang Mountains in Linzhou. Climbers, who must be under 60 and have no history of heart problems, are often subjected to a battering from the wind, rain and passing birds as they twist and turn their way to the top.

Underwater Park

➡ Summer divers at Grüner See (Green Lake) in Styria, Austria, find things they would not expect at the bottom of most lakes, such as grassy meadows, flowerbeds, paved paths, benches and a bridge.

In winter, the lake is only 6½ ft (2 m) deep and the surrounding area is a country park, but in spring the snow on the surrounding mountains melts, causing the whole area to fill with melt water. By summer, the lake is 40 ft (12 m) deep and the park is submerged. The underwater grass and foliage make the water appear a beautiful emerald green, giving the lake its name.

high pressure At the bottom of the deepest point on Earth, the Mariana Trench in the Pacific Ocean, the water pressure is equivalent to an elephant wearing high heels and standing on your head.

cemetery bones Heavy rain in January 2013 caused human bones from the cemetery at St. Mary's Church, Whitby, England, to be washed down the cliff into the town. The scattered bones were gathered up and reburied in the 900-year-old cemetery, which was used by author Bram Stoker as the setting for his novel *Dracula*.

church skaters Every day between December 16 and 24, streets in Caracas, Venezuela, are closed to traffic until 8 a.m. so that people can rollerskate to church for a traditional early morning service called Misa de Aguinaldo. Before children go to bed during this period, they tie one end of a piece of string to their big toe and hang the other end out of the window of their house. The next morning, passing skaters tug on any string they see to remind the children to get up for church.

hanging parts The Igreja Nosso Senhor do Bonfim—a church in Salvador, Brazil—has a Room of Miracles where wax or plastic replicas of body parts, including arms, feet, heads, hearts, spines and breasts, that represent people who have been cured over the centuries, hang from the ceiling.

no island Sandy Island—midway between Australia and New Caledonia—was charted on marine charts and world maps for more than a century, but when scientists from the University of Sydney went to check it out in November 2012, they found clear water and no sign of any island. Sandy Island was quickly removed from National Geographic Society and Google maps.

the eruption that never was

→ On the bright morning of April 1, 1974, the townspeople of Sitka, Alaska, awoke to see the snow-covered peak of their local volcano, Mount Edgecumbe, spewing a plume of thick black smoke. The volcano had been dormant for thousands of years and panic started to spread. A coastguard helicopter was summoned to take a closer look and what the pilot saw made him cry with laughter. A pile of 70 rubber tires was burning fiercely and spray-painted in the snow in huge letters were the words, "April Fool." A local prankster and his friends had spent years planning the practical joke, patiently waiting for exactly the right April Fool's Day weather conditions to make Mount Edgecombe "erupt."

snoring museum In The German town of Alfeld there is a museum dedicated to snoring. Doctor Josef Alexander Wirth has collected more than 400 devices and medications used to cure snoring, including nosepins, electroshock machines, leather chinstraps with attached mouth coverings, and heavy cannonballs that were sewn into the insides of snoring soldiers' uniforms during the American Revolutionary War to prevent the snoring soldiers turning onto their backs and disturbing the rest of the men with their noise.

seaweed rain It rained seaweed over the village of Berkeley in Gloucestershire, England, in August 2012. Residents collected entire bucket loads of the green slime from their gardens after a freak twister had swept up the debris from a beach 20 mi (32 km) away and then deposited it on the village.

caffeine pollution Water tested by scientists off the coast of Oregon has been found to contain high levels of caffeine. High rainfall can cause sewage pipes to overflow so that human waste is flushed out into the ocean—and the region is noted for its population's love of coffee.

green policy To make people feel more positive and convince them that spring was just around the corner, officials in Chengdu, China, gave nature a helping hand by painting the city's grass green in February 2013. Locals spotted the trick when they walked on the grass and paint came off on their shoes.

prison hotel People are paying to stay in one of Holland's most feared prisons—after it was converted into a luxury hotel. The 150 cells at Het Arresthuis have been stylishly transformed into 36 spacious rooms and seven suites. The establishment has been voted the best hotel in the town of Roermond.

cow stampede At the centuries-old Ekadashi religious festival in Madhya Pradesh, India, dozens of male villagers volunteer to lie on the ground and wait to be trampled upon by a herd of rampaging cows.

WINE FIGHT

→ Every year on June 29, thousands of people climb a mountain near Haro, Spain, to take part in a three-hour mass wine fight. For the La Batalla de Vino de Haro event, which dates back 300 years, trucks are filled with thousands of gallons of red wine. With around a gallon (4 l) of wine allocated per person, the combatants proceed to soak each other using water pistols, buckets, hollowed-out gourds and even old boots. All participants start out wearing white shirts, but by the end of the evening the whole town is a lighter shade of grape.

MAN LEAVES TAP RUNNING FOR THREE MONTHS

■ Have you ever wondered what would happen if you left the tap running at home? Well, this spectacular waterfall was created accidentally by a Chinese man who decided to leave his hot tap on all winter! The last remaining resident in a building due for demolition in Jilin City, China, Wen Hsu was worried that uninsulated water pipes running up through the empty apartments below him would freeze, leaving his seventh-floor home without running water. So, to make sure the temperature remained above freezing, he switched on the tap and then diverted the warm water to flow down the side of the building, where it promptly froze, turning it into a giant icicle.

heat blast The Sun's core is so hot that a piece the size of a pinhead would emit enough heat to kill a person 100 mi (160 km) away.

robot jellyfish A 5-ft-long (1.5-m) robot jellyfish is to patrol U.S. coasts with a view to mapping ocean floors, studying marine life and monitoring ocean currents. Developed by a College of Engineering team from Virginia Tech, battery-powered Cyro has electric motors that enable it to swim underwater just like a real jellyfish.

mud day The Westland suburb of Detroit, Michigan, hosts an annual Mud Day where hundreds of children wallow and play in a giant pit containing more than 200 tons of dirt mixed with 16,700 gal (76,000 l) of water. Events include mud limbo, wheelbarrow races and the contest to crown the King and Queen of Mud.

big nickel Since 1964, a 30-ft-high (9-m) Canadian nickel has stood on the grounds of the Dynamic Earth Museum in Greater Sudbury, Ontario—a big nickel–mining city.

stag calls Elvis Afanasenko won the 2012 World Bolving Championships, held in Exmoor, England, where competitors imitate the bellowing sounds made by rutting red deer stags. A four-time winner, his mimicry is so accurate that his mating calls are returned by jealous stags out in the wild.

gun law Military-age men in Switzerland are each issued a gun to keep at home in case the country is ever invaded.

nerves of steel The Stairway to Nothingness, a new Austrian tourist attraction, allows visitors with a head for heights to walk down 14 steps to a glass-bottomed platform perched 1,300 ft (400 m) directly above the Dachstein glacier.

wild ride The Texas SkyScreamer swing ride, which opened at the Six Flags Over Texas theme park in San Antonio on May 26, 2013, towers 400 ft (120 m) above ground and swings riders in a 124-ft (38-m) circle at speeds of 35 mph (56 km/h).

ship shed A wooden shed, 30-ft-long (9-m), 15-ft-high (4.5-m), in the shape of the H.M.S. Victory, Admiral Nelson's flagship at the Battle of Trafalgar in 1805, was built in Clare Kapma-Saunders garden in Southampton, England.

rat catchers Authorities in the South African township of Alexandra, Johannesburg, offer a free cell phone to any citizen who catches 60 rats.

swallowed gems A 25-year-old man, arrested as he waited to board a plane from Johannesburg, South Africa, to Dubai, had swallowed 220 diamonds worth $2.3 million in an attempt to smuggle them out of the country.

too old Mzee Julius Wanyondu Gatonga was told in 2012 that he could not receive Kenyan medical insurance coverage because his I.D. showed that he was 128 years old and the computer system only recognizes birthdates after 1890, six years after he was apparently born. If his date of birth is genuine, it would make him the oldest person to have ever lived.

christmas babies In 2012, Hamima Juma from Coventry, England, gave birth to her second Christmas Day baby in three years, defying odds of more than 130,000-to-one. Both daughters had a due date of December 19.

british invasion There are only 22 countries in the world that Britain has not invaded—Guatemala, Bolivia, Paraguay, Sweden, Liechtenstein, Luxembourg, Belarus, Andorra, Monaco, Vatican City, São Tomé and Príncipe, Uzbekistan, Mongolia, Kyrgyzstan, Tajikistan, Mali, Ivory Coast, Chad, Central African Republic, Burundi, Republic of Congo, and the Marshall Islands.

FAT PIG → With a pineapple in its mouth, a sacrificed pig—the unlucky winner of a fattest pig festival—is paraded outside the Tsuhsih Temple in Sanxia, Taiwan. The temple holds an annual "Pigs of God" contest to raise the fattest pig, with the 2013 victor weighing 2,112 lb (960 kg).

Eye Popping

➔ A Sufi holy man pokes his own eye with a sharp object during the annual Urs religious festival in Ajmer, India. Each year, thousands of Sufi devotees from different parts of India take part in a procession to mark the death of Sufi saint Khwaja Moinuddin Chishti and some show their devotion by performing eye-watering feats such as this, using pointed knives, sticks and spears to make their eyeballs protrude alarmingly.

Indiana Bones and the Jeweled Skeletons

➔ **Thousands of 400-year-old human skeletons, each adorned in gold, silver and precious gems, were hidden away in church vaults, storage units and containers all over Europe before being recently discovered by Paul Koudounaris, a Los Angeles historian dubbed "Indiana Bones."**

The skeletons were dug up from Roman catacombs in the 16th century and, on the orders of the Vatican, were given fictitious names and certificates identifying them as early Christian martyrs. They were then sent to Catholic churches in Germany, Austria and Switzerland to replace religious relics that had been destroyed in the wake of the Protestant Reformation.

There, the skeletons were dressed in ornate costumes and lavishly decorated, mostly by nuns because such was their supposed status they could be handled only by someone who had taken a sacred vow to the church. Some corpses took five years to decorate with hundreds of sparkling jewels and several pounds of gold and silver. The jewels alone are worth thousands of dollars.

Many were true works of art. To construct the relic of St. Deodatus in Rheinau, Switzerland, a wax face was molded over the upper half of the skull and a fabric wrap was used to create a mouth in order to make the corpse look more lifelike.

Known as the Catacomb Saints, they became holy shrines even though none of them had actually been canonized. In fact, few of the skeletons are thought to have belonged to anyone of religious significance.

By the 19th century, the fake saints had been exposed and were considered an embarrassment to the Catholic Church. Most of them were removed from display, stripped of their honors and locked away in containers for safe keeping. There they remained, largely forgotten, until Paul Koudounaris found their secret hideaways during his three-year trawl of European churches and ossuaries. He hunted down and photographed dozens of the skeletons to tell the amazing story of the jewel-encrusted skeletons of the Catholic Church.

The skull of "St. Deodatus" was covered with wax and given fake eyes and a veil to make it appear more lifelike.

The skeletal gold-encrusted hand of St. Valentin, or St. Valentine, was found in Bad Schussenreid, Germany. There have been eleven St. Valentines recognized by the Catholic Church, but the one that the Church believes to be the real St. Valentine resides in Terni, Italy.

The jewel-encrusted relic skeleton of St. Benedictus was found in the church of St. Michael in Munich, Germany.

ALIEN ISLAND → Described as "the most alien place on Earth" on account of its sci-fi landscape, the remote island of Socotra in the Indian Ocean has examples of a plant species that is 20 million years old. The island, which was separated from mainland Africa some seven million years ago, is home to 800 rare species of flora and fauna, a third of which cannot be seen anywhere else on the planet. The trees and plants, including the dragon's blood tree, whose red resin was used in medieval magic, have evolved to adapt to the hot, dry climate. Although Socotra has some 40,000 inhabitants, its first roads were built just a few years ago.

thawed moss Catherine La Farge, a biologist at the University of Alberta, collected some frozen moss that had been buried under the ice in northern Canada for 400 years and brought it back to life in her laboratory.

instant freeze Temperatures fell to –58°F (–50°C) in Siberia in December 2012. It was so cold that when a man in Novosibirsk threw a pot of boiling water from his balcony on one of the top floors of an apartment block, the water turned into a shower of frozen droplets.

mighty mississippi An amazing 7,000 rivers feed into the Mississippi, giving it a vast catchment area of around 1.15 million sq mi (2.98 million sq km), roughly 37 percent of the land area of the continental U.S.A.

acid soil Pollution from 19th-century factories has left Bleaklow Moor, east of Manchester, England, with peat soil that is more acidic than lemon juice.

saturn storm On December 5, 2010, a storm was detected on Saturn that quickly grew to eight times larger than the entire surface of planet Earth.

pumice island An island of floating pumice measuring 300 mi (482 km) long and 30 mi (48 km) wide—larger than the area of Israel—was spotted off the coast of New Zealand in 2012. The island was probably spewed to the surface by an underwater volcano, as pumice forms when volcanic lava cools rapidly.

MOUNTAIN MIRRORS

→ Located in the shadow of the Gaustatoppen Mountain, the Norwegian town of Rjukan never saw any sunlight in winter until, in 2013, three 183-sq-ft (17-sq-m) computer-controlled mirrors were placed on top of a nearby peak to redirect winter light and keep the town square bathed in sunlight during the day.

diamond planet Astronomers have discovered a planet twice the size of Earth and made largely of diamond. The surface of 55 Cancri e, some 40 light years from Earth, is thought to be covered in graphite and diamond with temperatures there reaching 3,900°F (2,149°C). The rocky planet orbits so fast that a year there lasts only 18 hours.

nice view A restroom on the 18th floor of New York City's Standard Hotel has 10-ft (3-m), floor-to-ceiling windows, which gives users amazing views of the Manhattan skyline, but also enables them to be seen on the toilet by people in other blocks or on the street below!

twisted tower The 75-story Cayan Tower in Dubai has a twist of 90 degrees from top to bottom so that residents in the lower part have views of Dubai Marina while those on the upper floors face the Persian Gulf. The concrete structure's columns rotate by just over a degree as they ascend from floor to floor.

Some of Rjukan's 3,500 inhabitants gaze up at the sunlight reflected by the mirrors, a scheme that ensures the town will no longer be totally without sunlight for six months a year.

The three giant mirrors that perch on top of a 1,300-ft-high (400-m) mountain have finally brought winter sunlight to Rjukan.

An ice-encrusted truck. The fire at the site was so intense that its heat and smoke even showed up on weather radar systems.

A Chicago firefighter becomes encased in ice while he tackles the fire. A third of the city's firefighters were on the scene at some point.

FREEZING FIRE

→ When a huge vacant warehouse on Chicago's South Side went up in flames on the night of January 22, 2013, freezing temperatures meant that the water spray from the firefighters' hoses encased everything in ice—including the building itself, trucks and even the crews.

Attended by more than 200 firefighters, the fire was the city's biggest blaze in seven years and was still smoldering 19 hours after it started, by which time the firefighters had inadvertently created an eerie winter wonderland.

Millions of gallons of water were pumped onto the burning building, but it froze instantly, turning the old warehouse into an ice castle.

ROCKET FESTIVAL →
Visitors to the Yanshui Beehive Rockets Festival in Taiwan wear protective helmets to protect themselves from the tens of thousands of firecrackers that are set off simultaneously. The nearby streets are left covered with so much firework debris that the asphalt is barely visible. The festival dates back to 1885 when people used fireworks to drive away a deadly cholera epidemic.

near miss On February 29, 2012, a real-life tornado came within 40 ft (12 m) of the Ripley's Believe It or Not! Odditorium in Branson, Missouri—a building deliberately designed to look like it has been hit by an earthquake! The 1,200-ft-wide (366-m) tornado tore the roof from the motel next door but, believe it or not, spared the Odditorium, the distinctive crumbling façade of which has made it a hugely popular building to be photographed. The unique building was erected in 1999 to commemorate the massive 1812 Missouri earthquake, which made the Mississippi River run backward for three days and made church bells ring in Philadelphia, nearly 1,000 mi (1,600 km) away.

long cables The cables of the iconic Golden Gate Bridge in San Francisco, California, are made from more than 80,000 mi (129,000 km) of steel wire.

fat blockage A 16-ton lump of festering food fat was found blocking an underground sewer in London, England, in 2013. The "fatberg," which was the weight of a double-decker bus, was so big it reduced the sewer to just five percent of its normal capacity and it took workers using a high-pressure jet hose three weeks to blast it away. The congealed mass was first discovered when residents complained that their toilets would not flush.

rat battle At the Festival of Dead Rats, held annually in El Puig, Spain, revelers hit a *cucaña*—a type of decorated container—that is filled with frozen rat corpses. When it breaks open, they hurl the dead rodents at each other. The mock battle dates back to when the *cucaña*s were filled with fruit, and rats that had infiltrated them were bludgeoned to death by festival-goers and thrown about the square.

smoked bodies Tribes in Papua New Guinea, Indonesia, preserve the bodies of respected relatives by smoking the corpses over a fire. The smoked corpses are then suspended in a bamboo frame, carried up a sacred mountain and placed on wooden poles so that they look out over the village hundreds of feet below.

tiny chapel The Cross Island Chapel in Oneida, New York State, sits in the middle of a pond and, with a floor space of 28 sq ft (2.6 sq m), seats only two people. For weddings, there is room only for the minister, bride and groom—the rest of the wedding party have to anchor outside in small boats.

office tree The office building of Cove Auto Towing and Recovery in Astoria, New York, was built around a living tree, which now grows right through the roof to a height of 50 ft (15 m).

PINK PIPES

→ These artistic-looking pink pipes snake through the center of Berlin, Germany, for more than 40 mi (60 km), disappearing around corners, looping above intersections, diving into bushes and suddenly appearing out of treetops. It's no wonder many of the city's residents are mystified by them. In fact they are water pipes, which, because Berlin is built on a swamp, suck water up from land being used for new building projects and pump it into rivers and canals. They twist and turn to combat thermal expansion and breakage in freezing temperatures, and were painted pink on the advice of a psychologist who said that children, young people and the young at heart really like this color.

FAT CONTEST

→ For six months, young men from the Bodi tribe, who live in southern Ethiopia's Omo Valley, gorge on only a stomach-churning drink made from cow's blood and milk in order to get fat and almost double their weight.

The area's scorching heat means that the men must drink the half-gallon (2-l) bowls quickly before the mixture coagulates. At the end of the six months, the men show off their bloated stomachs in a New Year's competition, where the fattest is declared the winner and is feted as a hero for life by the rest of the tribe. The cows, which are sacred to the Bodi, are not killed to provide the blood for the ritual. Instead it is taken by making a hole in a vein with a spear or an axe, then the wound is sealed with clay.

kitty kindergarten
The Kindergarten Wolfartsweier building in Karlsruhe, Germany, is constructed in the shape of a cat. Children enter by the mouth and exit by the cat's tail, which takes the form of a slide. The classrooms and dining room are in the cat's belly.

boeing home
Bruce Campbell lives in woods near Hillsboro, Oregon, in a Boeing 727 jet airplane that he spent over a decade converting into a home. He bought the plane for $100,000 and now uses the cockpit as a reading room, complete with a newly installed computer in the middle of the instrument panel.

professional sleeper
The Hotel Finn in Helsinki, Finland, advertised in 2013 for a "professional sleeper" to stay as a guest for 35 days, testing the hotel's rooms and writing an Internet blog about the experience.

pellet spit
In the traditional South African game of Bokdrol Spoeg, competitors spit lumps of antelope poop as far as they can. A poop pellet of an impala or kudu is first placed in a shot glass that has been filled with alcohol to sterilize some of the bacteria. Then the player downs the shot, catches the pellet in his teeth and spits it as far as possible—sometimes up to 50 ft (15 m) away.

high rider
Ethan Schlussler from Sandpoint, Idaho, can ride his bicycle up a tree. Tired of climbing a ladder to reach his 30-ft-high (9-m) tree house, he devised a bicycle-powered, pulley-system elevator, which allows him to pedal up in under 30 seconds. He uses an old water tank as the counterweight, adjusting it by adding or removing water.

false economy
Liechtenstein, which is the sixth smallest country in the world, is in fact the world's largest producer of sausage casings and of false teeth.

judge bean
The Efik people of Nigeria traditionally used the highly toxic calabar bean in criminal trials—if you died after eating the bean, you were said to be guilty.

native language
Indigenous peoples of Paraguay account for only about five percent of the population, but their Guarani language is spoken by about 90 percent of the people. This makes Paraguay the only country in the Americas where an indigenous language is spoken by a majority of the population.

47

RAINBOW TRUNK → After shedding their bark, these rainbow eucalyptus trees on Kauai, Hawaii, resemble brilliantly colored works of art. The trees shed patches of bark at different times throughout the year to reveal a bright green layer beneath. This inner bark then darkens and matures into vivid shades of orange, blue and purple.

tree protest Australian environmental campaigner Miranda Gibson spent 449 days living at the top of a 200-ft-high (60-m) eucalyptus tree in Tasmania in a protest against logging. She climbed the tree in December 2011 and stayed there until March 2013 when smoke from a bushfire forced her to come down.

oldest water Water found pouring out of boreholes 1½ mi (2.4 km) below ground at a remote copper and zinc mine in Timmins, Ontario, has been trapped there for as much as 2.64 billion years, making it the oldest free-flowing water discovered anywhere in the world.

great survivor A spiderwort plant has been growing inside a bottle without air or water for more than 40 years. David Latimer of Surrey, England, planted it inside a large globular bottle in 1960 to find out whether it could flourish in a self-contained environment. It had its second and last drink in 1972, after which he sealed the bottle neck with a bung that has not been removed since.

glass rain On a planet known as HD 189733b, located 63 light years from Earth, it rains glass particles, sideways, in howling 4,500-mph (7,240-km/h) winds. The distant planet's atmosphere reaches a scorching temperature of 2,000°F (1,093°C) and the glass rain gives it a blue color.

tree tuggers In 2012, residents of League City, Texas, decided to move a 100-year-old, 518,000-lb (235,000-kg) oak tree to a new location rather than cut it down. Using heavy machinery, it took ten hours to transplant the tree a quarter of a mile away to make way for a road-widening project.

new language Scientists in 2013 discovered a new language in northern Australia. Called Light Warlpiri, it blends elements of several other languages and is spoken by only about 300 people in a remote desert community 346 mi (557 km) from the town of Katherine in the Northern Territory.

underground hotel A 19-story hotel being built near Shanghai, China, will have 16 of its floors below ground level, up to 300 ft (90 m) beneath the Earth's surface. The 380-room InterContinental Shimao Shanghai Wonderland is being built into the side of an abandoned quarry and will feature an underwater restaurant and a 33-ft-deep (10-m) aquarium.

time zones The tiny island of Märket in the Baltic Sea is only 1,000 x 260 ft (300 x 80 m) in area—yet it has two time zones. Sweden and Finland each own half of the island, so one half keeps to Swedish time and the other to Finnish time, which is one hour ahead.

foam storm Residents of Mooloolaba in Queensland, Australia, woke on the morning of January 28, 2013, to find the beach town covered in up to 10 ft (3 m) of foam. Rough weather had whipped up the foam from the ocean and then carried it ashore.

dry island There are no rivers, streams or lakes on the 122-sq-mi (316-sq-km) Mediterranean island of Malta.

ALGAE SEA

→ Visitors to a beach in Qingdao, China, in 2013 romped in thousands of tons of thick green algae. Luckily the algae—*Enteromorpha prolifera*, or sea lettuce—is harmless, edible and rich in nutrients that are said to improve skin and lower blood pressure. Even so, 20,000 tons of the algae were removed in just a few days because if left to decompose and rot, it could produce large amounts of highly toxic hydrogen sulfide gas. It is not the first time the beach has suffered a green invasion. In 2008, the area was swamped by 20 sq mi (52 sq km) of algae, but 10,000 volunteers cleared it so that Qingdao could host the Beijing Olympics sailing events.

gold nugget In 2013, an Australian amateur prospector in Ballarat, Victoria, unearthed a massive gold nugget weighing 12 lb (5.5 kg) and worth an estimated $315,000. It is one of the biggest nuggets ever found in the area in the 162 years since Ballarat's original gold rush.

martian twinning The remote village of Glenelg in the Scottish Highlands has been twinned with its namesake on Mars—a rocky valley 140 million mi (225 million km) away.

hidden house Following 60-mph (96-km/h) winds in the region, Josh Pitman of Midland, Texas, found that his house was almost completely obscured by hundreds of tumbleweeds stacked on top of each other.

lightning strikes Alexander Mandón from Sampués, Colombia, was struck by lightning four times in six months and survived each strike. Believing he must be positively charged to attract lightning, local healers had him buried neck deep in the ground in an attempt to draw out the charge from his body.

RIPLEY'S RESEARCH

The underwater bubbles occur in the winter when the lake is completely covered in ice that's about 10 in (25 cm) thick. Plants on the lakebed release methane gas, which then freezes as it rises toward the cold surface. Where the gas is allowed to escape through a hole in the ice, the methane is highly flammable.

Methane Bubbles

➜ **Each winter, man-made Abraham Lake on Canada's North Saskatchewan River is host to a rare natural phenomenon—stacks of huge underwater ice bubbles composed of trapped methane gas.**

Released by plants, the gas bubbles are frozen in time and place, and keep stacking up for as long as the lake remains solid—until the spring thaw.

WORLD WAR I

➜ On July 28, 1914, World War I began. It involved more than 20 countries and extended from France to Russia to the Middle East and to naval battles in the Atlantic Ocean and the North Sea. By the time the war ended on November 11, 1918, 70 million soldiers had been mobilized, of which one in seven had been killed. A total of 16.6 million people, including civilians, were killed and the war had claimed 1 percent of the global population.

hard hats When World War I began in 1914, none of the countries involved issued protective steel helmets to their troops.

forgotten land Andorra declared war on Germany during World War I but wasn't included in the 1919 Treaty of Versailles that ended the war. It didn't sign a peace treaty with Germany until September 25, 1939.

war horses More than 16 million horses were used in the war, and it's estimated that half of them died. Britain used so many horses at the Western Front, more than one million, that there was a shortage in England, and circus elephants were enlisted to plow fields and pull heavy machinery for the war effort.

foot soldiers During the 1915 Battle of Loos, France, members of the 1st Battalion London Irish Rifles kicked a football during a charge on German positions. Before they could score a goal on the enemy trench, a piece of barbed wire deflated the ball on the German front line.

field medicine Army doctors applied garlic to wounds to stop gangrene and septic poisoning.

battle movies Scenes in the French movie *J'Accuse* (1919) were filmed in the middle of the Battle of Saint-Mihiel. In 1917, filmmaker D.W. Griffith also went to the French front to film his movie, *Hearts of the World*.

home front American women donated their corsets to the war effort, contributing 28,000 tons of steel—enough metal to build two battleships!

ambulance artists The writers Ernest Hemingway and Somerset Maugham, and the composers Maurice Ravel and Ralph Vaughan Williams, all drove military ambulances for the Allies.

war writers English fantasy authors and friends C.S. Lewis and J.R.R. Tolkien both survived the Battle of the Somme in World War I.

indestructible officer Legendary British officer Sir Adrian Carton de Wiart was injured eight times during the war, including being shot in the head at the Battle of the Somme and in the hip at Passchendaele. He removed his own fingers after being shot in the hand at Ypres because a doctor refused to amputate. He had previously been injured in the Boer War (1899–1902) in South Africa and lost an eye fighting in Somalia. He went on to fight in, and survive, World War II, despite being taken prisoner. He died in 1963. When writing about his experiences in World War I, he revealed, "Frankly, I enjoyed it."

plastic pioneer In 1917, the physician Sir Harold Gillies performed the first plastic surgery on British sailor Walter Yeo after his face was burned in the Battle of Jutland.

own sinking The German Navy—captured and interned in Scapa Flow, Scotland, at the end of the war in November 1918—sank 52 of its own ships in June 1919 to prevent the Allies from using them. Many of the ships were later raised and sold for scrap, but some still remain on the seabed.

squawking sentries During World War I, parrots were kept on the Eiffel Tower in Paris, France, to warn of approaching German aircraft. Owing to their acute sense of hearing, the birds could detect enemy planes long before they came into the range of human lookouts.

frozen combat Austrian and Italian troops fought battles in the mountains and glaciers of the Alps. In recent years, melting glaciers have revealed the frozen remains of soldiers who have been on the mountains for almost a century.

paris gun Germany's Paris Gun, a World-War-I artillery cannon, could bombard the French capital from 70 mi (112 km) away and could be fired so high that the Earth's rotation affected its trajectory.

christmas soccer During the Christmas of 1914, soldiers on the Western Front in World War I crossed lines to exchange presents and play soccer.

bird battalion More than 200,000 pigeons sent messages across enemy lines during World War 1. In 1918, a bird named Cher Ami carried a note that saved a U.S. battalion that was surrounded by Germans. She was shot by the enemy but continued to headquarters, where medics worked to save her life and fit her with a wooden leg. She was later stuffed and placed in the Smithsonian Institution in Washington D.C.

chemical warfare Mustard gas, a terrible chemical weapon that causes chemical burns, was first used in the war in 1917. After the war ended, studies of soldiers killed by the gas revealed that it may help fight cancer, and 30 years later a form of mustard gas was used as the first anti-cancer chemotherapy drug.

war hero Sergeant Alvin C. York was one of the most highly decorated U. S. soldiers of World War I. In 1918, he was part of a detachment that came under heavy fire when sent behind enemy lines to capture a machine gun nest. Alvin dodged bullets, killed 21 Germans singlehandedly and shocked the remaining enemy troops into surrender. He had silenced more than 30 German machine guns and captured 132 prisoners with just seven men. For his heroic actions he was promoted to Sergeant and awarded the Medal of Honor, as well as the French Legion of Honor and Croix de Guerre. He returned home in 1919 to a hero's welcome and a ticker tape parade in New York.

air war Zeppelins—giant, inflatable airships—were invented by German General Ferdinand von Zeppelin in 1900. The airships could be as long as 700 ft (213 m) and were capable of speeds of up to 80 mph (130 km/h). They were filled with flammable hydrogen gas inside the stitched intestines of thousands of cows. So many cows were needed for the airships—250,000 for a single Zeppelin—that sausages, also made with intestines, were banned in parts of Germany. German Zeppelins made 50 attacks over Britain during the war, bombing indiscriminately and killing hundreds of civilians. Their construction made them vulnerable to anti-aircraft guns and enemy airplanes, and more than half were shot down.

gentleman's agreement In 1916, British prisoner of war Captain Robert Campbell was given leave by the German authorities to visit his ill mother in England, as long as he promised to return to Germany. He kept his word, returning to the prison camp after two weeks, and remained captive until the end of the war.

boy soldiers Many young boys, excited about the war, lied about their age in order to enlist. The youngest soldier, Momčilo Gavrić of Serbia, fought for his country at the age of nine. British Private Sidney Lewis ran away to join the army and fought at the Battle of the Somme. He was removed from the war after his mother wrote to the War Office and revealed he was only 12 years old.

surrender flag The final truce flag of World War I was actually a tablecloth!

big bertha "Big Bertha" was a 75-ton, 16.5-in (42-cm) German artillery gun that fired 2,100 lb (950 kg) shells at a range of 9 mi (14 km). Soldiers operating the gun kept to a 900-ft (274-m) perimeter when the gun was firing, such was the power of the blasts. It was so big that it could be transported only on railway tracks.

late charges Although fighting in World War I finished in 1918, the war did not officially end until October 3, 2010—92 years later—when Germany finally settled its war debt by paying $90 million, which was the last instalment of the reparations imposed on it by the Allies. Germany was forced to pay compensation toward the cost of the war by the 1919 Treaty of Versailles.

CANINE SERGEANT

Stubby, a pit bull mix kept by the U.S. 102nd Infantry Regiment, was made a Sergeant after attacking a German spy. After the war he met President Coolidge at the White House and received a number of medals.

PIGEON CAMERA

The German army experimented with pigeons fitted with cameras for aerial surveillance behind enemy lines.

Snow Art

→ British map designer and artist Simon Beck is making his mark on the landscape of the French Alps by creating art in the snow simply by using his feet!

Using geometric designs created by working with an orienteering compass (right), Simon can spend from ten hours to two days on each piece, braving the icy climate and "drawing" his picture with snowshoes. Some of his pieces are as large as six football fields, but they are short-lived, usually only lasting a day or two until the wind blows, or the next snowfall.

sliding building When a historic building in Anda, China, had to be moved to make way for a railway line in the winter of 2013, engineers transported it to its new location 790 ft (240 m) down the road by sliding it on ice. They sprayed water underneath the structure and along its route until they created an ice bed that was strong enough to support the building. Then they inserted large rollers and gently slid it down the road—an operation that took more than two weeks.

no cars M-185 on Mackinac Island, Michigan, is the only U.S. state highway that prohibits motor vehicles. The restrictions date back to the 1890s—since then, only emergency vehicles have been allowed to use it.

big bonfire For the annual Slinningsbålet Midsummer Festival in Ålesund, Norway, around 40 people helped build a massive bonfire from wood pallets stacked over 132 ft (40 m) high.

wet spot The wettest place in the world, Mawsynram, a village in northeastern India, receives almost 39 ft (12 m) of rain in an average year.

biggest volcano The world's largest volcano—roughly the size of New Mexico—has been discovered on the floor of the Pacific Ocean 1,000 mi (1,600 km) east of Japan. Believed to be inactive, having last erupted about 145 million years ago, the Tamu Massif covers 120,000 sq mi (310,000 sq km), rising over a mile above the ocean floor and boring 18 mi (30 km) into the Earth's crust. It is a staggering 60 times bigger than Hawaii's Mauna Loa, the world's largest active volcano.

SKULL PODS

→ The *Antirrhinum* gets its common name of snapdragon from the flower's resemblance to a dragon's head—but when the flower dies, its seedpod looks even more macabre, just like a human skull. With such eerie pods, it's no wonder that in the Middle Ages people thought the plant possessed supernatural powers and could offer protection from witches.

enormous building The world's biggest building by volume is the Boeing Airplane Plant in Everett, Washington State. At 472 million cubic ft (13 million cubic m), it is so huge that Disneyland could fit inside. When the plant was first built in 1967, moisture in the air rose to the top of the building to form rainclouds near the ceiling.

sheep-killing plant The "sheep-eating plant," *Puya chilensis* of the South American Andes, has barbed leaves that ensnare passing sheep—and as the animals starve and slowly decompose, the plant uses them as fertilizer.

remote location The Zanskar region in India's states of Jammu and Kashmir is located high in the Himalayas mountain range and is cut off by snow from the rest of the world for more than half of the year.

vampire alert In November 2012, the mayor of Zarožje, Serbia, warned that a vampire was on the loose and that local residents should put garlic on their doors. Legendary vampire Sava Savanović reputedly lived in an old wooden mill where he sucked the blood of millers, but when the mill recently collapsed, local villagers believed that the vampire was roaming the mountains looking for a new home.

last speaker Gyani Maiya Sen, 76, from Nepal is the last fluent speaker of the Kusunda language, which is uniquely unrelated to any of the world's major language groups. Academics are trying to document Kusundu so that when Gyani dies, the language will not die with her.

Simon says that designs created in powdery snow, ideally around 9 in (23 cm) deep, make the best pictures. He likes to work on a level site with an even amount of snow.

Using designs inspired by mathematical patterns or even crop circles, Simon starts by plotting his art on graph paper. He then spends a couple of hours surveying and carefully measuring his site with a compass, before starting to walk. He can walk up to 25 mi (40 km) when creating a piece, and often listens to Beethoven to keep himself going.

dead dances Approximately every seven years, in a ritual known as famadihana, people in central Madagascar remove their dead ancestors from graves, spray them with perfume, wrap them in new cloth and dance with the corpses before reburying them.

snow boulders Hundreds of snow boulders—each weighing up to 75 lb (34 kg)—washed ashore along a 100-ft (30-m) stretch of coast at the Sleeping Bear Dunes National Park in northern Michigan in February 2013. They were formed by chunks breaking off from floating sheets of ice in nearby Lake Michigan before crashing waves molded them into smooth, round shapes that were washed ashore in high winds.

bone chapel The 19th-century Chapel of Bones in Faro, Portugal, was constructed almost entirely from the remains of more than 1,200 monks. Not only is it decorated with thousands of human bones and skulls, including a complete golden skeleton, but the walls of the chapel are actually built using femurs mixed with mortar.

ancient calendar Archeologists excavating a field in Aberdeenshire, Scotland, found a lunar calendar dating back 10,000 years. Twelve pits unearthed at Crathes Castle appear to represent the phases of the Moon and lunar months.

water spout A burst water main sent a 250-ft-tall (76-m) fountain of water—the height of a 20-story building—soaring over a suburb of Melbourne, Australia, in October 2012. The waterspout lasted an hour, during which time it shot over half a million gallons (approximately 2 million liters) into the sky over Glen Waverley, flooding streets and homes.

valuable doorstop Donna and George Lewis discovered that the rock they had been using for years as a doorstop at their home in Pineville, Kentucky, was a valuable, 4½-billion-year-old meteorite. The family had picked out the 33-lb (15-kg) rock from a cow pasture in the 1930s.

RAINBOW MOUNTAINS → It looks like a fairy tale landscape created by an animation studio, but these beautiful striped mountains in all the colors of the rainbow are a natural phenomenon that can be found at the Zhangye Danxia Landform Geological Park in China. The dazzling spectacle has been created by layers of different colored sandstones and minerals that have been pressed together and shaped over a period of 24 million years, by a combination of water erosion and tectonic movement. At different times of day, and in different seasons, the colors change, making the "Seven-Color Mountain," as it is known locally, more magical than ever.

NO-FLY ZONE

→ In 1,426 days, just under four years, Graham Hughes from Liverpool, England, visited all 201 nations of the world—without once flying! Instead, he used trains, buses, taxis and cargo ships—and did it all on a budget of $100 a week.

Traveling a total of 155,000 mi (250,000 km), Graham said that his most hazardous journey was a four-day ocean crossing in a leaky wooden canoe from Senegal to Cape Verde. He was imprisoned for a week in the Congo and ate live octopus in South Korea. He literally had to cross a minefield to reach the border in Western Sahara, only to be told he needed a visa from a town 1,250 mi (2,000 km) away—and he was arrested trying to sneak across the border into Russia!

ISRAEL

BAHAMAS

AFGHANISTAN

AUSTRALIA

CAMEROON

SUDAN

SOUTH SUDAN

BENIN

ESTONIA

CANADA

SOLOMON ISLANDS

RUSSIA

CENTRAL AFRICAN REPUBLIC

FIJI

Graham's trip in numbers

201 nations visited
193 of them U.N. members
67 of them visited more than once
59 of them were islands
18 bonus territories (for good measure)
Traveled: over 155,000 mi (250,000 km)
Average money spent: $100 a week
Hours of video footage: 352
Blog entries: 736
Blog wordcount: 584,886
Days spent in jail: 12
Days spent at sea: 196
Number of ships: 157

SRI LANKA

REUNION

GABON

INDONESIA

U.S.A.

MICRONESIA

Ripley's
Believe It or Not!®
www.ripleybooks.com

CHINA

EGYPT

THAILAND

ICELAND

TIBET

FRONTIER
GUINEE E

EQUATORIAL GUINEA

ITALY

THE RULES

I CANNOT FLY

I MAY NOT DRIVE

I MUST USE SCHEDULED GROUND TRANSPORT

I MUST STEP FOOT ON DRY LAND

TOGO

KENYA

SWAZILAND

PALAU

TONGA

NEW CALEDONIA

CHAD

REPUB
UNI
DEPARTE
SOUS-PR
POSTE CO

OMAN

MEXICO

PAPUA NEW GUINEA

WEST PAPUA

TANZANIA

NIGER

IRAN

VANUATU

SERBIA

NEPAL

WESTERN SAHARA

ENGLAND

PACIFIC OCEAN

NORTH KOREA

KIRIBATI

VENEZUELA

MARSHALL ISLANDS

BACK HOME!

55

swallows trees Created from a collapsed underground cavern, the 750-ft-deep (230-m) Assumption Parish sinkhole near Bayou Corne, Louisiana, swallowed several 20-ft-tall (6-m) trees and large areas of land in under a minute.

salt layer If all the salt in the world's seas and oceans were spread evenly over the land, it would form a crust 500 ft (150 m) thick.

store storm Lakeisha Brooks was struck by lightning while standing inside a store in Houma, Louisiana. The lightning bolt hit the roof, traveled through the sprinkler system and up through a metal plate on the floor. Lakeisha had gone into the store only to escape the storm.

worlds apart Windsor, Ontario, was just about the safest city in Canada in 2011, while Detroit, Michigan—only half a mile away—was branded the most dangerous city in the U.S.A. Windsor recorded just one murder while near-neighbor Detroit had more than 340.

flight simulator Aeronautics enthusiast Laurent Aigon from Lacanau, France, spent five years building a replica of a Boeing 737 cockpit in his children's bedroom. The simulator, which has five computer screens and was assembled with parts from around the world, can re-create flights to such far-flung destinations as Sydney, Australia, and Rio de Janeiro, Brazil.

sacred bell A temple bell in Liuzhou, China, weighs 120 tons, stands 30 ft (9 m) tall, measures 20 ft (6 m) in diameter at its widest point and is engraved with 92,306 Chinese characters.

slim house A house in Warsaw, Poland, is just 5 ft (1.5 m) wide at its broadest point and 3 ft (0.9 m) at its narrowest. Squeezed by architect Jakub Szczesny into an alley between another house and an apartment block, Keret House is fully functioning, despite only having 46 sq ft (4.3 sq m) of floor space. It is so squashed that the upstairs bedroom has to be reached via a metal ladder bolted onto a wall. The bathroom comprises a toilet and a shower, and the kitchen fridge is so tiny that it has space for just two drinks.

musical bridge Officials brightened up a drab bridge in Shijiazhuang, China, by painting huge piano keys and musical notes all over it.

inflatable room Architect Alex Schweder created an inflatable hotel room in Denver, Colorado, that rises a staggering 22 ft (6.7 m) in the air courtesy of a scissor lift on top of the van on which it is perched. The 5 x 7 ft (1.5 x 2.1 m) aluminum and vinyl room has a chemical toilet, a shower, a sink, curtains and an inflatable bed and couch.

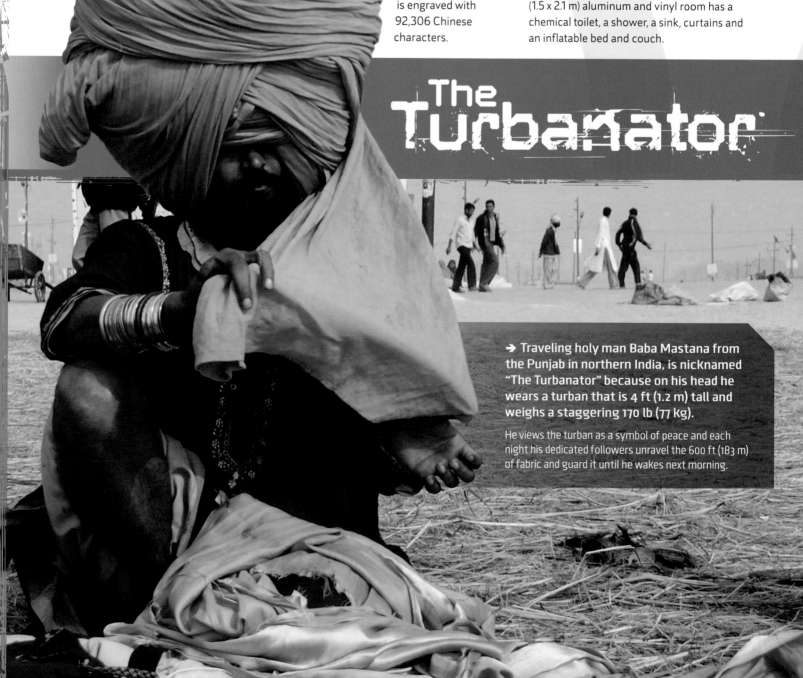

The Turbanator

➔ Traveling holy man Baba Mastana from the Punjab in northern India, is nicknamed "The Turbanator" because on his head he wears a turban that is 4 ft (1.2 m) tall and weighs a staggering 170 lb (77 kg).

He views the turban as a symbol of peace and each night his dedicated followers unravel the 600 ft (183 m) of fabric and guard it until he wakes next morning.

RIPLEY'S RESEARCH

A rainbow is an optical phenomenon caused by sunlight reflecting in water droplets in the Earth's atmosphere. The water most commonly takes the form of rainfall but, provided the sun is in the right position, spray from a waterfall can be equally effective. The Sun must shine from behind and be low in the sky, such as at dawn or in late afternoon, because the angle governs the direction the light travels in after it hits the water droplets and that determines whether or not we will see a rainbow.

RAINBOW WATERFALL ↗

→ Photographer Justin Lee from British Columbia captured the brief moment when the late-afternoon sunlight caught fine water spray to form a spectacular rainbow at the bottom of Bridalveil Fall in Yosemite National Park, California. The 620-ft-high (189-m) waterfall takes its name from the mist that sometimes drifts off it in a breeze and resembles a bride's flowing veil.

green house Agricultural lecturer Sheng Xiugi has turned the exterior of his house in Yiwu, China, into a five-story orchard. The walls of his huge house are covered entirely in crops such as grapes, eggplants and plums, so that if he wants fruit or vegetables all he has to do is open a window and pick some.

mini taj As a monument to his late wife, 77-year-old retired mailman Faizul Hasan Kadari set about building a miniature 5,000-sq-ft (465-sq-m) replica of the Taj Mahal in the garden of his home in Bulandshahr, Uttar Pradesh, India.

big school The City Montessori School in Lucknow, India, is populated with 47,000 pupils, 2,500 teachers, 3,700 computers and—to house them all—1,000 classrooms.

tears for hire In the Indian state of Rajasthan, professional female mourners called *rudaali* are hired to cry in public on behalf of the family members of a dead man.

wall of dust A towering wall of dust a mile high engulfed Phoenix, Arizona, on August 26, 2013, leaving the city blanketed in grit. Arizona's storm season produces massive dust storms called haboobs, which can stretch over 100 mi (160 km).

dead dialects The world's first Akkadian-language dictionary was completed in 2011 at the University of Chicago, Illinois, although the language's dialects of Assyrian and Babylonian haven't been spoken in around 2,000 years.

bus driver king Barry Watson, a former bus driver from Chepstow, Wales, is revered as a king among the Yanadi tribe of Andhra Pradesh, India, and has over 130 subjects who faithfully walk ten paces behind him. The father-of-four was given the title after helping the impoverished tribespeople to construct new homes, thereby fulfilling their ancient prophecy that one day a white man would come and build them a village.

dress code Under crime prevention laws, convicted robbers in Manchester, England, can be banned from wearing hoods within 160 ft (50 m) of shops, banks and cash delivery vans, and from wearing false mustaches and beards in public.

melting cars During the summer of 2013, the Sun caused such a bright glare reflected from a new 37-story skyscraper in London, England, that the metal roofs of vehicles parked in the street below began to melt.

AQUARIUM WALL

→ Turkish businessman Mehmet Ali Gökçeoğlu has replaced the metal fence around the front of his luxury, beachfront villa in Çeşme with a 160-ft-long (50-m) aquarium filled with hundreds of fish and octopuses. He acquires the marine creatures in his living aqua-fence from the nearby Aegean Sea, to which it is connected via a 1,300-ft-long (400-m) buried pipeline in order to ensure that the water is changed regularly and that the aquarium's occupants remain healthy.

Antarctic Hero

➜ In the era of heroic polar exploration, Sir Ernest Shackleton (1874–1922) spent 18 months leading the crew of his ship, the *Endurance*, to safety after a disastrous journey to Antarctica. Their survival, in the most extreme conditions on Earth, was a feat of unbelievable endurance, celebrated for Shackleton's leadership and the fact that every single member of his crew survived.

One hundred years ago, in August 1914, Shackleton and his crew left British waters to embark on the most ambitious polar expedition of all time—the Imperial Trans-Antarctic Expedition to cross Antarctica from one side to the other via the South Pole. He took 26 men and 70 dogs onboard but, unfortunately for his crew, their safe return was far from assured, and it would take them over two years to get home.

MEN WANTED

For hazardous journey. Small wages. Bitter cold. Long months of complete darkness. Constant danger. Safe return doubtful. Honor and recognition in case of success.

↗

Although polar expeditions were incredibly tough, there was never a shortage of men willing to risk everything for glory. Replying to an ad that may have read something like this one, more than 5,000 men applied to join Shackleton's Imperial Trans-Antarctic Expedition in 1914.

August 8, 1914
Endurance leaves British waters

→

December 5, 1914
Endurance leaves South Georgia headed for Antarctica

→

January 19, 1915
Endurance becomes stuck in ice

Perce Blackborow

➜ Eighteen-year-old Perce Blackborow had traveled from Wales to Argentina looking for work on a polar ship, but was refused a position on the *Endurance* as he was considered too young. Desperate for adventure, he ignored this refusal and stowed away. Discovered after three days, he was brought before a furious Shackleton, who told him, "Do you know that on these expeditions we often get very hungry, and if there is a stowaway available he is the first to be eaten?" Blackborow replied, "They'd get a lot more meat on you, sir." At this, Shackleton relented and made him the ship's steward.

1 Shackleton planned to use the *Endurance* to reach Antarctica, where he would land at Vahsel Bay and cross the continent on foot via the South Pole. However, things did not go as planned.

2 In December 1914, the *Endurance* left the remote South Atlantic island of South Georgia and soon entered pack ice in the Weddell Sea. Six weeks later, she became stuck in the ice. Shackleton decided they would spend the winter onboard the ship, hoping that she would eventually be released from the ice to continue her voyage in the spring. To make more space in their "winter station," the crew made igloos on the ice for the dogs.

4 Unfortunately, as the ice started to break up and move in the September springtime, it put tremendous pressure on the ship's hull and, on October 24, the *Endurance* was crushed and water poured in. Shackleton ordered everything to be removed from the wrecked ship and the weakest animals to be shot—three weeks later, the *Endurance* finally sank.

5 The crew left the *Endurance* with just three lifeboats and lived for five months on the constantly changing, precarious ice. On April 9, the ice floe they were camping on broke in two, and Shackleton ordered them into the lifeboats. Five days later, and five months after abandoning ship, the boats landed at Elephant Island— 346 mi (557 km) from the sunken vessel, and the first time they had set foot on solid ground for 16 months.

November 21, 1915
Endurance sinks

April 14, 1916
Crew arrive at Elephant Island

May 20, 1916
Shackleton arrives at South Georgia whaling station

August 30, 1916
Crew rescued from Elephant Island

3 For nine long months over the winter, the crew continued to live onboard the ship in the inhospitable environment of the Antarctic, slowly moving north as the *Endurance* traveled with the ice floe. The men's spirits remained high, despite the fact that they had to eat, sleep and live in very close and cramped quarters.

6 Shackleton realized there was no hope of rescue on this small spit of land, so he started to plan the 920-mi (1,500-km) journey back to a whaling station on South Georgia. Two weeks after reaching Elephant Island, he set off with five men on the Southern Ocean—one of the most dangerous oceans in the world—in the *James Caird*, a lifeboat just 22 ft (6.7 m) long.

7 After 17 days of strong gales, freezing cold, and giant waves, the *James Caird* reached South Georgia. However, the ordeal was not over yet—Shackleton had been forced to land on the uninhabited side of the island, and the whaling station was an arduous 32-mi (51-km) away, over icy slopes, snowfields and unpredictable glaciers. Upon finally reaching the whaling station, Shackleton was met by the station manager who reacted with disbelief at their journey across the island, let alone at their incredible tale of survival over the previous year.

8 It took four attempts and a further three months for a rescue ship to reach the rest of the crew on Elephant Island, on August 30, 1916. Amazingly, all of the 22 men left behind had survived, although a number were missing toes from frostbite. They were taken to Chile before making the long journey home to England. Shackleton's courage, ingenuity and determination had prevailed, and as a result he has always been remembered as a hero and as one of the great leaders of the 20th century.

ice tsunamis Over one weekend in May 2013, at two North American locations, 600 mi (960 km) apart, strong winds caused the formation of terrifying ice tsunamis that swept ashore from inland lakes and destroyed everything in their paths. On May 10, a wall of ice 30 ft (9 m) tall rose out of Dauphin Lake, Manitoba, in a matter of minutes and wrecked 27 homes in the town of Ochre River, forcing residents to flee for their lives. The following day, a huge ice floe, propelled by 40-mph (64-km/h) winds, engulfed 10 mi (16 km) of shoreline adjacent to Mille Lacs Lake, Minnesota, breaking through the front doors of homes and causing extensive damage.

safety check In Denmark, the law states that before starting a car's engine, drivers must check under their car for children who may be sleeping there.

extreme ride The Giant Canyon Swing at Steve Beckley's Glenwood Caverns Adventure Park, Colorado, swings riders at super-speeds of 50 mph (80 km/h) out over a 1,300-ft (400-m) sheer drop to the Colorado River below.

tree house Horace Burgess from Crossville, Tennessee, spent 11 years building a 97-ft-tall (30-m) tree house. Covering an area of 10,000 sq ft (930 sq m), the house encompasses seven trees and was built entirely from scrap lumber and donated materials, held together by an estimated 258,000 nails.

RARE SNOW ➜ In December 2013, snow fell in Cairo, Egypt, for the first time in 112 years. As the residents had never experienced snow in a city that averages less than an inch of precipitation a year, hundreds stopped to take pictures of the wintry scene. The snow covered much of the Middle East, with a couple of inches falling in Jerusalem (see above)—the heaviest snowfall recorded for 60 years.

panda hotel Jian Qin has opened a panda-themed hotel at Emei Mountain in China's Sichuan Province. All of the Panda Hotel's facilities are panda-related, including the towels, slippers and pajamas, and the staff dress in giant panda suits.

invisible room The Treehotel in Harads, Sweden, has a separate, elevated room called the Mirrorcube that is clad externally in mirrors to reflect its forest surroundings. As a result, when viewed from a distance with the naked eye, the hotel appears invisible.

oval office Presidential memorabilia collector Ron Wade has installed an exact replica of the Oval Office in his Longview, Texas, home at a cost of $250,000. Some 250 workers labored on the project, which took 2½ years to design and eight months to build. Ron's collection also includes 10,000 political buttons, and a rocking chair that once belonged to J.F.K.

FROST FLOWERS ➜ When temperatures plunge to around –8°F (–22°C), small cracks or imperfections in young sea ice can result in beautiful ice crystals—or frost flowers—sprouting up from the surface. These Arctic blooms grow several inches tall and contain high levels of salt and marine bacteria. In fact, there is more bacterial life in the frost flowers than in the frozen water beneath them.

parking price Lisa Blumenthal paid $560,000 for two parking spaces near her home in the Black Bay neighborhood of Boston, Massachusetts. When she bought the spaces, at an auction, each one cost almost as much as the price of an average family home in the state.

moon tracks Since the Moon has no atmosphere to erode them, tracks from astronauts and rovers at Moon landing sites are still visible and undisturbed after decades.

Underwater Wonderland

➔ To capture this magical underwater scene, Russian amateur photographer Yuri Ovchinnikov stuck his head through a hole in the frozen Tianuksa River and took pictures of what he saw.

The idea came to him after his son accidentally put his foot through the ice and discovered the winter wonderland beneath the surface. The natural light creates a range of colors as air pockets up to 2 ft (60 cm) deep extend down to transparent ice columns and crystalline shapes. Beneath the air pockets, water still flows.

bargain basement A luxury underground hotel worth $3.8 million sold for just $1,020 at an auction in 2012. Opened in 2004 in Airolo, Switzerland, La Claustra has 17 rooms, and a restaurant, library, spa and swimming pool, but few people attended the auction, allowing Lucia Filippi to grab a bargain.

animal buildings Buildings shaped like a dog and a sheep sit side by side along a road in Tirau, New Zealand. The large, corrugated Sheepdog houses the local tourist information center, while the Big Sheep is home to a wool gallery. Both were designed to promote tourism in the area.

lightning strikes Melvin Roberts from Seneca, South Carolina, has survived being hit by lightning seven times since 1998—and an eighth bolt missed him by just a few inches while he was inside his house. The strikes have sparked hallucinations and left him with scars all over his body.

03

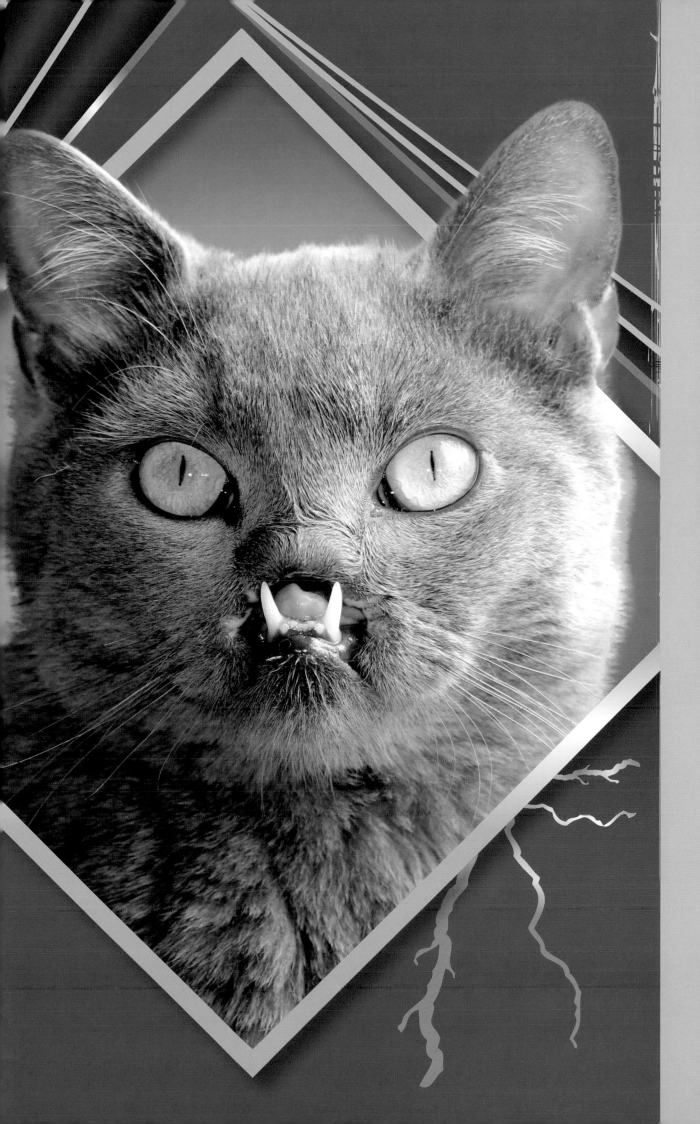

ANIMALS

Life with the Lions

→ In the early 1970s, Hollywood actress Tippi Hedren and her family, including her then 14-year-old daughter Melanie Griffith, invited a full-grown lion, called Neil, into their Californian home for a photo-shoot. Tippi and her husband Noel Marshall were in the process of sourcing a large number of exotic big cats for their movie Roar, an experience that would change their views on keeping exotic animals forever.

Tippi hired Neil from Ron Oxley, who lived in Soledad Canyon. She wanted to make a family movie, entitled *Roar*, using 25 lions, tigers and other big cats, and in order to get to know lions, she and her family invited a number of young cubs to live at their house. Even small lions can be dangerous, however, and one scratched Melanie Griffith's face with its claws. They also tore up the house. Melanie later said, "She didn't mean to hurt me, but after seven years growing up with lions, I forgot you have to be careful. Just a blow can pop your head like a Ping-Pong ball."

The family then moved, with the lions, to a mountain ranch to film *Roar*. It was a painful experience. Tippi had her arm badly scratched by a leopard, and director of photography Jan de Bont survived a particularly dangerous incident. The cameramen had positioned themselves in a camouflaged pit over which the lions were to run for a shot of stampeding big cats, protected with football helmets. When the lions rushed by, one of the lions saw movement and lashed out with its paw, tearing off de Bont's scalp—he had removed his helmet to get a better shot. The original plan was to shoot *Roar* in nine months, but filming the big cats eventually took five years, and the film was not released until 1981.

Tippi's experience with big cats during the filming of *Roar* convinced her that such animals should not be in close contact with humans, so she turned the ranch where it was filmed into the Shambala Preserve, dedicated to the protection of exotic animals rescued from private collections. Since opening, Shambala has rescued 230 such animals. Although the lions in the pictures here appear to be tame, Tippi now warns that there is no such thing, they never lose their predator's instinct and can attack at any time.

Tippi playing with Neil at her home in Sherman Oaks, California.

Melanie Griffith jumps into the pool, while Neil playfully grabs her leg.

A lion's paws are powerful enough to break a zebra's back—something to bear in mind when playing with them as pets.

Tippi and Melanie invited lions into their home at a time when the dangers of keeping such animals were not fully understood. Their experience taught them that even big cats are always extremely dangerous and should not be kept as pets. Since 1990, 254 big cats have escaped from captivity, with 143 killed, and exotic cats have killed at least 21 people in captivity. Today, Tippi campaigns against the exotic animal industry and is lobbying the United States Congress to introduce laws restricting the breeding and buying of exotic predators by individuals, which is still legal in the United States.

new legs After losing his rear hooves to severe frostbite in Augusta County, Virginia, Hero the calf was able to walk again thanks to a pair of new prosthetic legs fitted by a company from New Jersey.

fake poodles Dog lovers in Buenos Aires, Argentina, paid $150 for what they thought was a bargain price for a fashionable toy poodle, only to discover that they had been sold a ferret instead. The ferrets had been given steroids at birth to increase their size and then had their coats fluffed up to make them look like poodles.

squirrel profit After 30 squirrels escaped from an enclosure at Japan's Inokashira Park Zoo, zookeepers combed surrounding parkland and recaptured 38!

pooch hooch Boneyard Brewery of Bend, Oregon, has created an alcohol-free beer for dogs. The brainchild of brewery taster Daniel Keeton, it is called Dawg Grog and is packed with vegetables, spices and honey to provide a nutritional, liquid treat for dogs.

cat hat Seattle, Washington State, designer Yumiko Landers has created a range of hats for cats that make them look like lions. The false mane—in a variety of colors—attaches around the cat's head with Velcro. Landers says: "Every cat believes they're the master of their domain. So I thought there's no better way to represent that than by making them look like a true lion."

manure freshener Indonesian high-school students Dwi Nailul Izzah and Rintya Aprianti Miki won first prize in the country's Science Project Olympiad with their air freshener made from cow dung. After leaving the manure to ferment for three days, they extracted the liquid and mixed it with coconut water to create a product from digested cow food that has a natural aroma of herbs.

BULLDOG COW ➔ It may have a head like a bulldog but, believe it or not, this is a calf that once belonged to Tom McVey of Madisonville, Texas.

goats arrest Three goats were arrested and detained in Chennai, India, for vandalizing a new police car. The goats—part of a gang of 12—were accused of climbing on top of the vehicle, denting it, damaging the windshield and wipers, and scratching the paintwork.

iron supplement Farmers sometimes feed their cows magnets that sit in their stomachs for their entire lives. The magnets attract any accidentally eaten metal, preventing it from causing harm to the cows.

working dog Misty, Elaine Prickett's border collie, works for the administrative team at a quarry in Cumbria, England, handling bank notes and credit cards and returning them to customers. She also waits at the window for customers to arrive, then takes their ticket and finds a staff member to process the paperwork.

unique noses Cows can be identified by their noseprints, which, just like human fingerprints, are unique.

extra baggage Bisou, a seven-year-old Persian cat, made an unscheduled 3,400-mi (5,470-km) airplane and car journey after sneaking into owner Mervat Ciuti's suitcase as she packed at home in Cairo, Egypt, to visit her sister in England. Bisou, who normally never leaves the house, passed through airport security undetected and was stacked into the hold of the plane with hundreds of other bags, but survived her ordeal unscathed.

surfing pig Every morning Matthew Bell takes his piglet Zorro surfing off the coast near Mount Maunganui, New Zealand. Matthew, who describes Zorro as a "phenomenal swimmer," first took him out on the waves when he was just three weeks old and plans to continue surfing with him until the pig is too big for the board.

two's company Rudi Saldia cycles around the streets of Philadelphia, Pennsylvania, with his tabby cat Mary Jane perched on his shoulder. Using a sports camera mounted on his bike, he's recorded "Mary Jane's Co-pilot Adventures" and posted them on YouTube, where they picked up more than 1.2 million views in the first six months.

mole dig Archeologists discovered a series of valuable 2,000-year-old Roman artifacts at an ancient fort in Cumbria, England, after the relics had been dug up by burrowing moles.

tortoise tunes Celebrated pianist Richard Clayderman performed a selection of romantic tunes to Galapagos tortoises in London Zoo, England, in an effort to encourage them to mate.

udderly beautiful An annual cow beauty contest—the German Holstein Show—takes place in Oldenburg, Germany. A dozen cow hairdressers use razor blades to groom more than 250 animals from across Europe in the search to find the most beautiful bovine.

SHREW "CARAVAN"

➔ To avoid getting lost, young Asian musk shrews form a "caravan" behind their mother, lining up behind her as she walks and holding on to the fur of the animal in front with their teeth. If they lose contact, they reattach themselves to any moving object—in this case a child's toy.

FLUFFY COWS

➜ Groomed and pampered dogs have long been a regular fixture in animal shows around the world, but now pampered cows are beginning to make their mark.

Phil Lautner of Lautner Farms in Iowa shows and sells his special-breed bovines at the National Western Stock Show, with one specimen being sold for an amazing $100,000. His cute cows undergo a meticulous beauty routine to create their unique look.

It takes months of special care, and up to two hours of preparation on the day, to get the cows ready for their moment in the spotlight.

Each cow has its coat shampooed, blow-dried and styled—with oil added for shine, and hairspray applied to keep the fuzzy look intact.

HUGE WASPS' NEST

➜ A wasps' nest discovered in an abandoned house in San Sebastian de La Gomera on the Spanish island of La Gomera in 2013 measured an incredible 22 ft (7 m)—half the length of a bus—making it the biggest wasps' nest ever recorded.

snakes alive! Police found a collection of 40 pythons—the biggest measuring a hefty 4.6 ft (1.4 m) long—in a motel room in Brantford, Ontario. The snakes, which were discovered in five plastic storage bins, belonged to a couple who had checked in for one night.

phoney names Struggling to think up names quickly for 101 new beetle species that have recently been discovered in Papua New Guinea, scientists found inspiration by looking through the local phone book and choosing human family surnames at random.

bootylicious fly In 2011, a previously unnamed species of Australian horsefly with an attractive golden lower abdomen was named *Scaptia beyonceae* after the singer Beyoncé.

A colony of **20,000 bats** moved into an empty Victorian house in Tifton, Georgia, in 2011.

A man who doused a rag in a flammable solvent and set it alight in a bid to smoke out a **wasp nest** from his house in Nottingham, England, in 2013 accidentally set fire to his neighbors' adjoining house, gutting the building.

In 2012, Germany was invaded by more than a **million raccoons** many of which nested in the attics of city houses.

For four years the Trost family saw their St. Charles County, Missouri, home invaded by **hundreds of venomous spiders** —the brown recluse spiders have a bite that can cause kidney failure.

In 2013, an estimated **100,000 Africanized bees** invaded a vacant home in Houston, Texas. The aggressive bees killed birds and a neighbor's German shepherd dog.

raining spiders Local people thought it was raining spiders when thousands of the creatures were found dangling from overhead power lines in one huge web in the Brazilian town of Santa Antônio da Platina in February 2013. The spiders had temporarily joined thousands of individual webs together to form a massive web that extended more than 26 ft (8 m) above ground and up to 10 ft (3 m) in diameter. Strong winds have been known to pick up such massive webs, along with the spiders, and carry them for miles until the wind drops, whereupon the web falls and it appears to be raining spiders.

Euryplatea nanaknihali, a newly discovered species in Thailand, is the world's smallest fly, with a length of less than 0.02 in (0.5 mm)—and it reproduces by laying its eggs inside some of the world's smallest ants.

bat cave A cave in Austin, Texas, is home to 10 million Mexican free-tailed bats, crammed together on the walls at 400 bats per square foot.

eager beaver In June 2013, a hungry beaver chewed through a fiber line and caused a 20-hour Internet and cell-phone outage in northern New Mexico, which affected more than 1,800 Web users.

lonely roaches Cockroaches can suffer from loneliness and show signs of depression when separated from each other. If young cockroaches are not in constant physical contact with one another they suffer isolation syndrome and take longer to develop into adults.

artful dodgers Ants can survive in the intense heat of a microwave oven because they are small enough to dodge the rays.

HOME INVADERS

TRAPDOOR SPIDER

➔ The trapdoor spider lives in an underground burrow, the entrance to which is a cunningly camouflaged trapdoor made of vegetation and soil and hinged on one side with silk.

While waiting for prey, the spider holds on to the underside of the door and as soon as one of the silk "trip" lines are disturbed above ground, the trapdoor springs open and the spider leaps out to snatch its meal.

Viewed from below

TWO-HEADED SALAMANDER

➔ This two-headed fire salamander survived for only six months with a private breeder who had tried to feed it through both mouths. On its death, he donated it to a German university for research. The salamander's condition is called bicephaly, where each head has its own brain and they share control of the creature's organs and limbs. When snakes are born with bicephaly, one head may attack and even attempt to swallow the other.

Viewed from above

hitchin' a ride While observing dolphins near Kalamos, Greece, in June 2012, researchers photographed an octopus riding on the belly of a dolphin as it leapt from the water.

mine seekers Bees in Croatia are being trained to detect unexploded land mines, which have littered the country since the Balkan Wars in the 1990s. During four years of fighting in Croatia, 90,000 mines were planted all over the country, but now honeybees are being taught to seek out the smell of the explosive by associating it with food.

rat catchers A group of urban hunters—the Ryders Alley Trencher-Fed Society—meet regularly in New York to hunt rats with their pet dogs on the streets of Manhattan.

noisy ants When a 75-year-old woman from Offenburg, Germany, called police at 3 a.m. one morning to say that she could not sleep because her doorbell was always ringing, officers found that the cause was an ants' nest right next to the doorbell. The ants had built such a large home that their nest pressed the switching elements together, setting off the bell.

sweet revenge When a fig wasp lays its eggs inside a fig but fails to pollinate it, the tree retaliates by dropping those unpollinated figs to the ground, killing the baby wasps inside.

baker bees When giant hornets invade Japanese honeybee colonies, the bees kill individual hornets by swarming into a ball and cooking the hornet to death with their body heat.

WolfMan

TOUGH NUT

➜ You might not fancy this little turtle's chances in the jaws of an alligator at the Okefenokee Swamp in Georgia, U.S.A., but it proved too tough a nut to crack. After trying in vain to pry open the shell with its powerful teeth, the gator eventually gave up, and when photographer Patrick Castleberry went over to see how the turtle was, he was delighted to find that it was still alive. So he flipped it over and it quickly swam off, none the worse for its brush with death.

homeward bound After going missing on a family vacation in Daytona, Florida, Holly, a four-year-old cat owned by Jacob and Bonnie Richter, returned exhausted to within a mile of their home in West Palm Beach, having traveled 190 mi (306 km) in two months.

third eyelid Woodpeckers have a third eyelid that keeps their two eyeballs in place as they ram trees with their beaks at great force at least twenty times a second.

croc escape After heavy rain allowed 15,000 crocodiles to escape from Rakwena Crocodile Farm in northern South Africa, one croc was found on a school rugby field 75 mi (120 km) away.

meerkat mimic The African drongo bird can imitate the warning sound of meerkats. When the real meerkats run to the safety of their burrows, it swoops down and steals any food they have left behind.

→ Former paratrooper Werner Freund has hand-reared and lived among wolves on his sanctuary in Merzig, Germany, for 40 years and is so close to them that they actually take meat from his mouth.

To show the 29 wolves that he is their leader, he makes sure he is the first to get his teeth into some raw meat—in this case a dead deer—at feeding time. The wolves wait obediently until he has finished, and because he has earned their respect, they play with him rather than attack him, regularly licking his face as a sign of subservience.

night crash A great horned owl somehow emerged unscathed from a 60-mph (96-km/h) nighttime collision with a truck on the Florida Turnpike. Driver Sonji Coney Williams thought the bird must have been killed by the impact, until she found it alive and well behind the front grill of her vehicle the following morning.

unrequited love After his long-term partner was killed, Whooper the swan took a fancy to a helicopter at Jersey Airport in the Channel Islands. Animal experts were so worried that his dangerous infatuation might lead to him coming to a grisly end in the rotor blades of the helicopter that they ordered his wings to be clipped.

snow trap Two sheep trapped by blizzards in Antrim, Northern Ireland, in April 2013 were found alive after spending 23 days covered in snow. They survived in an air pocket in a ditch beneath 6 ft (1.8 m) of snow.

blown away When a deer became trapped on thin ice in Antigonish Harbor, Nova Scotia, Canada, helicopter pilot David Farrell remembered an old trick and used the wind created by the chopper's rotor blades to blow the stricken animal across the frozen water to safety.

life saver When her boxer puppy Lola suffered an instant allergic reaction to a bee sting, Emma Harris from Plymouth, England, saved the dog's life by performing CPR. As the dog collapsed, 20-year-old kindergarten assistant Emma pounded Lola's chest for over two minutes until she started breathing again.

OVERSTUFFED BIRD → After attacking and devouring a small bird in Long Beach, California, this juvenile red-tailed hawk realized that it had eaten so much it was unable to fly. The bird of prey took half an hour to consume the bird, and then managed to waddle just a few yards before falling flat on its back. Luckily, photographer Steve Shinn was on hand to call a local wildlife center and by the next day the hawk had recovered once it had fully digested its heavy meal.

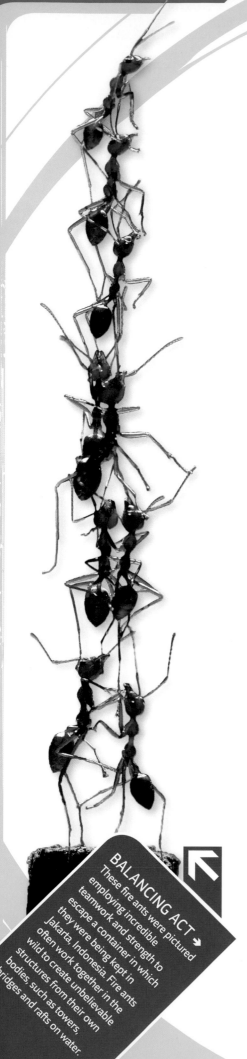

duck escort The busy A3 highway in Surrey, England, was closed during rush hour on August 15, 2013, causing a long traffic jam, while 50 mallard ducks were given a police escort. The ducks were walked along the road before being steered with handfuls of corn to the safety of a nearby shed.

miracle milk Despite never having had puppies, Ba Boo, a three-year-old Shar-Pei dog owned by Sherry Brandt from Kodak, Tennessee, not only adopted an abandoned kitten, but also nursed it with her own milk.

head hunter Charlie Perito has a pet cat named Nicholas who sits on his head when they go out for walks together through the streets of New York City. Nicholas learned to perch on Charlie's shoulder as a three-month-old kitten and became so confident amid the busy traffic that he now jumps straight up from the ground onto his owner's head and expects to stay there so he can keep a lookout for low-flying pigeons.

porker walker When piglet Chris P. Bacon was born with a congenital defect that meant he had no use of his hind limbs, his owner, Dr. Len Lucero of Sumterville, Florida, built him a two-wheeled harness out of a K'Nex building set. Now the little pig gets around in his cool customized wheelchair, has his own Facebook page with thousands of followers and has even become an inspiration to humans who have disabilities.

bear rescue A 100-lb (45-kg) young bear spent at least 11 days with his head stuck in a plastic jar before being freed by a team of rescuers in Jamison City, Pennsylvania. The bear had apparently been attracted to the jar because it had once contained cooking oil.

cash guzzler Sundance, a 12-year-old golden retriever owned by Wayne Klinkel of Helena, Montana, ate $500 in cash (five $100 bills) when left alone in the car during a Christmas visit to Denver, Colorado.

pooch smooch Every Valentine's Day, the Planet Dog Company store in Portland, Maine, holds a dog-kissing contest, where owners let their pets kiss their faces—including their lips—for as long as possible. The 2013 winners were Linda Walton and Beau, a Yorkie and dachshund mix, with a kiss of 45.8 seconds.

skunk heaven Deborah Cipriani shares her home in North Ridgeville, Ohio, with 50 skunks. The animals are free to wander around her five-bedroom house—called Skunk Haven—and even sleep on her bed.

BALANCING ACT → These fire ants were pictured employing incredible teamwork and strength to escape a container in which they were being kept in Jakarta, Indonesia. Fire ants often work together in the wild to create unbelievable structures from their own bodies, such as towers, bridges and rafts on water.

survival instinct When their boat's engine exploded off the coast of Oregon, Mark and Cynthia Schneider had to jump into the ocean and leave their two cats, Jasper and Topaz, on the doomed vessel, but then the cats, too, dived into the water and swam 100 yd (90 m) through debris to rejoin their owners on the rescue boat.

killer worm Workers at an aquarium store in Surrey, England, were mystified by the disappearance of dozens of fish—until they found that a 3-ft-long (1-m) bobbit worm had been hiding in the tank for years. The sinister worm usually lives deep in the ocean, but had been unwittingly introduced to the aquarium in a large rock and had been eating the fish ever since.

lady tarzan A 14-year-old girl from Jharkland, India, talked to elephants that had settled in a residential area in 2013 and persuaded them to return to the forest. Nirmala Toppo, who is known as "Lady Tarzan," began talking to elephants after her mother was killed by a herd. She learned the techniques for driving them away and says elephants understand her tribal language.

costly wool Wool from the South American vicuña, which cannot be farmed and is sheared only every other year, costs $150 per pound—200 times the price of sheep wool.

family abandon snake-infested home

→ A dream home in Idaho amid fields of rolling farmland turned into a nightmare for a young family when hundreds of snakes moved in with them. The five-bedroom house was just what they had been looking for when Ben and pregnant Amber Sessions moved in with their two small sons. However, the house came with secret lodgers—behind the skirting, beneath the floor, in the walls and in the roof space. Lying in bed at night they could hear the garter snakes—some up to 2 ft (60 cm) long—scurrying around in the walls. Sometimes there were so many snakes on the lawn it looked like the ground was moving. The house had been built on a hibernaculum, a place where the snakes come from miles around to curl up together for warmth when hibernating in winter and to breed in the springtime. The family abandoned the house after just three months.

Insect Replica

➚ This grasshopper in Indonesia took 40 minutes to cast off its exoskeleton—a hard outer shell—as it went through one of the stages in its two-month transformation from a nymph, which has no wings, into a fully grown adult grasshopper. As the nymph grows, the exoskeleton cannot stretch to match, so the young grasshopper must get rid of up to six different casings before it can grow wings.

gator guest A 2-ft-long (60-cm) alligator was found living under an escalator at Chicago's O'Hare International Airport. A startled maintenance worker discovered the reptile, which was captured when a police officer trapped it in a trash can.

celebrity cow Big Bertha, a cow owned by Irish farmer Jerome O'Leary, died in 1993 aged 49—over three times the average lifespan of a cow. She produced 39 calves and became a local celebrity, leading noisy St. Patrick's Day parades after being given whiskey to calm her nerves. Following her death, she was stuffed and is now on display at Beaufort, County Kerry.

ballistic bug The froghopper bug can leap 100 times its own length and accelerates from the ground faster than a ballistic missile. It accelerates with a force 400 times greater than gravity, whereas humans jump with a force just three times that of gravity.

both ends Despite being unremarkable to look at, woodlice can drink from both ends of their body—either through their mouth or their anus. They have tubelike structures on their posterior called uropods, which use capillary action to pull water up and into the anus.

green giants Adult male mountain gorillas of East Africa can eat up to 75 lb (34 kg) of vegetation every day—equivalent to the weight of an 11-year-old boy in leaves.

resurrected frog Using cloning technology, scientists in Australia are bringing back to life the southern gastric-brooding frog, which became extinct in 1983. A few samples of the long-dead frog were found in a freezer, and this was enough to enable researchers to produce tadpole embryos.

mother's sacrifice The female Japanese foliage spider allows her young to eat her to give them sufficient nutrients to survive.

dozy owl As a romantic gesture at her wedding to Andrew Mattle in Wiltshire, England, bride Sonia Cadman hired a trained barn owl to swoop down during the ceremony with the rings attached to its feet. Alas, despite repeated attempts to coax it down, the bird fell asleep in the church rafters for an hour, forcing the minister to use a pair of backup rings.

dog boots Police dogs in Germany have been issued Velcro-fastening shoes to protect their paws from broken glass during riots.

GONE FISHING

➔ The raft spider of Europe, which has a 3-in (8-cm) leg span, can dive beneath the surface to catch fish such as sticklebacks, and can walk on water. The spider gets its name from the way it waits for its prey like a raft on the surface of the water—the minute hairs that cover its legs spread the spider's weight so it doesn't sink.

life raft If one dolphin becomes distressed, the other members of the pod will often join forces to form a raft with their bodies and keep the injured dolphin above the water so that it can breathe and regain its balance.

aerial view Alphie, a tabby kitten owned by Vanessa Waite of Sheffield, England, made a full recovery after swallowing a 6-in-long (15-cm) TV aerial. He needed emergency treatment when the metal antenna, which was almost as long as his body, became lodged in his throat and stomach.

designer doghouse A St. Bernard dog named Wellington lives in an exact replica of his owner's home. Julian Kite, a former bricklayer, spent nearly £2,000 ($3,350) building Wellington's luxury kennel at a scale of 1:3 to his own detached house in Derbyshire, England. The 6½-ft-high (2-m) doghouse boasts stylish windows, a slate roof, fully functional guttering, and even hanging baskets and potted shrubs outside. The interior has fully insulated floors and walls to keep out the cold, electric lighting and a fitted carpet to protect the pooch's paws.

monkey business Sika deer on Japan's Yakushima Island find food by eavesdropping on the calls of feeding macaque monkeys.

DEATH GRIP ➜ Sloths can retain their grip on tree branches even after death. As they spend most of their lives in trees—sleeping, mating and giving birth while hanging upside down from branches—their claws and muscles have been developed for climbing, albeit slowly. This has made their grip so strong that sometimes when they die they are found still hanging from the branch hours later.

star pig Ramona Flowers, a two-year-old female potbellied pig owned by Luis Bojorquez from Tijuana, Mexico, has furrows in her brow that make her look just like the character Yoda from *Star Wars*.

party piece Jack, an Australian cattle dog owned by Nicole Lee of San Francisco, California, can balance an incredible range of objects on his head—including a soup can, a soccer ball, books, fruit, an egg and even a kettle. Nicole and her boyfriend Trey started out by balancing popcorn on Jack's nose while watching a movie and now he allows them to stack anything on his head as long as it's not too heavy. They have also trained him to shut the kitchen cabinets and open the refrigerator.

life saver When 17-year-old Ben Rees was home alone in the shower in Llanelli, Wales, his pet cockatiel Cookie flew into the bathroom, squawked noisily and dive-bombed him repeatedly to let him know that the house was on fire. Ben managed to escape through thick smoke, but sadly his feathered savior died in the fire and was later buried in the garden.

drunken pig A pig drank 18 cans of beer left outside at a campsite near Port Hedland, Western Australia, and then went on a drunken rampage during which it tried to fight a cow and swim across a river, before finally passing out.

fur extensions An online company in the U.K. called Poochie Plumes offers hair extensions for dogs! Provided the dog's fur is at least an inch long, owners can pay £11 ($19) for extensions made from colored feathers. The plumes, which are attached individually using a micro ring, can be left in for six weeks, but the company warns that the bright colors may run on white dogs.

fish frame When Einstein the goldfish developed swim bladder disease, causing him to turn upside down and sink to the bottom of his tank, his owner, Leighton Naylor from Blackpool, England, built him a special life jacket to enable him to swim again. The jacket came in the form of a floating frame made from recycled tubing, fitting perfectly over the fish's body.

feline felony A black-and-white cat was caught trying to smuggle illicit cell phones to prisoners inside Correctional Colony No. 1 at Verkhny Chov, Russia. Guards spotted the cat walking along the prison fence with a suspicious package strapped to his stomach, and closer inspection revealed that he was carrying two phones and two adaptors, destined for inmates.

million-dollar sheep A single Wagir sheep can fetch more than $1.5 million at animal auctions. The sheep, native to Asia, is pure white with huge ears and there are only about 1,000 of them in the world.

sign language Angi and Don Holt-Parks from Toledo, Ohio, learned sign language and taught it to Rudi, their deaf pit-bull mix, so that they could communicate with the dog.

skateboarding goat Happie, a Nigerian dwarf-cross goat owned by Melody Cooke, has spent hours riding around a parking lot in Fort Myers, Florida—on a skateboard. Happie took to skateboarding like a natural and has ridden the board nonstop for 25 seconds, covering a distance of 118 ft (36 m).

pet armor To protect his vulnerable guinea pig Lucky, doting owner Sean McCoy from Fairfax, Virginia, made the pet a tiny suit of armor, consisting of an authentic miniature steel helmet and a chain-mail suit.

lion passenger A motorist who spotted an escaped lion roaming the streets of Kuwait lured it into the back of his car and then slammed the door shut to keep it secure. The man then got into the car with the angry lion to call the police.

> **DECAPITATED FLATWORMS REGROW THEIR OLD MEMORIES ALONG WITH THEIR NEW HEADS.**

athletic collie Jumpy, an Australian border collie owned by Omar Von Muller of Los Angeles, California, lives up to his name by performing more than 20 agile tricks, including skateboard jumps, surfing, backflips, leaping off walls, playing Frisbee and riding a scooter.

interspecies transfusion Kate Heller, a veterinarian from Tauranga, New Zealand, saved the life of a cat by giving it blood from a dog! When Rory the ginger tom became dangerously ill after eating rat poison, a suitable donor could not be found quickly enough to save the hapless cat. So Heller gambled by taking 4 fl oz (120 ml) of blood from Macy the labrador and transferred it to the cat—which quickly started to recover.

blind faith When their blind, eight-year-old dog Abby went missing from their home in Fairbanks, Alaska, during a heavy snowstorm, the Grapengeter family thought they would never see their beloved hound again—but a week later she turned up at the home of a local veterinarian 10 mi (16 km) away, having survived freezing temperatures of –40°C (–40°F) without even a hint of frostbite.

FLAT FACE

→ With his cute pie face and huge brown droopy eyes that give him a permanent air of innocence, Snoopybabe, a cat from Chengdu, China, has his own Facebook page and around half a million fans online.

His owner, Miss Ning, regularly uploads dozens of new pictures of him, often dressing him in a range of designer outfits and even jewelry. Snoopybabe gets his distinctive appearance from his parents—he is a cross between an American short-hair and a Persian cat.

WOMAN PERFORMS CPR ON BLIND CHICKEN

■ Roberta Rapo spent 3½ hours successfully resuscitating her daughter Rayna's blind pet chicken, Chooky Wooky, after a gust of wind had blown the bird into the family pool in Sydney, Australia, leaving it to drown. Finding the stricken chicken floating lifelessly in the pool, Roberta pulled it out and started mouth-to-mouth resuscitation and CPR, pumping the frail bird's heart until it finally began to revive. A grateful Chooky Wooky was later given a clean bill of health by a veterinarian and then laid a celebratory egg. Rayna, pictured here with Chooky Wooky, now describes her bird as a "miracle chicken."

wonder web In the movie *Spider-Man 2*, the superhero shoots a web to prevent a runaway train from plunging to disaster—and a team of U.K. scientists has shown that this is not Hollywood exaggeration. The Darwin's bark spider, from Madagascar, creates webs that are ten times stronger than Kevlar and, if scaled up to Spider-Man proportions, its silk would be strong enough to halt a four-car subway train traveling at full speed.

rubber tail Mr. Stubbs, an alligator at an animal sanctuary in Scottsdale, Arizona, has been given a 3-ft-long (0.9-m) rubber tail after losing his natural one in a fight. Before the prosthetic tail was fitted, he tended to walk in circles, but with the extra weight he is now able to move in a straight line.

subway shark A dead shark was found on a New York subway train! Passengers were asked to leave the train at Queens so that a conductor could remove the carcass from beneath a row of seats. The 4-ft-long (1.2-m) shark had first been discovered washed up on the beach at Coney Island before 31-year-old Chris Landros from Brooklyn decided to display it to a wider audience by taking it for a ride on public transit.

pig whisperer Veterinarian Kees Scheepens from Brabant, Netherlands, hypnotizes pigs to measure their stress levels. An expert in pig body language and grunts, he estimates that he has seen more than five million swine while visiting stables in every country in Europe. To win the animals' trust, he sometimes eats from their troughs!

skin surgery Veterinarians in Tualatin, Oregon, carried out an operation to remove 2½ lb (1.1 kg) of loose skin from a previously obese dachshund that had lost weight. Obie had once weighed a whopping 77 lb (35 kg), but after he shed 40 lb (18 kg) on an eight-month diet, the loose skin started to drag and so owner Nora Vanatta had it cut off.

cleanest cat Murli the cat ended up with an unexpected wash and blow-dry after being wedged behind the bumper of his owner's car when he drove it through a car wash. Reinhold Pratl of Hartberg, Austria, drove 15 mi (24 km) to the car wash and took the vehicle through the full cleaning cycle before he realized that his cat had come along for the ride. Cut free from the car, Murli was none the worse for her ordeal apart from the fact that she was soaking wet and smelled of shampoo.

waiting game After her six-month-old pet chicken Sarah swallowed a $450 diamond earring while perched on her shoulder, Claire Lennon from Berkshire, England, learned she might have to wait eight years to retrieve the gem. The earring is trapped inside the bird's stomach and an operation to remove it could prove fatal, meaning that Claire will probably have to wait until Sarah dies of old age.

COLOR CHANGE

➜ A dull olive-green color the rest of the year, the male Indian bullfrog (*Hoplobatrachus tigerinus*) dresses to impress in the mating season. To attract a female, his skin dramatically turns bright yellow while his prominent vocal sacs become a vivid blue. The Indian bullfrog has one other idiosyncrasy: despite being relatively large, it can jump over the surface of water the same as it does on land.

Poop Disguise

→ **Predatory birds and wasps usually give the bird-dung spider of Singapore a wide berth because its body looks like an unappetizing dollop of poop.**

The squat brown spider hunts by night, but spends most of its day huddled motionless on an exposed leaf or branch, and so needs its disguise to avoid being eaten.

record brood
In 2013, a mallard duck at a wildlife reserve in Arundel, England, successfully hatched no fewer than 24 ducklings—which is three times the average number of hatches and the largest brood ever recorded.

squirrel rampage
A gang of ten gray squirrels caused $21,000-worth of damage at a lawn bowling club in Edinburgh, Scotland, by eating part of a clubhouse. The rampaging rodents gnawed through 6-in-thick (15-cm) wooden joists and electrical wiring, causing the ceiling to collapse.

power purr
Merlin, a cat owned by Tracy Westwood from Devon, England, purrs at an incredible 100 decibels—as loud as the sound of a subway train and around 180 times louder than the average cat's purr.

whistling caterpillars
Walnut sphinx caterpillars frighten off predatory birds by whistling from breathing holes in their sides. They pull their heads back to compress their body and then force air out of their abdominal spiracles as a whistling sound. Each whistle can last up to four seconds.

peed on bomb
Juliana, a Great Dane, was awarded the Blue Cross Medal after she extinguished a Nazi incendiary bomb dropped during a World War II attack on the U.K.— by urinating on it. The bomb fell through the roof of her owner's house in April 1941, and burst into flames, but Juliana put out the fire by standing over the bomb, lifting her leg and emptying her bladder.

> **NEWBORN OPOSSUMS ARE SO TINY THAT 20 OF THEM COULD FIT ON A SINGLE TEASPOON.**

star signs
Dung beetles use the Milky Way galaxy to navigate in straight lines at night. Needing to chart a straight course for fear of ending up back at the dung pile where another insect would steal their prize, they orientate themselves by looking up at the stars as they roll their balls of poop along the ground.

barking mad
A zoo in Luohe, China, tried to pass off a large dog as a lion because it was unable to afford the real thing! The deception was exposed when the Tibetan mastiff that was posing in the lion cage as the king of the jungle barked loudly in front of baffled spectators. Elsewhere, visitors found a mongrel dog in the wolf enclosure, a fox in the leopard's den and, in the reptile house, two giant sea cucumbers masquerading as snakes.

jet pets
Italian fashion designer Valentino has six pet pug dogs—Mary, Maude, Milton, Monty, Molly and Margot—and each has its very own seat on board the designer's private jet.

indestructible ants
Ants can survive a fall from any height—because they have so little body mass relative to their air resistance that they fall very slowly. Even when dropped from an airplane, an ant's terminal velocity is only approximately 4 mph (6 km/h) compared to a human's of at least 125 mph (200 km/h).

thieving parrot
While Scottish tourist Peter Leach stopped to take pictures at Arthur's Pass on New Zealand's South Island, a kea parrot flew through the open window of his campervan and stole $900 in bank bills from the dashboard.

spoiled shells Fewer than 300 of Madagascar's ploughshare tortoises are living in the wild, prompting some conservationists to mark the animals' beautiful shells in order to reduce their value to poachers.

agent swan An Egyptian man arrested a swan and took it to a police station because he thought the bird was a spy. He became suspicious when he noticed the swan was carrying an electronic device, but it turned out to be a wildlife-tracking instrument.

silk thread The silk used to form a silkworm's cocoon is actually hardened saliva that has been secreted from its mouth, and it can unravel into a single thread up to 1 mi (1.6 km) long.

sinister skull The pink underwing moth caterpillar of Australasia and North America has sinister face markings on its head that look uncannily like a human skull so that it can scare off predators.

shark diver Hawaiian free diver Ocean Ramsey swims and rides with great white sharks up to 17 ft long (5.2 m) in order to prove they are nothing like the terrifying man-eater from *Jaws*. She travels the globe in search of sharks and has so far swum with more than 30 different species.

six-clawed lobster A mutant six-clawed lobster was caught off the coast of Massachusetts in 2013. Donated to the Maine State Aquarium in Boothbay Harbor, 4-lb (1.8-kg) Lola has a normal claw on one side, but instead of a singular claw on the other, she has five claws like a hand. The extra claws are either a genetic mutation or an unusual regrowth from a damaged or lost claw.

larger female The female blanket octopus can be 40,000 times heavier and 100 times larger than a male—that's the equivalent to an average human standing next to a walnut. The female can reach 6½ ft (2 m) in length and weigh 22 lb (10 kg), but the male often measures just 0.9 in (2.4 cm) and weighs no more than 0.009 oz (0.25 g).

stalking croc New Zealand kayaker Ryan Blair was trapped on Governor Island off the coast of Western Australia for two weeks by a giant crocodile that he thought would eat him if he tried to escape. Having been taken to the remote location by boat, Blair had intended to kayak the 2.5 mi (4 km) back to the mainland, but every time he tried to paddle away, the 20-ft-long (6-m) crocodile stalked him, forcing him to return to the island. Desperate for water, he finally shone a light to alert a rescuer.

soccer-playing fish Ilana Bram of Poughkeepsie, New York, spent two months training her pet cichlid fish Erasmus to play soccer in his tank with a miniature ball. The talented fish can also weave his way through a slalom course and perform a limbo dance.

■ The wood frog survives a Canadian winter by effectively dying for weeks. Covered in ice, it looks dead, but has simply frozen itself solid on the forest floor to cope with the intense cold, and when the temperature eventually rises, it thaws out and springs back to life.

FROZEN

DEFROSTED

RIPLEY'S RESEARCH

In winter, up to 65 percent of the wood frog's body water becomes extracellular ice. Frozen crystals grow between the skin and muscle layers of the body, in the bladder and in the lens of the eye. A large mass of ice also fills the abdominal cavity, encasing all of its internal organs, leaving the frog with no heartbeat or brain activity. The frog can shut down completely because the formation of ice crystals on its skin triggers its liver to produce large amounts of glucose, which protects its vital organs.

FREAK LOBSTER

➜ Jeff Edwards from Owl's Head, Maine, caught this half-brown, half-orange lobster—a one-in-50-million genetic freak resulting from a lack of pigmentation. The two-tone lobster is currently on display at the Gulf of Maine Research Institute in Portland. In a bizarre coincidence, a year earlier, fisherman Dana Duhaime caught a similar specimen off Beverly, Massachusetts. Split-color lobsters are often hermaphrodites, but Duhaime's catch was entirely female, making it even more rare.

spinning pet Chica, a guinea pig belonging to Marilyn Jones from New Plymouth, New Zealand, emerged unscathed after spending 30 minutes inside a running laundry dryer. Chica ended up in the dryer after becoming entangled in a bedsheet but somehow survived an intense cycle at temperatures of 160°F (71°C).

color change Reindeer change their eye color, from gold in summer to blue in winter. The blue color reduces the amount of light that is reflected out of their eyes, and this has the result of boosting their vision for the dark winters.

two-tone lamb A lamb named Battenberg was born with black markings on one side of his face and white on the other—and while his front right and back left legs are black, the other two legs are white. His distinctive coloring helped save his life by ensuring that he was spotted in deep snow shortly after he was born in the Brecon Beacons National Park in Wales.

stretch jelly Although its body is usually only about 6 ft (1.8 m) in length, the lion's mane jellyfish has tentacles that can grow up to 120 ft (37 m), making it longer than a blue whale.

fiery shrimp *Acanthephyra purpurea*, the fire-breathing shrimp, blinds and distracts its would-be predators by spewing out a blue-glowing bacterial cloud.

snake bite Working at Werris Creek cemetery in New South Wales, Australia, 66-year-old Jake Thomas killed a venomous red-bellied black snake by cutting it in half with his shovel—but, amazingly, 15 minutes later the dead snake bit him on the hand and he had to spend two days in a hospital intensive-care unit.

eagle selfie A sea eagle snatched a video camera that was positioned to take pictures of crocodiles in Western Australia and then recorded its two-hour flight, along with taking a couple of selfies. The 6-in-long (15-cm) camera vanished from a spot next to the Margaret River, but wildlife rangers had no idea of the thief's identity until the camera was retrieved 70 mi (112 km) away. When finally the film was played, the feathered culprit was seen poking its face into the lens.

Death Trap

➜ Measuring as much as 5 ft (1.5 m) in diameter and built up to 6 ft (1.8 m) above ground, the conjoined web of female red-legged golden orb spiders is so large, and is woven from such strong silk, that it can ensnare bats and even birds.

This bird—a seafaring lesser noddy—was photographed by Isak Pretorius after it became trapped in a web on Cousine, an island in the Seychelles. Luckily for the bird, it was saved, but most perish. After a struggle, the web will eventually break, but as the birds fall to the ground their wings are still tangled in the web fibers, and they can't fly. They soon die from a combination of exhaustion and dehydration.

1. LURE!

2. ATTACH!

3. EAT!

BEETLE ↗ REVENGE: PART 1

➔ Frogs and toads consider beetle grubs to be a tasty snack, but Epomis ground beetle larvae have turned the tables and are able to eat amphibians many times their size. The baby beetle performs a dance with its antennae to lure the toad into launching an attack, but at the last minute it dodges out of the way and quickly latches onto the toad with its spiked jaw. It then sucks the toad dry, eventually reducing it to just a pile of bones.

guardian angel A faithful dog has been trained to sniff out peanuts for seven-year-old Meghan Weingarth, from Suwanee, Georgia, who suffers from a serious nut allergy. Meghan breaks out in hives and could go into shock if she eats anything containing peanuts but LilyBelle the goldendoodle now checks all of her food first and raises a paw to warn her if she is about to eat nuts.

late lunch Baby adders go into hibernation shortly after they are born and often do not have their first meal until they are one year old.

hungry birds Hummingbirds burn so much energy that, to avoid starving to death, they must eat their body-weight in food each day and slow down their metabolism as needed.

split personality A two-headed turtle named Thelma and Louise was born at San Antonio Zoo, Texas, in June 2013. The baby turtle ate with both heads but displayed a split personality, the right side being curious while the left was more aggressive.

dolphin's dinner A dolphin caught a huge 10-lb (4.5-kg) cod and then appeared to give it to a human family for their supper! Lucy Watkins and her grandparents were kayaking off the coast of Devon, England, when the dolphin surfaced with the fish and dropped it close to Lucy's boat. The friendly dolphin then nudged it to within 5 ft (1.5 m) of her before reappearing with its own dinner, a sea bass.

super snake Titanoboa, a snake that lived in South America 58 million years ago, grew up to 50 ft (15 m) long and had a mouth large enough to swallow a crocodile—whole.

falling tree While Lydia Bigras was walking with friends through Goldstream Provincial Park, British Columbia, her four-year-old Australian terrier Roo suddenly ran back the way they had come. The humans followed and seconds later a 60-ft (18-m) cedar tree crashed down where they had been standing. None of them had noticed that the tree was falling.

killer catfish European catfish 5 ft (1.5 m) long living in the River Tarn in southwestern France have been seen lunging out of the water, snatching pigeons from the bank and then returning to the river to devour their prey.

deadly fish There are over 1,200 species of venomous fish—outnumbering the world's venomous snakes and all its other venomous vertebrates combined.

← BEETLE REVENGE: PART 2

➔ The adult Epomis ground beetle continues this unusual behavior, biting, paralyzing and eating frogs larger than themselves.

Ripley's
Believe It or Not!®
www.ripleybooks.com

Sea Monster

➜ Members of the Catalina Island Marine Institute hold an 18-ft-long (5.5-m) oarfish that washed up off the coast of Southern California in 2013—a sea monster so huge that it needed 16 people to drag it ashore.

The dead oarfish was spotted floating underwater, having drifted up from the deep. Oarfish live at depths of up to 3,000 ft (915 m) and are therefore rarely seen. They can grow up to 60 ft (18 m) in length and can weigh 600 lb (272 kg). Known in Japan as "Messengers from the Sea God's Palace," they are one of several animal species believed to have warned humans of impending natural disasters by a change in their behavior.

ANIMALS THAT CAN PREDICT NATURAL DISASTERS

Twenty oarfish stranded themselves on beaches in northern Japan shortly before the 2011 **earthquake and tsunami** As deep-sea fish living near the ocean bed, it is thought that they are more sensitive to the active faults that mark the start of a quake than those living closer to the ocean surface.

12 hours before **Hurricane Charley** hit Florida in 2004, eight sharks that had been tagged in Pine Island Sound fled abruptly to the open ocean. It is believed sharks sense the air and water pressure changes caused by an impending storm.

Just before the massive 2004 **earthquake and tsunami** devastated the Indian coast, elephants were seen breaking their chains and fleeing to higher ground.

A few hours before **Hurricane Jeanne** battered Gainesville, Florida, in 2004, butterflies in the University of Florida's experimental rain forest went into hiding, wedging themselves under rocks and disappearing into tree hollows. Eardrum-like organs on their abdomens may have alerted them to seek shelter when they sensed a marked drop in air pressure.

Common toads that had been breeding in a shallow Italian lakebed suddenly moved uphill in 2009—five days before a strong **earthquake** struck the region. The toads returned to the pool as soon as the quake's last aftershock had occurred.

Earthworms pour out of the ground before a **major flood** as they seek to escape rising groundwater.

Southern Buller's albatrosses often change their flight direction 24 hours in advance of a weather system so that they can take advantage of **strong winds**

walking shark A previously unknown species of small shark, *Hemiscyllium halmahera*, uses its fins to walk along the ocean floor. The 30-in-long (76-cm) shark, which was recently discovered off the coast of Indonesia, wiggles along the seabed so that it can hunt for small fish and crustaceans.

dogged determination After his owner John Dolan of Bay Shore, Long Island, was admitted to hospital, Zander, a white Samoyed-husky mix, missed him so much that he sneaked out of the house and tracked his scent to the hospital 2 mi (3.2 km) away, crossing a highway and a stream to get there. Zander's amazing sense of smell enabled him to make the long trek to find his master. Huskies have up to 300 million scent glands, whereas humans have just five million. Also certain breeds of dog develop a special bond with humans that can act as a sixth sense.

ram raiders A flock of 80 sheep invaded a ski shop in the Austrian resort of St. Anton. It is thought one sheep saw its reflection in a mirror and went in to investigate and, being sheep, the rest of them decided to follow.

FLYING WHIPPET

Davy Whippet, a three-year-old dog owned and trained by Lara Sorensen at Thorhild, Alberta, ran and caught a Frisbee thrown a distance of 402 ft (122.5 m). Thrower Rob McLeod launched the Frisbee, and Davy, starting alongside him, sprinted the distance in about 10 seconds—that's nearly 25 percent faster than Usain Bolt—to catch it before it landed. Lara has a big field for Davy to run about in yet she says: "He is a couch potato 99 percent of the day, but when you ask him to work, he is completely switched on."

odd couple Every day a cat in Kunming, China, hitches a ride to the local stores on the back of his best friend—a large dog. The animals' owner Xu Wan noted that whenever he took the dog out for a walk the cat miaowed as if it wanted to come, too. He bought a small lead for the cat, but it quickly tired of walking and decided that it was easier to travel by dog.

artistic chimp Brent, a 37-year-old chimpanzee who paints colorful pictures with his tongue, earned $10,000 for the Chimp Haven sanctuary in Keithville, Louisiana, by winning first prize in a national art contest.

cobra alert In April 2013, police in Hanoi, Vietnam, arrested the driver of a car who was traveling with 53 live king cobras as passengers.

flab lab Mike, an obese 133-lb (60-kg) labrador, lost 37 lb (17 kg) in seven months at a rescue center in Leicestershire, England, by going for regular walks in a tank of water—even though he was too big to fit in it at first. Before the hydrotherapy treatment, Mike was so heavy and unfit that he damaged a ligament in one of his legs and would be gasping for breath after waddling just short distances.

STARTLED LOOK

→ With two unusual, diagonal black markings on his forehead, Sam, a former stray cat from New York, looks as if he has eyebrows—and his distinctive, permanently startled appearance quickly made him an Internet sensation. He has his own website and more than 100,000 followers on picture-sharing site Instagram.

pet capybara Melanie Typaldos and Richard Loveman keep Gary, a 110-lb (50-kg) capybara, as a pet at their home in Buda, Texas. They adopted the giant rodent after seeing capybaras while on vacation in Venezuela. They even let their pet sleep in their bed.

oh deer! The city center of Nara, Japan, is home to a herd of more than 1,000 sika deer who happily roam the streets among the busy traffic and pedestrians.

skateboarding dogs Biuf, a skateboarding bulldog, has become such an Internet star, with thousands of followers on Facebook, that his owner, Ivan Juscamaita, has opened a school in Lima, Peru, to teach other dogs to skate.

elastic nests Long-tailed tits are small songbirds that deliberately weave stretchy spiders' webs into their nests to allow the structure to expand as their chicks grow.

miraculous survival Wasabi, a two-year-old cat owned by Stephanie Gustafson, survived a fall from the 11th floor of an apartment block in Juneau, Alaska, after chasing a mosquito out of a window. Landing in the parking lot, she escaped with a fractured leg and broken bones, which surgeons repaired in an operation.

new species There are believed to be tens of thousands of olinguitos—relatives of raccoons—living wild in the treetops of Colombia and Ecuador, but until recently no one knew they even existed. In 2003, Dr. Kristofer Helgen of the Smithsonian's National Museum of Natural History found some misidentified bones and skin in storage at a Chicago museum, but it took another decade for these to be identified and officially unveiled as the first new mammal species to be discovered in the western hemisphere for 35 years.

TWO HEADS → Yuri Yuravliov of Kiev, Ukraine, has a six-year-old female Central Asian tortoise with two heads, two hearts, one heart-shaped shell and six legs. The two heads even have different tastes in food. The left head is more dominant and opts for green vegetables, like lettuce, while the other prefers brightly colored food, such as carrots.

Trunk Snap

→ **Looking for a quick bite, this ambitious Nile crocodile clamped its powerful jaws onto the trunk of a young elephant as it drank water from a pool in Zambia's South Luangwa National Park.**

The startled elephant trumpeted loudly, shook itself free and ran off into the bush, leaving the croc to search for a more modest meal. Lodge worker Ian Salisbury, who took the photo, said the same crocodile had earlier attacked a buffalo. The scene is a case of life imitating art, after the Rudyard Kipling story about the elephant that got its trunk when a crocodile bit it on the nose and stretched it.

warm nest After crawling into a rabbit burrow to make a kill, the European stoat will sometimes use the dead rabbit's carcass as a warm furry nest in which to raise its own young.

batmobile The New Zealand batfly cannot fly and does not even have wings—it hitches rides on bats instead.

light bones Sharks do not have a hard bone skeleton. Instead, their skeleton is made from light, flexible cartilage—the same material that supports a human outer ear.

rubber flippers Yu, a loggerhead turtle that lost her front fins to a shark attack, swims around the Suma Aqualife Park in Kobe, Japan, wearing a pair of artificial flippers. The rubber limbs are attached to a vest slipped over the turtle's head.

inflatable snake Burmese pythons' hearts enlarge by up to 40 percent after they've eaten, and many of their organs, including the long digestive tract, double in size to enable them to swallow and digest large prey.

tiger trainer Animal trainer Randy Miller spends his days being attacked by a fully grown, 400-lb (181-kg) tiger—and he usually walks away without a scratch. Randy, who runs a facility in Big Bear, California, has trained big cat Eden to leap 15 ft (4.6 m) through the air at him and then pin him to the ground. The terrifying attacks are so realistic that Randy's animals have appeared in movies including *Gladiator*, *Transformers 2* and *The Last Samurai*.

RIPLEY'S RESEARCH

Although only ½ in (12 mm) long, dermestid beetles can strip the flesh off a bear's skull in less than 24 hours in a process called skeletonization. Their voracious appetites have made them popular with law enforcement agents who use the beetles to expose skeletons in homicide cases where the application of harsh chemicals might destroy vital evidence. Museum curators and taxidermists also buy dermestid beetles to clean skeletons before they are exhibited. In the wild, the beetles eat dead animals, but in North American homes, where they can lurk in walls or under floorboards, they devour old books, carpets or clothes.

Flesh-eaters

→ Skulls Unlimited, a company based in Oklahoma City, Oklahoma, used thousands of tiny dermestid beetles to remove the flesh from this beached, dead, 40-ft-long (12-m) humpback whale before reconstructing it as a skeleton.

The bones of the whale had to be separated and placed in containers for the beetles to be able to do their work. The whale was then degreased and chemically whitened, making the bones sanitary and ready to display at the Museum of Osteology, also in Oklahoma.

Flesh-eating bugs!

GUARD CROCS → Instead of guard dogs, Awirut Nathip uses two adult crocodiles to protect his house in Thailand—and unsurprisingly he has not been burgled in 15 years. He keeps Nguen under the house in a ditch because he is so aggressive, while Thong patrols the yard, often lying in front of the door as an extra deterrent.

greedy shark A Greenland shark that was found in distress in a harbor in Newfoundland, Canada, had bitten off more than it could chew—in the form of a moose. The shark almost choked to death on its gargantuan meal, but fortunately two people on the beach spotted the creature with the 2-ft-long (0.6-m) piece of moose flesh sticking out of its mouth. They managed to dislodge the meat from its jaws, before pushing the shark back out to sea.

athletic dog Boogie the Labrador received a medal for completing a 13-mi (21-km) half-marathon for humans in Evansville, Indiana. After escaping from his leash the night before, he was found running in the race, which he finished ahead of more than half the competitors, before being reunited with owner Jerry Butts.

what a snitch! Driver Guillermo Reyes was arrested in Mexico City after his pet parakeet told police he was drunk. The officers had stopped Reyes during a routine check, but as he got out of his car to be tested the bird inside the vehicle squawked: "He's drunk, he's drunk." Guillermo subsequently failed the breathalyzer test.

light language There are more than 2,000 species of fireflies in the world—most of which emit flashing lights—and each flashing species has its own unique flashing-light language.

riding raindrops A mosquito being hit by a falling raindrop is like a person being hit by an SUV—but the insects survive the impact by "riding" the raindrop for a fraction of a second.

tough guy The grasshopper mouse of North America can eat the highly poisonous Arizona bark scorpion without any ill effects because it is immune to the scorpion's venom, which instead acts as a painkiller to the mouse.

stealth location Some moths hear so well that the barbastelle bat, which feeds on them, needs to make its echolocation calls up to 100 times softer than normal so as not to scare away its prey.

jellyfish invasion A mass invasion by jellyfish forced one of the world's largest nuclear reactors to shut down on September 29, 2013. Operators of the Oskarshamn nuclear plant in Sweden had to scramble the reactor after tons of jellyfish blocked the pipes that bring in cool water to the plant's turbines.

guilty locust In 1866, a locust was put on trial in Croatia for the damage caused by its swarm. It was sentenced to death by drowning.

seal crossing An elephant seal weighing more than half a ton stopped traffic for over an hour in the Brazilian beach city of Balneário Camboriú after waddling out of the Atlantic Ocean and across a busy street. The 10-ft-long (3-m) seal actually used a pedestrian crossing while police officers and firefighters splashed water on the animal to keep it cool.

BIZARRE BUG

→ With its striped body and long "hair" sticking out of its rear, this planthopper insect looks just like a troll! The unnamed ¼-in-long (7-mm) creature may be a new species, one of 60 discovered by Conservation International researchers during a three-week trek through the South American rainforest in Suriname. The planthopper's hair-like excretions, which may serve to distract predators, are actually made of wax and are produced by specialized glands in the bug's abdomen.

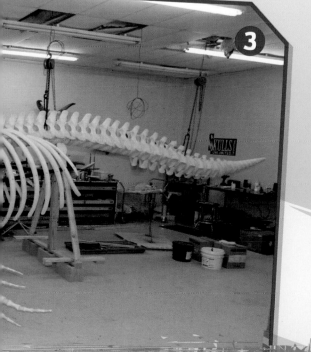

[YOUR / UPLOADS]

BIKER BIRD

No, your eyes are not deceiving you—Myles Bratter of Dover, New Hampshire, regularly rides his motorcycle at speeds of up to 80 mph (128 km/h) with Rainbow, his pet ruby macaw parrot, perched on his shoulder. Myles sent Ripley's this picture of him with speed-loving Rainbow, who is not tied down in any way, on the bike. The talented bird can speak over 160 words and phrases and has been photographed with dignitaries including George H.W. Bush as part of her fundraising work to help homeless people. Although she was born back in 1995, Rainbow has plenty of air miles left in her yet, as macaws can live to be over 100 years old.

EASY RIDER

→ In *Ripley's Believe It or Not! Download the Weird*, we told you about Norman, a shaggy Briard dog owned by the Cobb family of Canton, Georgia, who has been riding a scooter since he was a puppy and can cover 30 yd (27 m) in under 30 seconds. Well now Norman, who has his own Facebook page and over two million fans on YouTube, has learned to ride a bicycle, resting his front paws on the handlebars and pedaling expertly with his back paws.

dog detour Hendrix, a six-year-old English springer spaniel, was supposed to be flying in cargo from New Jersey to Phoenix, Arizona, but instead ended up some thousands of miles away, across the Atlantic in Ireland, after the airline put him on the wrong flight.

doctor parrot Barbara Smith-Schafer from Lincolnshire, England, has a guardian angel watching over her in the form of her husband's African gray parrot, Dominic. Barbara has been diagnosed with a sleeping disorder called sleep apnea, which causes her breathing to be blocked, but Dominic has learned to recognize the heavy snoring that marks a possible attack and when he hears it, he wakes her by flapping his wings and pecking at her shoulder.

devoted dog For more than two months after his owner died, Tommy, a 12-year-old German shepherd dog, turned up every day at the church she used to attend. The dog headed to the church in San Donaci, Italy, as soon as the bells began to ring each afternoon, just as he had done for years when his owner was alive. Tommy even attended his owner's funeral, following her coffin as it was carried into the church. The local priest was so impressed by his devotion that he allowed him to sit in front of the altar during services.

abstract artist Forced to stop racing after damaging a knee in 2009, racehorse Metro Meteor has since found fame as an abstract painter. Adopted by artist Ron Krajewski from Rocky Ridge, Maryland, the horse has sold more than 200 paintings for a combined sum of $20,000, and in 2013 was the best-selling artist at Gallery 30 in Gettysburg, Pennsylvania. For his large paintings, which can sell for up to $2,000, there is a waiting list of 120 customers.

fox text A fox that stole a cell phone from 16-year-old Lars Andreas Bjercke in Norway ran off with it and then used it the next day to send a text message to Lars' friend!

long fur Colonel Meow, a Himalayan–Persian mix owned by Anne Marie Avey and Eric Rosario of Los Angeles, California, has hair that is an astonishing 9 in (23 cm) long. The cat, who has his own website, Facebook page and YouTube channel with more than two million views, has such long hair that it takes two people to brush it, which Anne Marie and Eric do three times a week.

traveling cat Ron Buss's cat Mata Hairi left her home in Portland, Oregon, for her usual short walk on September 1, 2012—and spent the next ten months traveling around the U.S.A. with a hitchhiker who picked her up in a café after thinking she was a stray. With Michael King, she hitched to California and Montana, becoming a local celebrity by riding on top of his backpack. It was only when she was taken to a veterinarian that a scan found a microchip, which led to her being reunited with Ron.

dog vacations The Paw Seasons holiday resort in Somerset, England, offers luxury two-week vacations for dogs— for a cool £47,000 ($70,000) a pet. The package includes a designer leash, collar and coat, a spa and grooming session, surfing on the beach, behavioral lessons, a custom-made doghouse in a replica of their owner's home, and screenings of *Lassie* and *101 Dalmatians* while chewing on dog-friendly popcorn.

killer croc Over a 20-year period, Gustave, a 20-ft-long (6-m) Nile crocodile living in Africa's Lake Tanganyika, is thought to have killed more than 200 people and has so far resisted all attempts to be killed or captured.

extra passenger Polly, a two-year-old tabby cat, traveled 1,700 mi (2,736 km) trapped underneath a speeding train—and survived. Without food and water, she spent two days hurtling through England and Wales at 125 mph (200 km/h) before her mewing finally alerted the train manager.

calming parrot Jim Eggers from St. Louis, Missouri, suffers from bipolar disorder, but whenever he feels an episode coming on, he relies on his pet parrot, Sadie, to calm him down with a few wise words. She now accompanies him everywhere, carried in a backpack adapted to hold her cage.

booming bark Charlie, a golden retriever owned by Belinda Freebairn of Adelaide, Australia, has a bark that has been measured at 113.1 decibels—that's louder than a rock concert or a pneumatic drill.

Vampire Cat

➜Lazarus, a kitten found wandering the streets of Johnson City, Tennessee, has a cleft palate that has left him looking like a vampire.

With no upper lip, his lower fangs protrude, and he appears to be missing a nose, too. Yet, despite his condition, he is so loveable that his new owner, Cindy Chambers, is using him as a therapy cat to help change people's perceptions about animals and people with disabilities.

COOKIE-MONSTER FISH

➜ This may look like Cookie Monster, the hungry Muppet, but it is in fact a trio of purple sea sponges (*Aplysina archeri*) that had fused together near Curaçao in the Caribbean to form what appear to be a pair of wide eyes and a gaping mouth. The sponge is about 3 ft (0.9 m) tall. You can close its "mouth" simply by squeezing it gently between your thumb and forefinger.

same place Using stealth and its powers of camouflage to hunt and avoid predators, the giant Pacific octopus spends more than 90 percent of its day in one place.

turtle pee The Chinese soft-shelled turtle urinates from its mouth. The urine travels through the reptile's bloodstream to its mouth, where it has strange, gill-like projections. The turtle then submerges its head in a puddle of water and spits out the pee.

split shell An injured endangered green sea turtle that was washed ashore at Key West, Florida, had its fractured shell repaired by local dentist Fred Troxel using denture adhesive. He used the acrylic resin to bond two metal orthopedic plates across the 10-in (25-cm) split on the turtle's shell.

eye candy Thailand has several species of bees that drink the tears of mammals, including people, to extract protein and salt for their diet.

slime defense A single hagfish can turn a bucket of water into slime in seconds. The fish is covered in slime glands and when attacked it releases the slime as a defense mechanism, choking the airways of predators as large as sharks.

musical fish Japanese researchers have found that, although famed for their short attention span, goldfish can distinguish between the music of Johann Sebastian Bach and Igor Stravinsky.

fish candle The eulachon, or candlefish, found on America's Pacific Coast, is so fatty during spawning that it can be dried, threaded on a wick and burned as a candle.

elusive hippo A hippopotamus spent over six months living in a sewage plant in Cape Town, South Africa, after escaping from a nature reserve. While on the run, the young male eluded capture for weeks in a city lake and also popped up in suburban gardens before setting up home in the sewage plant. He was finally caught and shipped to a game reserve.

TURTLE TEARS

➜ This yellow-spotted river turtle in the western Amazonian rain forest is being mobbed by butterflies that have come to drink its tears. In a region where salt is rare, the turtles have a plentiful supply of the vital mineral sodium through their diet, prompting dozens of butterflies to flutter around the reptiles' heads for a fortifying drink. If no turtles are around, the butterflies will get their salt fix from animal urine or sweaty humans.

Ripley's
Believe It or Not!®
www.ripleybooks.com

WALKING TALL

→ In the 19th century, a giraffe called Zarafa rode on the back of a camel before walking 560 mi (900 km) across France from Marseille to Paris.

As the first giraffe ever to be seen in France, she was greeted by huge crowds throughout her epic 44-day walk. When she finally arrived in Paris, 100,000 people turned out to see her.

Captured in the Sudan in 1826, Zarafa was a gift from the viceroy of Egypt, Muhammad Ali, to the King of France, Charles X. The one-year-old giraffe was taken to Khartoum loaded onto the back of a camel. She was then transported down the Nile and across the Mediterranean Sea in the cargo hold of a ship. A hole cut into the ship's deck allowed her long neck to poke through.

After 32 days at sea, she then had to walk from Marseille to Paris. She set off on hoof on May 20, 1827. All along her route people marveled at this strange 12-ft-tall (3.7-m) creature.

In Paris, fashionable ladies arranged their hair into towering styles, and spotted fabrics became all the rage.

Zarafa remained the star attraction at the Jardin des Plantes zoo until her death in 1845.

Zarafa became such a sensation when she arrived in France that her image was painted on plates and embroidered into tapestries.

GIRAFFE Femelle.
Âgée de 2 Ans et demi.

jamaican icon Biologist Paul Sikkel of Arkansas State University discovered a new species of parasite in the coral reefs off Jamaica's coast and named it *Gnathia marleyi* to honor Jamaican reggae musician Bob Marley.

branching out Two days after going missing from Cynthia Weeks' home in Davenport, Iowa, Laddy, a seven-year-old border collie, was found safe and well two blocks away—10 ft (3 m) up a tree.

walking upright Born with bones missing from his front legs, Harvey, a kitten at an animal rescue center in Glasgow, Scotland, learned to get around by crawling on his "elbows" or by walking upright on his back legs.

rent-a-goat In August 2013, the historic Congressional Cemetery in Washington, D.C., hired 58 goats for a week at a cost of $4,000 to act as lawn mowers and eat invasive plant species up to 7 ft (2.1 m) high.

bumper ride A lucky black kitten nicknamed Pumpkin suffered nothing worse than a broken paw after being trapped for 22 hours and traveling about 100 mi (160 km) along upstate New York roads wedged behind the bumper of Stacey Pulsifer's Jeep.

dung roamin' Several species of frogs in Sri Lanka use mounds of fresh elephant dung as a moist, temporary home.

STRANGE MARKINGS → It is difficult to work out how many heads or legs Evita, a giant anteater at San Francisco Zoo, really has! The markings on her front legs could be mistaken for a panda's head. What is certain is that if the newborn baby on her back grows up to look like mom, she'll be easy to recognize.

nasty shock The shock from an electric eel is so powerful that it can knock a horse off its feet. The eels can generate an electrical charge of up to 600 volts—five times the power of a standard U.S. wall socket. Their bodies contain electric organs with cells that store power like tiny batteries, and when the eel feels threatened or is in attack mode, these cells discharge simultaneously.

snake stash Discovering nine eggs in the yard of his home in Queensland, Australia, three-year-old Kyle Cummings put them in a plastic container and stashed them in his closet. By the time his mother found the container, seven of the eggs had hatched into venomous eastern brown snakes. The bite from these snakes, even as babies, can be fatal.

snake intruder Police investigating a break-in at a charity store in Queensland, Australia, found the culprit was a 19-ft-long (5.7-m) python. Seeing a roof panel cut in half, clothing knocked over and crockery smashed, officers naturally suspected a human intruder until they discovered a smelly pool of vomit and the snake lying next to a wall. It is thought the 37-lb (17-kg) python entered the store through the roof, which was damaged in a cyclone in 2011.

panda video Inexperienced female giant panda Colin kept rejecting male Yongyong until conservationists at the Panda Breeding and Research Base in Chengdu, China, played the pair a video of pandas mating to show them how it was done. "Colin took great interest in the film," said a vet at the center. "After that they mated successfully."

beefy beetle The 6-in-long (15-cm) Hercules beetle of South America can lift 850 times its own body weight—the equivalent of a human lifting a 65-ton object. The male beetle also has fighting horns that are longer than its body.

curly tusks The tusks of the babirusa pig of Indonesia grow up and curve backward over its eyes, often reaching a length of 12 in (30 cm)—so long that they sometimes pierce its forehead.

wayward moth A giant Atlas moth, which has a 12-in (30-cm) wingspan, was discovered by a family in their garden in Lancashire, England—more than 6,000 mi (9,600 km) from its Southeast Asian habitat.

fake spider A newly discovered species of small spider in Peru makes large fake spiders in order to ward off predators. It forms the decoy arachnids—right down to their eight legs— from pieces of debris and then vibrates its web to make the big spider seem alive.

cat candidate Hank, a Maine Coon cat, received over 6,000 votes in the 2012 United States Senate election in Virginia. Owners Matthew O'Leary and Anthony Roberts nominated Hank as a protest against regular political campaigns. Finishing third, Hank, who advocated spay and neuter programs, raised $60,000 for animal shelters.

SQUIRTING BLOOD

→ The short-horned lizard, which lives in the deserts and prairies of North America, shoots blood out of its eye as a defense mechanism to scare off predators. The blood is propelled from ducts in the corner of the eye and can spurt a distance of 3 ft (1 m). As well as warding off predators, the blood contains a chemical that is noxious to wolves and coyotes.

cat burglar Wandering from house to house through neighbors' cat flaps, tabby Milo stole 26 sets of house and car keys from houses in London, England. Her crimes were uncovered when her owner Kirsten Alexander spotted her coming through the cat flap with a set of keys dangling from her magnetic collar.

stowaway fish In the wake of the 2011 Japanese tsunami, a striped beakfish, native to Asia, crossed the Pacific Ocean to Washington State in the U.S.A. aboard a small drifting boat. The fish survived the 5,000-mi (8,000-km) journey by feeding on organisms in the vessel.

crowd pleasers Fighting male crickets are more violent—and more expressive in their victory dance—if other crickets are watching.

Snake Ball

→ Emerging from hibernation in spring, European grass snakes form "mating balls," where up to eight males and one or two females congregate for as long as two hours in a tight, writhing, reproductive mass.

The males attempt to uncoil the female with a constant intertwining of their bodies through hers until their sexual organs are aligned for mating.

snake invasion In May 2013, the Louisiana State Capitol building in Baton Rouge was invaded by water snakes migrating from nearby Capitol Lake. Baby snakes were found curled up in closets, crawling across committee-room carpets and coiled in the corner of a bathroom.

huge hairball Ty, a 392-lb (178-kg) tiger at Wildlife Rescue and Rehabilitation in Seminole, Florida, underwent surgery to remove a hairball the size of a basketball from his stomach. The 17-year-old tiger had been unable to hack up the 4-lb (1.8-kg) hairball because it was so big, and hadn't eaten for two weeks.

wrong cat Karen Jones of Kent, England, was heartbroken after the funeral of her beloved pet cat Norman, only to discover that she had buried the wrong animal. She was sure it was her black cat that she had found lying dead on a busy road, but a day after the backyard burial Norman turned up in the kitchen and began eating his tea.

avian marvel In January 2013, Wisdom, a Laysan albatross of the North Pacific, gave birth to her 36th chick—at age 62! The average Laysan albatross dies at less than half her age.

SPORTS

THE MIGHTY ATOM

→ Joseph Greenstein was born prematurely in Poland in 1893. A small child, he never grew over 5 ft 4 in (163 cm) in height and weighed just 145 lb (65.7 kg).

However, his small stature did not prevent Joseph from becoming 'The Mighty Atom,' one of the strongest men in the world—perhaps even the strongest, pound for pound.

In his youth, Joseph was befriended by a Russian wrestler and circus strongman who helped him become a top wrestler billed as "Kid Greenstein,"—a name that would take him to Asia, where he honed his physical prowess and developed the mental powers he would later use in his strong man performances. He believed that the power of the mind was just as important as the power of physical strength.

It was in America that Joseph became the Mighty Atom, and made his name devising unique and seemingly impossible feats of strength for his comparatively small stature. He could lift 500-lb (225-kg) weights with his teeth, bite nails in two, and bend iron bars into different shapes.

In 1934, he broke a rib during an act in New York, but when the ambulance was called he offered to pull it to the hospital with his hair. He performed at Atlantic City and Coney Island, and, after wowing crowds with his brawn, he would sell them tonics that promised to maximize their own muscle power. His other feats included changing a car tire with no tools, and lying on a bed of nails while supporting a 17-piece band on his body.

The Mighty Atom could bend iron bars using his hair.

MIGHTY ATOM FEATS

Breaking a chain by expanding his chest

Lying on a bed of nails while supporting ten members of his family and, on another occasion, a 17-piece band

Pulling a hammered nail out of a board with his teeth

Tying horseshoes into knots

Pulling five cars with only his hair

Biting steel chains in two with his teeth

Changing a tire with no tools

Pulling a 32-ton truck

Two gentleman help the Atom bend an iron bar over his nose.

The Atom lying on a bed of nails, with the added weight of 17 members of a band!

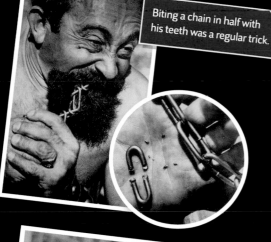

Biting a chain in half with his teeth was a regular trick.

→ **The Mighty Atom** had a surprisingly long career, given the extreme demands placed on his body, and he continued to perform into old age, appearing at Madison Square Garden, New York, in his eighties. His incredible story is thought to be the basis for the long-running DC Comics character "Atom," who first appeared in 1940.

Breaking a chain purely by the expansion of his chest.

An iron grip, strength and concentration helped the Mighty Atom bend steel bars as if they were wire.

URBAN SKIING

→ Karl Fostvedt (far left) was one of several skiers in Detroit, Michigan, that used the city's derelict buildings and structures as a private ski park. With the aid of ramps made from scrap materials, they performed spectacular twists off walls and ledges and jumped down flights of steps and through open windows. If there is not enough snow for their routines, they simply truck some in.

lucky bounce Former National Football League quarterback Brad Johnson is the only person in the league's history to complete a touchdown pass to himself. He did it playing for the Minnesota Vikings against the Carolina Panthers in 1997 when he caught his own deflected pass and then ran three yards for a unique touchdown.

big bounce Thirty-year-old Jay Phoenix completed 150 bungee jumps in 21½ hours from a 130-ft-high (40-m) crane in Brisbane, Australia, averaging seven jumps an hour. He maintained his energy levels by snacking between jumps and, as he found he was often still chewing on the way down, he discovered that he could swallow while bouncing.

stair slalom Urban skiers Matt Wild and Logan Imlach skied from top to bottom through an abandoned five-story military block in Whittier, Alaska. They carried piles of snow into the building and then climbed to the top before slaloming down the stairs and leaping out through windows.

killer ball In 1920, Ray Chapman of the Cleveland Indians died after the ball pitched to him struck him on the head—he is the only player to be killed by a baseball during a Major League game.

garden course Desperate to build a snowboarding course in the back garden of his home in Aviemore, Scotland, Mikey Jachacy and nine friends made several trips 2,000 ft (600 m) up the Cairngorm Mountains and collected eight tons of snow. They then built a 200-ft-long (60-m) course, complete with ramps, jumps and even a cable-operated ski lift, which ran off an old motorcycle engine.

skateboard speedster

→ Daredevil South African professional skateboarder Decio Lourenco hit a top speed of 68 mph (109 km/h) as he raced down a hill and through traffic on a busy Cape Town highway, passing within just a few feet of oncoming vehicles. His high-speed stunt angered the police, who say he triggered a speed camera in an area where the limit is just 37 mph (60 km/h).

team toilet In 2012, Toronto Maple Leafs fan Jim Vigmond paid $5,300 for a toilet from the hockey team's locker room at their old Maple Leaf Gardens arena.

flying high Professional kiteboarder Jesse Richman from Maui, Hawaii, was towed by a boat and lifted an unprecedented 790 ft (240 m) into the air above the Columbia River Gorge in Oregon—more than 20 times the height that kiteboarders usually reach when their kite is caught by the wind.

rare card As an investment for his son, Jason LeBlanc of Newburyport, Massachusetts, paid $92,000 at a 2013 auction in Maine for a 148-year-old baseball card. The 1865 card showed a photograph of the all-conquering Brooklyn Atlantics amateur baseball club.

helping hand Brazilian soccer team Aparecidense were thrown out of the Fourth Division play-offs in 2013 after club masseur Romildo da Silva stepped onto the field from behind the net and blocked two goalbound shots in the dying minutes to prevent opponents Tupi from snatching victory. Da Silva, who was chased from the field by enraged Tupi players, was fined $250 and suspended for 24 matches.

40 marathons Double leg amputee and Paralympian gold medalist Richard Whitehead from Nottinghamshire, England, ran 40 marathons in 40 days on his prosthetic blades while traveling the length of Britain in 2013.

piglet prize The winner of the Carrera Ciclista del Cochinillo cycle race, held in Huércal-Overa, Spain, each December is traditionally presented with a live piglet, which he is expected to eat for Christmas dinner.

ditch plunge Extreme kayaker Ben Marr from Mallorytown, Ontario, somehow kept upright as he paddled furiously down a steep concrete drainage ditch called the Lions Bay Slide in British Columbia at nearly 35 mph (56 km/h) before splashing into a reservoir.

global run Starting and finishing at Sydney Opera House, Australian athlete Tom Denniss circumnavigated the world on foot by running the equivalent of a marathon a day for 622 days. Visiting five continents and going through 17 pairs of shoes, he ran 16,250 mi (26,000 km) in just under 21 months from December 2011 to September 2013. His scariest moment came during his run over the Andes mountain range, when he slipped on a snowcap and nearly fell down a 1,000-ft (300-m) ice cliff.

batting marathon Overcoming fatigue, muscle pain and hunger, 52-year-old baseball fanatic Mike Filippone, president of the North Babylon Youth League, New York, batted for 24 hours straight in June 2013, during which he hit close to 10,000 balls.

oldest player Armenian-born Artin Elmayan from River Plate, Argentina, age 96, is the world's oldest professional tennis player. He plays three times a week against younger opponents.

UNARMED BARBIE

→ Even though she lost both her arms when she was just two, Barbie Thomas from Phoenix, Arizona, has been competing in fitness contests against able-bodied women for over ten years.

Her arms were burned to the bone by a supercharged electric shock after she had climbed onto a transformer and grabbed the wires with both hands. "They were like charcoal," she said. "They were completely dead and had to be amputated at the shoulders."

Young Barbie was not expected to live. However, not only did she survive against the odds, she also quickly learned to adapt by holding out her legs to hug her mother and using her legs and feet to get dressed. As a young girl, she entered dance and swimming competitions, as well as playing soccer, before turning to fitness. Now the inspirational mother-of-two trains at the gym six days a week, doing weights and leg exercises and practicing her routine, which includes splits, high-kicks and an incredible ninja kip-up where, from lying on her back, she bounces straight up into a standing position.

Ripley's ask

What made you become a fitness fanatic? I've always been "fit." I was very active growing up, but got serious about my fitness after I had my first baby.

How often do you train? I'm in the gym six days a week. I also go to gymnastics practice three to four days a week.

What is your favorite part of the competition? Performing a routine. It's the most challenging part for me, but it's so much fun!

What inspires you? Knowing that I'm inspiring others and hearing their stories. Also people who have it harder than I do—they inspire me!

Do you have particularly dextrous feet? My feet ARE my hands. I wish my toes were a little longer, but yes... they have a lot of dexterity, especially my right foot. I'm right footed!

What has been your greatest challenge, and how did you overcome it? Besides backflips, caring for my boys when they were babies, especially when they were newborn. The first time I learned by trial and error, but by the time I had my second baby it was a piece of cake.

GREASY POLE ↘

→ Every August in St. Julian's, Malta, hundreds of brave young men attempt to climb a 65-ft-long (20-m) greasy pole and retrieve a flag at the end for a game called gostra, which dates back to the Middle Ages. Some competitors prefer to run along the wooden pole as fast as possible in the hope of grabbing a flag before inevitably slipping off into the water below.

tree throwing Every January, people living near Weidenthal, Germany, get rid of their old Christmas trees by staging a competition to see how far they can throw them. There are three disciplines in the World Christmas Tree Throwing Championships—*weitwurf* (javelin-style), *hammerwurf* (hammer-style) and *hochwurf* (high-jump-style)—and all trees must first be stripped of lights and other decorations.

hybrid sport Originating in the Netherlands, footgolf is a new sport where players kick a soccer ball into holes on a golf course in as few shots as possible—and in June 2012 the first Footgolf World Cup was held in Budapest, Hungary, attracting players from countries as far away as the U.S.A., Argentina and Mexico.

ping-pong rally Max Fergus and Luke Logan, students at Stoughton High School, Wisconsin, played a table-tennis rally that lasted 8 hours 30 minutes 6 seconds, hitting the ball back and forth without stopping.

pudding race At the Yorkshire Pudding Boat Race in Brawby, England, competitors paddle giant traditional Yorkshire puddings—made of flour, water and eggs and coated in varnish—across a lake.

ALL FOURS → Running on all fours, Japan's Kenichi Ito scrambled 100 meters in a speedy 16.87 seconds at Tokyo's Olympic athletic track in November, 2013. He beat six other competitors in an all-fours 100-meter race and said that he's been developing his distinctive running style, which is based on the movements of the African Patas monkey, for more than a decade.

atlantic flight Bernard Chambers released his prize-winning racing pigeon Percy in Brittany, France, expecting him to fly the 303 mi (485 km) home to Staffordshire, England—but instead the bird turned up 3,200 mi (5,150 km) away in Quebec, Canada.

veteran racer Hershel McGriff from Portland, Oregon, drove in a NASCAR West Series race at Sonoma Raceway, California, on June 23, 2012, at the age of 84. He finished a respectable 18th in a field of 30 drivers.

high scoring Four Nigerian soccer clubs were suspended on suspicion of match-fixing after vital 2013 play-off matches produced scores of 79-0 and 67-0. Plateau United Feeders scored 72 of their goals against Akurba FC in the second half—nearly two goals per minute—while Police Machine FC scored 61 times in the second half of their mauling of Bubayaro FC.

sand skier Henrik May from Germany prefers to ski on sand rather than on snow, and has reached a top speed of 57 mph (92 km/h) on a dune in the Namibian Desert.

highest paid There are only 11 states in the U.S.A. where the highest-paid public employee is not a sports coach—Alaska, Nevada, Montana, North Dakota, South Dakota, New York, Maine, Vermont, New Hampshire, Delaware and Massachusetts.

apt names When Hartlepool beat Notts County 2-1 in an English Football League Division One soccer game in February 2013, their goalscorers' names were Hartley and Poole!

marathon man Chuck Engle of Arlington, Virginia, has won more than 150 marathons since he began running them in 2000, including winning at least one marathon in each of the 50 U.S. states.

RAM RACE

→ In a novel twist to the 100 meters, competitors in Yiwu County, China, race along a course while carrying a full-grown sheep whose legs are bound to prevent escape. The "Running with Sheep" event is part of an annual harvest celebration, which also includes a sheep beauty contest.

unlucky strike A man in Jupiter, Florida, accidentally shot himself in the leg while bowling. He was carrying a gun in the pocket of his shorts and the weapon fired off a round when he struck his thigh with his bowling ball.

blind vaulter Fifteen-year-old pole-vaulter Charlotte Brown from Emory, Texas, qualified for the 2013 state championships even though she is blind. She has cleared a height of 11 ft 6 in (3.5 m) and is able to vault by counting her steps on her run-up and listening to her coach yell when it is time to launch. She also places an 80-ft (24-m) strip of dark artificial turf adjacent to the approach lane to create a light/dark contrast she can follow in order to keep running in a straight line.

wheely crazy! Originating in the U.S.A., the sport of extreme mountain unicycling, described as a cross between mountain biking and rodeo riding, sees thrill-seekers pedal, pivot and bunny-hop from rock to rock as they try to ride all the way down steep mountain faces on their custom-made unicycles without falling into deep chasms.

explosive targets The traditional Colombian sport of tejo involves throwing metal disks at gunpowder-filled targets that explode on impact.

sibling rivalry When John Harbaugh's Baltimore Ravens defeated Jim Harbaugh's San Francisco 49ers in Super Bowl XLVII in 2013, it was the first time in Super Bowl history that teams coached by two brothers had met.

tank biathlon The Russian military staged a tank biathlon in 2013 where teams from Russia, Kazakhstan, Armenia and Belarus had to steer their tanks across an obstacle course and shoot at targets in the fastest possible time.

36 off A referee at a junior league soccer match in Paraguay between Teniente Fariña and Libertad brandished 36 red cards—sending off the substitutes as well as all the players—after a mass brawl broke out in the closing minutes.

BUBBLE SOCCER

→ For the exciting new British sport of bubble soccer, players are encased in zorbs—huge inflatable bubbles—and instead of tackling for possession of the ball, they simply bounce into each other.

The game, devised by Lee Moseley, is played by two teams of seven and is safer than it looks, because although players are easily flipped on their backs like turtles, they bounce straight back up.

wrong route Of the 5,000 runners that took part in the 2013 Marathon of the North in Sunderland, England, only one competitor—Leicester's Jake Harrison—completed the correct course. Organizers accidentally sent everyone else on a wrong route, which meant that their total run was in fact 289 yd (264 m) short of the full 26 mi 385 yd (42.2 km) marathon distance.

tough nut Amateur goalkeeper Duško Krtalica carried on playing in a soccer match in Sarajevo, Bosnia-Herzegovina, despite being shot in the head with a rifle. He was accidentally hit by a bullet fired into the air at a nearby wedding celebration.

EVEREST BASE JUMP

→ In May 2013, Russian extreme sports star Valery Rozov BASE jumped off the north face of Mount Everest 23,688 ft (7,220 m) above sea level. He flew for nearly a minute at 125 mph (200 km/h) along the north face before landing safely on the Rongbuk glacier at an altitude of 19,521 ft (5,950 m). He made his daring jump to celebrate the 60th anniversary of the conquest of Everest.

moving target As a stunt, Japanese soccer star Shunsuke Nakamura curled a football with his left foot into an open window on a moving bus—on the first attempt.

three generations Bob Banhagel, 67, his son Rob Banhagel, 44, and his grandson, Jacob Blankenship, 18, are all pole vaulters—and the three of them participate together in U.S. sporting meets.

happy dad When 19-year-old soccer player Ryan Tunnicliffe came on as a substitute for Manchester United in their 2012 Capital One Cup tie against Newcastle, it earned his dad Mick £10,000 ($16,000). The proud father had placed a £100 bet when his son was nine that he would one day play for Manchester United—at odds of 100 to one.

safe hands Cincinnati Reds fan Caleb Lloyd caught two home-run balls in the same inning during the Reds' win over the Atlanta Braves in May 2012.

miles ahead Sixty-nine-year-old Larry Macon from San Antonio, Texas, completed an unprecedented 255 marathons in 2013, averaging three a week, which made a total of over 4,110 mi (6,614 km). He wears out 13 pairs of running shoes a year and, working as a full-time attorney, has even held conference calls while running.

no fear Peter Sheath from Southampton, England, has been water-skiing for over 25 years despite being blind since the age of 30. Now aged 74, he still takes to the water twice a week and says that his disability helps him in the sport because, as he is unable to see, he never feels scared.

oldest winner Sixty-five-year-old Bill "Spaceman" Lee of San Francisco, California, became the oldest pitcher to win a pro baseball game when his San Rafael Pacifics beat the Maui Na Koa Ikaika on August 23, 2012.

FLAMING FOOTBALL

→ Played in parts of Indonesia to celebrate the holy month of Ramadan, sepak bola api is just like soccer—except all the players are barefoot and the ball is a red-hot fireball! The ball is actually an old coconut shell, which has been soaked in 5 gal (20 l) of kerosene for up to a week to ensure it will stay alight for the duration of the game. So that players can kick and even head it without suffering severe burns, they undergo a pre-match ritual that is supposed to make them impervious to fire and includes a 21-day fast and avoiding eating any foods cooked with fire.

helicopter drop In July 2013, Zack Hample of New York City caught a baseball dropped from a helicopter flying 1,050 ft (320 m) above him at Lowell, Massachusetts. The ball plummeted toward him at 95 mph (152 km/h) on its 12-second journey into his mitt.

mass backflip While holding hands, 30 skiers skied down a slope and performed a simultaneous backflip at the resort of Mont Saint-Sauveur, Quebec, in April 2013.

golden foot Japanese jeweler Ginza Tanaka has cast a solid gold replica of the left foot of Argentine soccer star Lionel Messi. The golden foot weighs 55 lb (25 kg), is 10 in (25 cm) tall and is valued at $5.25 million.

baseball card To herald spring training in 2013, sports trading card manufacturer Topps created a giant baseball card nearly 90 ft tall and 60 ft wide (27 x 18 m) depicting an image of Detroit Tigers' Prince Fielder.

$92,613!

RED SOCK → A bloody sock worn by Boston Red Sox pitcher Curt Schilling in the 2004 World Series sold for $92,613 at an auction in February 2013.

pig carrying As part of the annual Hercules strongman competition in Hengyang, China, contestants race over a 98-ft (30-m) course carrying two live pigs, each weighing 44 lb (20 kg).

mine hazards U.S. Army soldiers at Camp Bonifas in South Korea built a one-hole golf course alongside the North–South demilitarized zone, featuring live land mines that mark the boundaries.

soccer hero Twenty percent of new babies born in the first half of 2013 in La Paz, Bolivia, were called Neymar in honor of the latest Brazilian soccer star.

giants stadium New York Giants fan Don Martini, 75, spent two years and $20,000 building a replica scale model of the team's old stadium in a garage behind his Blairstown, New Jersey, bagel shop. He made 65,000 seats and even included working lights and elevators in the model, which measures 20 ft (6 m) long and 17 ft (5.2 m) wide.

quick change During the 2012 Formula-1 German Grand Prix, the McLaren team changed all four tires on driver Jenson Button's car in just 2.3 seconds.

unique feat After winning the men's doubles at Wimbledon in 2013, U.S. brothers Bob and Mike Bryan became the first pair ever to hold the U.S., Australian, French, Wimbledon and Olympic titles at the same time—tennis' Golden Grand Slam.

skateboard ride In December 2012, Taiwan's Wu Meng-lung traveled more than 186 mi (300 km) on a skateboard in 24 hours— that's about the distance from New York City to Philadelphia and back. He has previously completed a 14-day, 684-mi (1,100-km) trip around Taiwan on skateboard and on foot.

virtual manager Azerbaijani Premier League soccer team Baku FC appointed 21-year-old Vugar Huseynzade as manager of their reserve team in 2012 even though his only previous experience was playing the computer game *Football Manager* for ten years.

floral jersey German Bundesliga soccer club Borussia Dortmund launched their new jersey for the 2013–14 season by planting 80,645 flowers—mainly yellow marigolds— to replicate the design on nearby parkland.

jacket potatoes At the Kiplingcotes Derby, a 500-year-old, 4-mi (6.4-km) cross-country horse race in Yorkshire, England, the amateur jockeys achieve the required riding weight of 140 lb (63.5 kg) by putting potatoes into their jacket pockets.

no runs The Detroit Tigers and Pittsburgh Pirates baseball teams played a pair of nine-inning scoreless games in three days in May 2013—only the fifth time this has happened in over 100 years of Major League history.

last dog The last hot dog and bun sold at the last Montreal Expos baseball game in 2004 sold for $2,605 on eBay—more than 700 times its original price.

Berry Boarding

→ **Believe it or not, this intrepid wakeboarder is being pulled through a bog of cranberries at the 2010 Red Bull Winch Sessions in Tomah, Wisconsin.**
To harvest cranberries, the beds are flooded with up to 1 ft (30 cm) of water above the vines, and because the berries are filled with air, they readily float to the surface and present a fresh, fruity challenge for wakeboarders.

05

Ripley's ask

Larry, what inspired your tattoos? I got tired of society's expectations—I didn't want to do what was expected of me, so I started to become a manimal—half man, half animal. My leopard tattoos have given me special leopard powers, such as seeing in the dark, running really fast and hunting at night.

What kind of reaction did you get when you first had them all done? My family has a military and Christian background so they didn't take to my tattoos very well. I was upset that they couldn't relate to my self-expression. What I saw as art, they saw as desecrating my body. It took them ten years to come round, but now we've got a better relationship. They can see I'm doing alright for myself.

Do you ever regret your tattoos? No. I'm proud of my tattoos—few people look like me. When I look in the mirror in the morning I like what I see. My tattoos will never be taken away from me. They could throw me in jail, but I'll always have this art on my body.

Do you have any plans for more body modification? I top up my facial tattoos several times a year as they fade in the sun. I'd like to get my eyelids tattooed too, but I don't want to do it myself. It's hard to tattoo your own eyelids. And having your private parts tattooed really hurts—I wouldn't recommend it—but to me the art is worth the pain.

Larry, seen here as a young boy, didn't always look like a leopard—he got his first tattoo at the age of 20.

Larry in full leopard persona out with a friend in Austin.

Tattoo artist Larry retouches his spots himself as they start to fade.

Larry Da Leopard

A tattoo artist from Austin, Texas, has covered his entire body in more than 1,000 spots to become half man, half leopard.

Born Lance Brieschke, the 40-year-old big cat enthusiast has even changed his name to Larry Da Leopard. He began getting leopard tattoos at age 20, had his face inked five years later, and is now covered head to toe in spots. In keeping with his character, he prowls the streets wearing little more than a Tarzan-like loincloth and a leopard-print jacket. If he goes out for walks with a friend, he is sometimes led around by a chain.

While many people love his look, his family cried when they first saw his spots and disowned him for ten years. He struggled to find a job, but now that he runs his own tattoo parlor he uses his distinctive body as an advertisement.

This leopard certainly has no intention of changing its spots. He tops up his tattoos every few months as they fade and claims that they have somehow given him some of the traits of a big cat.

Larry stalks the streets of Austin, Texas, in little more than a leopard-skin loincloth!

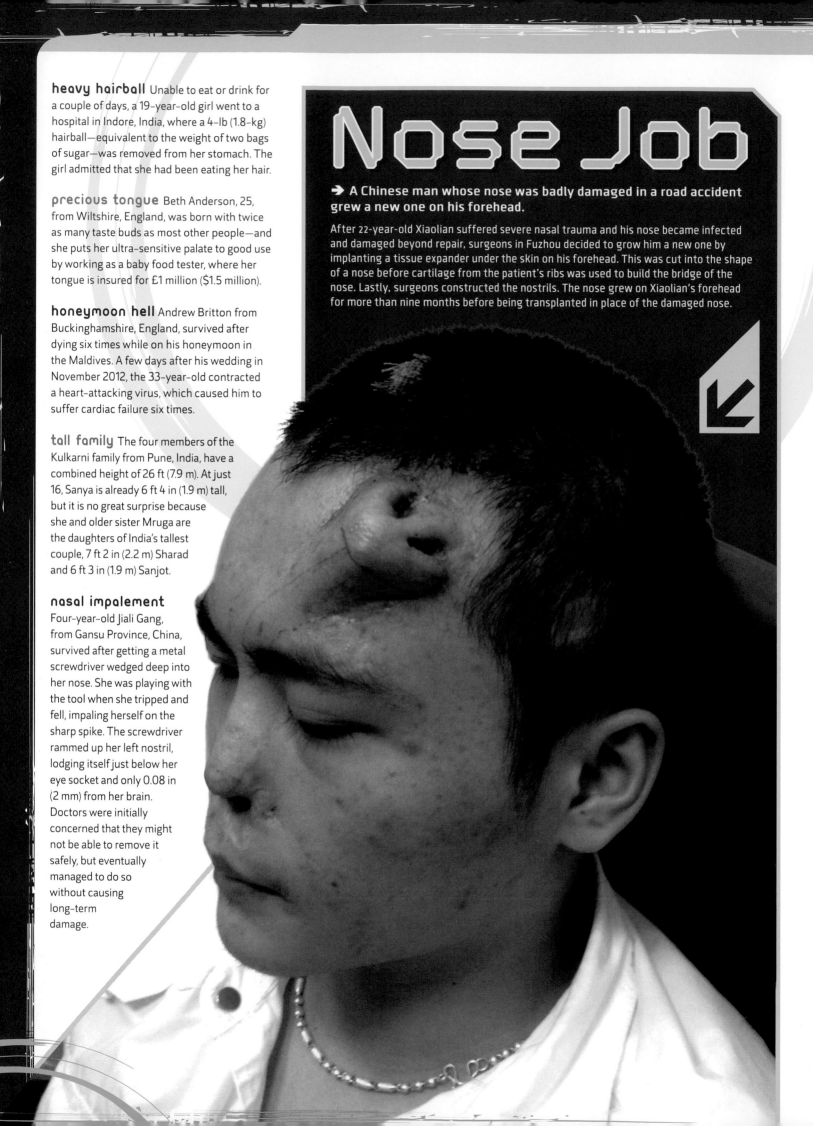

heavy hairball Unable to eat or drink for a couple of days, a 19-year-old girl went to a hospital in Indore, India, where a 4-lb (1.8-kg) hairball—equivalent to the weight of two bags of sugar—was removed from her stomach. The girl admitted that she had been eating her hair.

precious tongue Beth Anderson, 25, from Wiltshire, England, was born with twice as many taste buds as most other people—and she puts her ultra-sensitive palate to good use by working as a baby food tester, where her tongue is insured for £1 million ($1.5 million).

honeymoon hell Andrew Britton from Buckinghamshire, England, survived after dying six times while on his honeymoon in the Maldives. A few days after his wedding in November 2012, the 33-year-old contracted a heart-attacking virus, which caused him to suffer cardiac failure six times.

tall family The four members of the Kulkarni family from Pune, India, have a combined height of 26 ft (7.9 m). At just 16, Sanya is already 6 ft 4 in (1.9 m) tall, but it is no great surprise because she and older sister Mruga are the daughters of India's tallest couple, 7 ft 2 in (2.2 m) Sharad and 6 ft 3 in (1.9 m) Sanjot.

nasal impalement Four-year-old Jiali Gang, from Gansu Province, China, survived after getting a metal screwdriver wedged deep into her nose. She was playing with the tool when she tripped and fell, impaling herself on the sharp spike. The screwdriver rammed up her left nostril, lodging itself just below her eye socket and only 0.08 in (2 mm) from her brain. Doctors were initially concerned that they might not be able to remove it safely, but eventually managed to do so without causing long-term damage.

Nose Job

→ **A Chinese man whose nose was badly damaged in a road accident grew a new one on his forehead.**

After 22-year-old Xiaolian suffered severe nasal trauma and his nose became infected and damaged beyond repair, surgeons in Fuzhou decided to grow him a new one by implanting a tissue expander under the skin on his forehead. This was cut into the shape of a nose before cartilage from the patient's ribs was used to build the bridge of the nose. Lastly, surgeons constructed the nostrils. The nose grew on Xiaolian's forehead for more than nine months before being transplanted in place of the damaged nose.

JAR OF NAILS

Richard M. Gibson of Lafayette, Louisiana, has been saving his fingernail and toenail clippings since 1978. He keeps them in a 10-fl-oz (300-ml) jar, which is now 99 percent full.

ACTUAL SIZE!

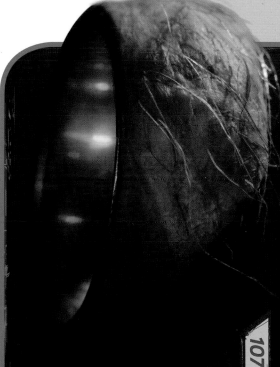

drank urine
Eighteen-year-old backpacker Sam Woodhead from London, England, survived for three days in searing 104°F (40°C) heat in the Australian Outback by drinking contact lens fluid and his own urine. Lost and disorientated after going for a jog from a Queensland cattle station, he shed 28 lb (12.7 kg) during his ordeal and was just hours from death when a search helicopter, which was just about to return to base because it was low on fuel, spotted a pair of brightly colored shorts that Sam had hoisted as a distress signal.

speared in mouth Elisangela Borborema Rosa came within a hair's breadth of death after being shot in the mouth with a spear gun as her husband cleaned the weapon in the kitchen of their home in Arraial do Cabo, Brazil. The spear went in through her mouth and pierced her spine, but if it had gone a fraction to either side she would either have been killed or left paralyzed for life.

mummified arm In early 2012, an anonymous donor gave a mummified arm to the National Museum of Civil War Medicine in Frederick, Maryland. It is believed to have come from the 1862 Battle of Antietam, and to have been found and preserved by a local farmer.

pee teeth Scientists in Guangzhou, China, have grown teeth from human urine. The urine was used as a source of stem cells, which were then implanted in mice, and within three weeks had developed into tiny toothlike structures with dental pulp and enamel.

endless tune For more than three years, Susan Root from Essex, England, has had an endless loop of the novelty song "How Much is that Doggie in the Window?" playing in her head. She suffers from a rare form of tinnitus where music and songs play in her head day and night—and the music she hears is often so loud it drowns out the sound of her husband Graham when he is speaking.

skin fall Teen sisters Emma and Stacey Picken from County Durham, England, shed all of their skin every day. They suffer from lamellar ichthyosis, a condition that accelerates their skin-cell turnover, causing the top layer to shed six times faster than with most people. They constantly need to vacuum up their fallen skin and the family washing machine keeps breaking down because it gets blocked with the residue of the skin cream they have to apply twice a day.

lennon clone After buying John Lennon's rotten tooth for $30,000 at auction in 2011, dentist Dr. Michael Zuk, from Edmonton, Alberta, says he is hoping to extract the DNA and clone the former Beatle!

sleep trek Joy Grigg from Cornwall, England, disappeared after climbing out of her kitchen window while sleepwalking—and was later found unharmed in a hedge 6 mi (10 km) away. Two months earlier, in January 2013, she had walked 5 mi (8 km) in her sleep. Her husband kept calling her cell phone until the vibration in her pocket eventually woke her up.

eye catching An assault trial in Philadelphia, Pennsylvania, was halted after the victim's prosthetic eye popped out in court while he was giving evidence. John Huttick was testifying about losing his eye in a fight when his prosthetic blue eye suddenly popped right out and he caught it as jurors gasped in shock.

SKIN RING ➔ Icelandic designer Sruli Recht has produced a gold ring covered in a slice of his own skin. Surgeons removed a 4¼-in (11-cm) flap of skin from his abdomen and the strip was then salted and tanned, and then mounted on the 24-carat gold ring.

WONDER BUTT

➔ Vanity Wonder, a 30-year-old model and former dancer from the U.S.A.'s Midwest, became addicted to having injections to enhance the size of her butt. In five years, she spent $15,000 on around 1,000 injections. In her first session she had nine silicone injections plugged with super glue in each buttock, but in later sessions she had a staggering 120 jabs in each cheek. However, the shots, which could have killed her, gave her an infection that left her butt looking like "a sack of oranges." To regain its rounded shape, she had to have extra silicone implants, and these caused her butt to end up bigger than even she had wanted, leaving her with a unique 34–23–45 figure. She vows that she will have no more injections.

blue body Jim Hall from Baltimore, Maryland, has his entire body covered in one huge bright-blue tattoo. When employed as a city planner, he kept his tattooed body hidden beneath his work suit, but once he retired in 2007 he was free to get his face and head inked, too. Over a 35-year period, Jim, who calls himself Blue Comma, has spent more than $135,000 on body modification.

shock diagnosis A 66-year-old Chinese man went to a hospital in Hong Kong seeking treatment for a swelling in his abdomen—and discovered that he was really a woman! The man's condition was caused by an extremely rare combination of two genetic disorders— Turner Syndrome, which causes women to lack some female features including the ability to get pregnant; and congenital adrenal hyperplasia, which makes the patient look like a man. Only six cases of a patient with both conditions have ever been reported.

forever airsick Since stepping off a plane in Turkey more than eight years ago, Catharine Bell from Northumberland, England, has been almost permanently airsick. She has been diagnosed with the neurological disorder Mal de Debarquement Syndrome, which leaves her with a spinning head and a churning stomach for months at a time.

handy app A Scottish company has created a prosthetic hand that can be controlled by a cell-phone app. Touch Bionics' "i-limb ultra revolution" features a powered rotating thumb for increased dexterity and 24 different grip options, each activated by a single tap of the screen. This allows the wearer to adjust the hand for different tasks, such as writing, typing or even tying shoelaces.

vampire saliva A new drug developed for treating stroke victims is made from Draculin, the saliva of vampire bats.

MIXER SURVIVES TO TELL TALE

RIPPED OPEN BY CEMENT

■ Construction worker Shaukei Oliveira from Chatham, Ontario, had miraculously survived when he was pulled into an operating cement mixer that ripped him open, crushing his bones and leaving his heart and a lung exposed. The 47-year-old had been scraping excess mortar from the edge of the mixing barrel when the paddle caught on his sweater and instantly dragged him inside the powerful machine. Luckily, his colleagues flipped the machine over and managed to free him before he was crushed to death. Even so, in just a few seconds he had suffered several broken ribs, a huge gash across his chest, serious cartilage and nerve damage and a collapsed lung. He was rushed to hospital and placed on a respirator, but remarkably two weeks later he had recovered enough to return home.

Horned Man

➔ Colombian body modification artist Cain Tubal shows off his silicone horn implants and his metal facial piercings at the third annual International Tattoo Convention in Medellin, Colombia.

The convention showcased unconventional body-shock artists from all over the world, the most extreme of whom were suspended by metal barbs in their back or on razor-sharp hooks pierced through their skin.

➔ "blind" barber Tian Hao, a hair stylist from Shaanxi Province, China, cuts his customers' hair with his eyes closed. He says he uses Zen meditation to feel the "aura" of the hair and to trim it perfectly while keeping his eyes shut. Once he has finished cutting the hair with sharp scissors, he uses a vacuum cleaner—rather than a blow-dryer—to style it.

anything to declare? British tourist Lee Charie survived a 22-ft (6.7-m) fall from a hotel balcony in Thailand—and then flew home with a quarter of his skull in his hand luggage. Lee, from Hertfordshire, England, smashed the left side of his skull in the fall and Thai surgeons were forced to remove a section of it to allow his brain space to recover. They gave him the missing piece in a box so that doctors in the U.K. could use it as a mold for designing a titanium plate to cover the gap.

brain implant Born deaf, three-year-old Grayson Clamp of Charlotte, North Carolina, finally heard his father's voice for the first time after becoming the first child in the world to receive an auditory brain-stem implant, a process that involved implanting a microchip in his brain.

rapunzel family Four members of the Russell family from Morris, Illinois, have long hair that measures a combined total of 14 ft (4.3 m). Mother Tere Lynn Svetlecich Russell has 74-in (1.88-m) locks that have been left to grow since she was a toddler; oldest daughter Callan, 11, has 37-in-long (0.93-m) hair; nine-year-old Cendalyn has 36-in (0.91-m) tresses; and Chesney, six, comes in at 26 in (0.66 m). Tere Lynn says the main downside to having such long hair is that she sometimes gets it caught in car doors or sucked up while she is vacuuming.

tapeworm trauma Sherry Fuller from Essex, England, nearly died after pork tapeworms burrowed into her brain. The infestation, picked up while working in Madagascar, left her with larvae the size of a dime inside her head and dreams that haunted her for two years. She suffered headaches and seizures, her right eye turned black, and when she was given a worming tablet to kill the larvae, her arms, legs and back swelled up.

snail facial The Ci:z.Labo beauty salon in Tokyo, Japan, offers live snail facials to customers. The snails are placed on the customer's face and allowed to move around at random, their trail of slime helps to get rid of dead skin, heal the skin after sunburn, and generally moisturize it.

eyes write! Tapan Dey of Kolkata, India, can write neatly by holding a pen with various parts of his body, including his eyes, nose, mouth and hair. He can also write with both hands and both feet simultaneously.

sight trick People who have been able to see during their entire life and are suddenly struck blind can develop Anton's Syndrome, in which they are mentally unaware that they have become blind.

DOUBLE VISION

Pavan Agrawal and his older brother, Amit, each have one blue and one brown eye. Pavan's right eye is blue, the left is brown; while Amit's eyes are the other way round. They live with 20 members of their family in Ahmedabad, India—none of whom have the same condition—and work in the family business.

baby blue Two-year-old Areesha Shehzad from Bradford, England, has to spend at least 12 hours a day under the glare of blue UV lights to save her from a one-in-four-million liver condition. Crigler-Najjar Syndrome means she is missing an enzyme that breaks down a toxic chemical found in red blood cells. Without the daily phototherapy treatment, she could succumb to fatal brain damage.

knife blade Billy McNeely of Fort Good Hope in Canada's Northwest Territories, wondered why he suffered back pain and set off metal detectors—until he learned he had a 2¾-in (7-cm) knife blade buried in his back.

bearded schoolgirl A 16-year-old Chinese schoolgirl grew a full beard and mustache after the life-saving drug medication she was given to tackle a rare form of anemia produced unwanted side-effects. As well as the tough black beard on her face, the girl's legs and arms became covered in thick hair—a condition called hirsutism.

flesh-eating maggots After going on vacation to Peru, Rochelle Harris returned home to Derby, England, and began to hear scratching sounds and experience painful headaches. One morning she woke to find her pillow covered in fluid. When doctors investigated they found a writhing mass of flesh-eating maggots living inside her ear. A New World screwworm had laid its eggs inside Rochelle's ear and the maggots had chewed a 0.5-in (12-mm) hole into her ear canal. Had the larvae reached her brain, the infestation could have been fatal.

back to her senses Thanks to a three-hour operation, 66-year-old June Blythe from Norfolk, England, can taste and smell things for the first time in nearly 40 years. She lost her senses in 1975 after suffering from chronic rhinosinusitis, a severe inflammatory condition of the nasal sinuses. Amazingly, she went on to win prizes for her cooking (which she couldn't taste) and became an aromatherapist, using fragrant plant oils (which she couldn't smell).

desert drama Stranded in the desert and without his wheelchair, coat, food and water, paraplegic Ricky Gilmore from Newcomb, New Mexico, somehow managed to drag himself 4 mi (6.4 km) along a dirt road in three days. Ricky, who had lost the use of his legs in a car crash 19 years earlier, was close to exhaustion when finally a passing driver stopped to rescue him.

huge tumor Gemma Fletcher of Sheffield, England, had her daughter Ava delivered by emergency cesarean section only 32 weeks into her pregnancy after doctors discovered she had a kidney tumor that was even bigger than her baby. Little Ava weighed 6.4 lb (2.9 kg) at birth, but the tumor weighed 7.5 lb (3.4 kg).

➜Nerina Orton has a waist that measures just 15¾ in (40 cm). The student from Birmingham, England, has shrunk her abdomen by tying herself into smaller and smaller corsets, a method known as "tightlacing," eventually displacing the intestines, stomach and liver.

Nerina wears a corset almost all day every day, even in her sleep, and removes it only to shower. She reports that when she takes the corset off, she can feel her internal organs moving back to their original position as her waist returns to a svelte 24 in (61 cm). Nerina, who first started wearing corsets as a teenager and now owns 78 of them, makes regular visits to a doctor to ensure that the extreme effect of the corset on her body is not causing long-term damage to her health.

Nerina Orton wears a corset for 23 hours a day.

ACTUAL SIZE!

TEENY WAISTS

15¾-inch (40-cm) waist!

MORE...

Queen of the Corset

Ethel Granger (1905–1982) of Peterborough, England, had possibly the smallest waist of all time, just 13 in (33 cm) around!

Ethel wore a corset for decades, but she did not come to public attention until the 1950s, and achieved her tiniest waist in the 1960s, by which time her natural size had shrunk by 10 in (25 cm). She would sleep in her corset and gradually tighten the laces over the course of each day, until her waist was so small that she had to make her own clothes.

Ethel in the garden of her home in Peterborough in 1957.

THE "VERY THING" FOR LADIES
FOR AN ELEGANT FIGURE & GOOD HEALTH.
HARNESS' ELECTRIC CORSETS
PRICE ONLY 5/6
POST FREE.

ELECTRIC CORSET
C.B HARNESS

THEY CURE WEAK BACK

FOR WOMEN OF ALL AGES.

HARNESS' ELECTRIC CORSETS
ONLY 5/6 POST FREE.

By wearing these perfectly designed Corsets the most awkward figure becomes graceful and elegant, the internal organs are speedily strengthened,
THE CHEST IS AIDED IN ITS HEALTHY DEVELOPMENT.
And the entire system is invigorated.
Send at once Postal Order or Cheque for 5s. 6d. to the Secretary, C Dept.
THE MEDICAL BATTERY CO. LIMITED.
ONLY 5/6 POST FREE.
52, OXFORD St LONDON. W.

Electric corsets were advertised as the latest miracle cure in the late 19th century. It was claimed that electricity running through the corset—actually magnets—could treat a wide range of medical conditions, strengthen the internal organs and "weak backs," and even cure obesity.

In Victorian times, the fashion for tight corsets led doctors to warn that the undergarments could pose a health risk. They advised on how to wear corsets to avoid rib damage.

THE FAMILY DOCTOR
AND PEOPLE'S MEDICAL ADVISER.
426
SATURDAY, APRIL 29, 1893.
PRICE ONE PENNY.
THE RIBS AND TIGHT-LACING
IN WELL-SHAPED CORSETS.

FIG. 1. FIG. 2. FIG. 3. FIG. 4.

Oval 24 in Natural waist
Round 20 in Well corseted waist
Round 15 in Extremely tight-laced waist
Treble views of all waists

Polaire (1879–1939), real name Emilie Marie Bouchard, was a French vaudeville performer famous in Paris in the early 20th century for her tiny 16-inch "wasp waist"—shrunk by years of wearing a corset for hours every day. When Polaire played on Broadway she was billed as "The Ugliest Woman in the World," yet was renowned in Europe for her beauty.

sleep eater Mother-of-three, Lesley Cusack from Cheshire, England, eats up to 2,500 calories a night—in her sleep. She suffers from a sleep-related eating disorder and has no control over what she eats while sleepwalking. Her nighttime feasts have included an entire bowl of fruit, Vaseline, cough syrup, raw potatoes, soap powder and emulsion paint!

frozen corpses The Alcor Life Extension Foundation in Scottsdale, Arizona, provides safe storage for more than 120 frozen people, which it hopes one day to bring back to life.

foreign bodies Every year, about 1,500 patients in the U.S.A. have objects accidentally left inside their bodies during surgery. They have included surgical towels, sponges, tubes, a 7-in (18-cm) surgical clamp, a 13-in (33-cm) retractor, a section of a fetal heart monitor and a surgical glove.

rare blood James Harrison of New South Wales, Australia, has donated his rare type of blood 1,000 times. It contains an antibody that has saved over two million Australian babies from Rhesus disease, a serious form of anemia.

> **IN 2008, BRITISH RESEARCHERS DISCOVERED A 60-YEAR-OLD WOMAN WHO COULD RECOGNIZE ONLY ONE VOICE—THAT OF JAMES BOND ACTOR, SEAN CONNERY!**

lucky fall After Kevin Brockbank collapsed with a heart attack at work in Dundee, Scotland, his life was saved when his 210-lb (94-kg) friend, Martin Amriding, reached out to grab him, but instead accidentally fell on him—and the impact kick-started his heart.

truck tattoo Fire-eater Miss Mena from Myrtle Beach, South Carolina, has a tattoo of a Ford F-150 truck on her upper arm—not because she likes them, but because she has been hit by one three times.

head ads Brandon Chicotsky from Austin, Texas, sells advertising space on his bald head. He has founded Bald Logo.com where, for $320 a day, companies pay him to walk around town with their logo or brand name temporarily tattooed on his head.

1,345-LB MAN

→ Weighing a colossal 1,345 lb (610 kg)—the same as five baby elephants—Khaled Mohsen Shaeri of Saudi Arabia was bed-bound for 2½ years. The country's King Abdullah took a personal interest in his situaton and ordered his evacuation to a hospital. This involved part of the apartment block where Shaeri lived being demolished so that he could be winched out of his home and wheeled onto a forklift truck before being airlifted to the hospital.

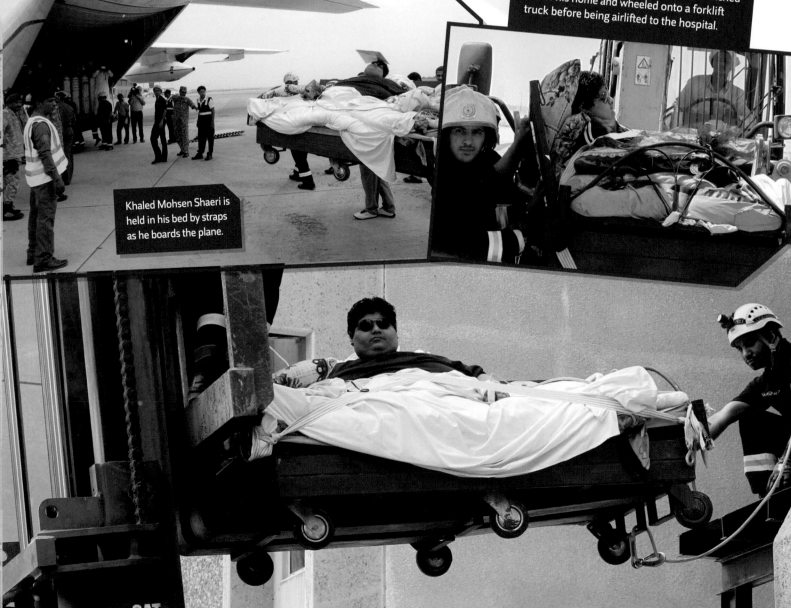

Khaled Mohsen Shaeri is held in his bed by straps as he boards the plane.

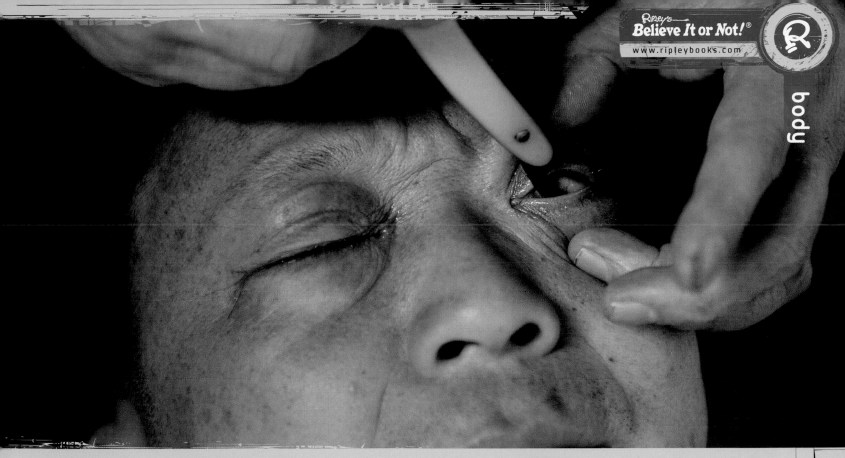

EYEBALL SHAVING

→ **In China's Sichuan Province, barbers charge 80 cents to scrape customers' eyeballs with a sharp blade.**

Liu Deyuan is one of a few barbers who still practice the centuries-old tradition of eyeball shaving, which is said to enhance a person's view of life. He dips the blade in water and gently scrapes the insides of both eyelids. Then he pokes a thin metal rod with a smooth ball-shaped end beneath the eyelids and slides it back and forth like a windshield wiper. The whole process takes approximately five minutes, during which time the customer dare not move a muscle. Liu says he has never had an accident, attributing his success to a steady hand.

eye watering When archeologists found the mummy of Ancient Egyptian Pharaoh Ramesses IV in Egypt's Valley of the Kings in the late 19th century, they found that his eyes had been replaced with onions.

scary scars It is customary for men living on the Sepik River in Papua New Guinea to have their backs cut to make deep scars that create the appearance of crocodile skin.

pin number Distracted by a phone call, an acupuncturist in Wiener Neustadt, Austria, locked up and went home, completely forgetting that a female patient was still in the treatment room covered in pins. Vivi Ziegler initially felt so relaxed that she fell asleep, but when she woke up alone in the dark and cold, she had to call police to rescue her through a window.

big eyes The eyeballs of people native to the Arctic Circle are 20 percent bigger than those of people from the Equator. This helps them to see better in a part of the world that receives little sunlight for large parts of the year.

severed arm When a Hungarian construction worker severed an arm in an accident in Purbach, Austria, he drove 10 mi (16 km) to the hospital—taking the arm with him. Despite blood pouring from his wound, he even stopped at traffic lights on the way. Then, he parked, walked into the hospital, placed his arm on the reception desk and asked for help.

tattooed mayor Ray Johnson of Campo, Colorado, is thought to be the U.S.A.'s most tattooed mayor. He has tattoos across his thighs, torso and arms.

bird poop A Japanese beauty treatment, the Geisha Facial, uses a cream made from rice bran mixed with Asian nightingale excrement.

whiskey drip Doctors in Taranaki, New Zealand, saved the sight of a patient—Denis Duthie—who was suffering from methanol poisoning, by tube-feeding a bottle of Johnnie Walker whiskey into his body after they had run out of the medical alcohol that they usually use for this treatment.

shooting baskets While in a meningitis-induced coma, Maggie Meier of Overland Park, Kansas, was unable to walk, talk or eat, but the comatose high-school basketball player could shoot baskets from her wheelchair! Her neurologist explained that because basketball was ingrained as one of her basic instincts, her body remembered how to do it before it could stand or walk.

HEAD TATTOO → Left completely bald by alopecia, 60-year-old grandmother Ann McDonald from Edinburgh, Scotland, got fed up with wearing a wig and decided to have a full head tattoo instead. The £720 ($1,150) tattoo took 12 hours and consists of spiral shading with a black background and curls to represent hair.

Black Scorpion

→ Performer Jason Black was born with the rare medical condition ectrodactyly (or lobster claw syndrome), which has left him with only two large pincerlike fingers, a thumb on each hand and three toes on each foot.

He has turned his deformity to his advantage, however, by reinventing himself as the Black Scorpion, and touring the United States as a dynamic magician and sideshow performer who swallows balloons, escapes from handcuffs and walks on broken glass.

As well as working for over 15 years at the Austin, Texas, news station KEYE-TV, he is the creative director, writer and performer with the 999 Eyes Freakshow, a surreal sideshow founded by Samantha X and Dylan Blackthorn. The sideshow features body-modified performers and Vaudeville-style artists such as sword-swallowers and human pincushions, as well as artists with genetic anomalies such as Black himself. All of the acts are set to live music by That Damned Band under the musical direction of Dr. Sick. On tour, the show exhibits its grotesque "Mutantstrosities" — an authentic American Dime Museum featuring Patches the two-headed cow, pickled punks and oddities from around the world.

Wearing his trademark multicolored bandit mask and proudly displaying his claws, the Black Scorpion aims to change people's perceptions by making them realize that "freaks" are no different from any of the members of the audience.

→ Black first got into performing after meeting Joe Hermann (aka The Amazing Mr. Lifto) at a friend's wedding. Black says: "He was the first person who'd ever made me feel good about my hands and feet. Before I met Joe I really didn't think of them as a gift, more as that little something that keeps me from living a normal life." Since he started touring with 999 Eyes, he has found that his fellow performers think his hands and feet are simply awesome. "Lifto was just the first person of many who pointed out how lucky I am."

These unlucky individuals managed to impale themselves on various objects in a catalogue of accidents... Happily, none did lasting damage.

Eight-year-old Veronica Valentine was pierced 3 in (7.5 cm) into her chest by a **pen** when she fell down the stairs at her home in Coral Springs, Florida, in 2001.

Thirteen-year-old Daniel Carr fell out of a tree and impaled himself on a 2-ft (0.6-m) **flagpole** in Suffolk, England, in 2005.

French long jumper Salim Sdiri was impaled in the side by a Finnish competitor's **javelin** thrown from the other side of the arena during a 2007 track-and-field meet in Rome, Italy.

Eleven-year-old Vignesh Nageshwaran from Delhi, India, impaled himself through the roof of his mouth with a **toothbrush** when he fell off his bicycle while cleaning his teeth in 2009.

Chicago Cubs' Tyler Colvin was impaled in the chest by a **broken baseball bat** while running from third base in a 2010 game against the Florida Marlins.

The right eye socket of 86-year-old Leroy Luetscher from Green Valley, Arizona, was impaled by a pair of **pruning shears** in 2011.

Eight-year-old Lewis Todd from Manchester, England, slipped while climbing a gate in 2013 and was impaled above the thigh on a **metal spike**

SPIKED ON A BIKE → Cyclist
Adrian Wood had an incredible escape when this 15-in-long (38-cm) tree branch skewered his neck. He was riding near Peterborough, England, when the wheel of his bike hit a tree root and he was flung out of the seat and impaled on the branch. The stick passed through a vein and came within a whisker of his vital carotid artery.

foreign accent After suffering a serious head injury more than eight years ago, Leanne Rowe, an Australian woman born and raised in Tasmania, now speaks in a French accent—even though she has never been to France and has no French friends. She is believed to be Australia's second-ever case of Foreign Accent Syndrome, a condition linked to damage to the part of the brain that controls speech.

lively eyes
The focusing muscles of the eyes move about 100,000 times a day. To give your leg muscles the same workout, you would need to walk 50 mi (80 km) daily.

perfect match When Jonathan Woodlief of Dallas, Texas, needed a kidney transplant, he discovered that his wife of less than a month, Caitlin, was a match, overcoming incredible odds.

million-dollar baby Rachel Evans of Sydney, Australia, was about to return home after a vacation in British Columbia when she went into premature labor at the airport. She gave birth to a daughter at a Vancouver hospital—and was presented with a medical bill for Canadian $1 million.

frog diet William LaFever, 28, survived for three weeks in Utah's Escalante Desert by eating raw frogs and roots. He had been attempting to walk the 150 mi (240 km) from Boulder, Utah, to Page, Arizona, but had covered less than a third of the distance when he began to suffer from starvation and dehydration in the intense heat. A rescue helicopter found him just in time as he would probably not have lasted another day.

pencil puzzle A 24-year-old Afghan man unknowingly spent 15 years with a pencil in his head following a childhood accident. After suffering for years from constant headaches, colds, and deteriorating vision in one eye, the man sought help from doctors in Aachen, Germany, and a scan showed that a 4-in (10-cm) pencil was lodged from his sinuses to his pharynx, damaging his right eye socket.

hand-walker Ten-year-old Yan Yuhong from Yibin, Hubei Province, China, has been walking on his hands for part of his journey to and from school every day for more than four years. Paralyzed by a childhood illness, he learned to walk on his hands when he was four and now finds it faster walking that way than if he uses crutches. He still has to get up earlier than his classmates, because his journey to school takes him 90 minutes each way.

throat threat A 55-year-old woman from Kattappana, India, suffering from a tickly throat, had a live, venomous centipede removed from her throat where it had been stuck for a week.

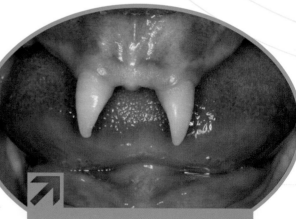

VAMPIRE FANGS

→ Sixteen-year-old Wang Pengfei from Chongqing, China, has grown two sharp front teeth that give him fangs like a vampire. He was born with very little hair and grew only these two pointy teeth from his upper gum and none on his lower jaw. His mother is desperate for him to undergo corrective surgery, but doctors say he must wait until he is an adult.

Nail Olympics

→ More than 200 competitors converged on Rome, Italy, to take part in the 2013 Nail Olympics— a two-day nail art competition showcasing outrageous designs featuring feathers and figurines on perfectly manicured fingernails.

Looking for Treasure by Cristina Bea boasted skulls, pirates, mermaids and even a ship. Other creations depicted 1920s dancers and Japanese geisha girls, while in the stiletto category acrylic nails were filed down to impossibly sharp points worthy of Freddy Krueger.

bouncing baby Two-year-old Maria Kohler had an amazing escape when she fell 30 ft (9 m) from a fifth-floor balcony in Munich, Germany, bounced off a canvas canopy and landed on grass without suffering even a bruise or a scratch.

back from dead Having been pronounced dead by doctors at a hospital in Syracuse, New York State, 39-year-old Colleen Burns was lying on the operating table about to have her organs removed for transplant when she suddenly woke up.

lucky break Zoe Sievwright of Dundee, Scotland, survived a fall from 3,500 ft (1,067 m) when her parachute failed during a skydive, suffering only a broken ankle.

wayward arrow While walking through a park in Moscow, Russia, Konstantine Myakush was shot through the neck by a sportsman's misfired arrow—yet survived. The 20-in (50-cm) arrow entered on the right side of his neck beneath his jaw and emerged through his throat on the left side. Surgeons removed the arrow successfully as it did not hit any major arteries.

leaking brain Joe Nagy of Phoenix, Arizona, thought he had a chronic runny nose for 18 months—only to learn that the clear liquid was actually his brain leaking! The brain, which is located directly above the nose, produces up to 12 oz (350 ml) of fluid a day and doctors found that the membrane surrounding Joe's brain had a hole in it, causing fluid to trickle out. Having located the leak, they repaired it with surgery.

touching shoulders Krystal Dickson from Boston, Massachusetts, is able to twist her body so that she can touch her shoulders together.

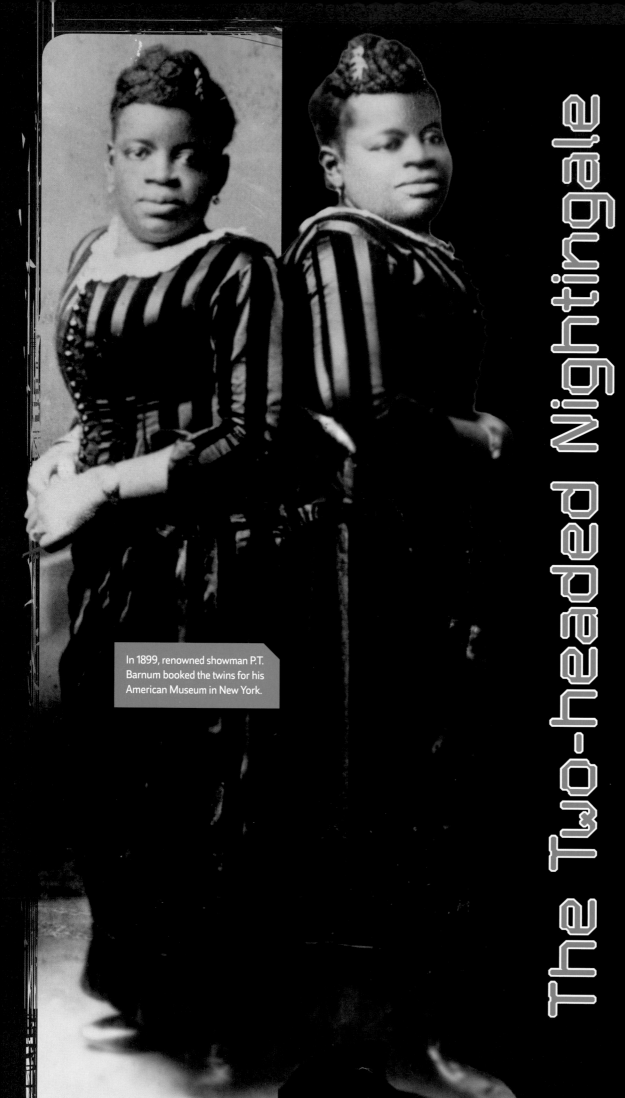

In 1899, renowned showman P.T. Barnum booked the twins for his American Museum in New York.

The Two-headed Nightingale

Millie and Christine McKoy were born joined at the hip to slaves on a farm in North Carolina in 1851, the eighth and ninth of 14 siblings.

While still toddlers, they were sold to a traveling show and traded between various showmen before Joseph Smith became their manager. In another trade gone wrong, the sisters were stolen and taken to England, where they were abducted at least once more, before Smith and the girl's mother Monemia tracked them down four years later.

When they were eventually returned to the U.S.A., Smith and his wife helped Millie and Christine learn to sing, dance, and play the piano and guitar, promoting them as the "Two-headed Nightingale"—one with a contralto voice, the other a soprano. The pair also mastered five languages and wrote their own poetry, talents that helped make the girls international stars.

At the height of their popularity, "Millie Christine"—the girls would often refer to themselves as a single person—was performing for thousands of people each day, and 150,000 spectators saw the pair when they visited Philadelphia. They soon earned enough money to buy a farm in North Carolina for their father Joseph—then a free man—and to support schools for black children. They performed at P.T. Barnum's famous American Museum in New York, appeared before Queen Victoria of England on a number of occasions and even received an invitation from the Pope.

They retired from show business in the early 1900s, and survived until 1912 when they contracted tuberculosis and died within 24 hours of each other. They are buried at Welches Creek cemetery, North Carolina, where their descendants held a ceremony in 2012 to honor the centenary of their death.

REMARKABLE HUMAN PHENOMENA!
THE AFRICAN TWINS.

(The Engraving by Permission of the Proprietors of the "Picture Times.")

The twins were exhibited in London when only five years old.

(CHRISTINA AND MILLY.)

These extraordinary Children, only Five Years old, and whom Nature has linked by an Indissoluble Band, about 16 inches in circumference, having excited the most intense interest, and created the greatest sensation wherever they have been witnessed, ARE NOW ON VIEW, for a brief period only, at the

EGYPTIAN HALL, PICCADILLY,

From TWO till FIVE, and from SEVEN till NINE o'Clock.

These extraordinary Children, only Five Years old... appointed by the Orphan Court of Philadelphia, United Slavery; and their Guardian, Mr. THOMPSON, of that City, who instantly freed them from their to appropriate the Children, who are at this moment Slaves on a North-American well as the strongest impulses of Curiosity, are therefore to in the Public Prints, they were feloniously abducted charge of them, and recovered in Dundee, having taken the warmest interest Appearance, and their with wonderful of a Duet, arising greatest, and most

The twins were so popular that they had their own music written for performances in England.

Millie and Christine performing at a fair in Leeds, England, in a photo believed to be from 1874.

RIPLEY'S RESEARCH

Conjoined twins occur when an egg that would normally divide in two to become identical twins fails to separate properly—a phenomenon seen in only 0.001 percent of births. Millie and Christine were joined at the pelvis, making them "Pygopagus" twins, a relatively rare form of the condition with two separate bodies (most conjoined twins share organs, or are joined at the head). With modern medical techniques, it is plausible that Millie and Christine could have been separated, and doctors who examined the pair did consider the possibility, but medical knowledge at the time was limited and the twins anyway were very happy to live together as one.

NIGHTINGALE MUSIC

WRITTEN COMPOSED AND ARRANGED FOR
CHRISTINE MILLIE
THE TWO-HEADED NIGHTINGALE.
BY
WILLIAM WILSON.

Nº1. THE DEAR, DEAR FRIENDS AT HOME 3/-
Nº2. (DUET) SISTERS WE, GAY & FREE. 4/-
Nº3. PUT ME IN MY LITTLE BED. 3/-
Nº7. THE SONG OF THE NIGHTINGALE 3/-
Nº4. NIGHTINGALE SCHOTTISCHE. 3/-
Nº5. NIGHTINGALE MAZURKA 3/-
Nº6. SONG) WHIP POOR WILL 3/-

"Carolina Twins,"
MILLIE AND CHRISTINA.

An early photograph of the teenage "Carolina Twins" in 1866, such "carte de visite"—visiting cards—of well-known personalities were popular before snapshot photography was possible.

bladder ball After Amlesh Kumar of Delhi, India, had suffered stomach pains for 20 years, doctors removed a 1-lb (0.5-kg) bladder stone the size of a baseball ball from his abdomen.

hypnotic mom Danielle Davies, from South Yorkshire, England, shed 84 lb (38 kg) and dropped ten dress sizes after her mother Bev hypnotized her into thinking she had been fitted with a gastric band.

oldest dad Ramajit Raghav, a farmer from Sonipat, northern India, claims to have fathered a child at age 96, making him the world's oldest dad. He says he practiced celibacy until he met his wife Shakuntala, who is 44 years his junior, in 2000. He fathered his first son in 2010 at age 94 and had another child two years later.

long locks Eighty-six-year-old Nguyen Van Chien, from Tien Giang, Vietnam, has not cut his hair since he was in 12th grade—over 70 years ago. His hair now measures more than 13 ft (4 m) long and weighs about 4.4 lb (2 kg).

permanent smile After suffering a stroke in 2004, Malcolm Myatt from Staffordshire, England, has been constantly smiling and laughing because he is no longer able to feel sadness. The stroke interfered with the part of the brain that regulates emotional responses, leaving him liable to start giggling at any time.

two toes Many members of the Vadoma tribe in Zimbabwe have only two toes on each foot. They suffer from a genetic condition called ectrodactyly, which results in their middle three toes being absent. The mutation does have one benefit—their feet help them climb trees easily.

MORE BIG BODY PARTS

Waist	Walter Hudson (U.S.)	119 in / 3.02 m
Fingernail	Melvin Boothe (U.S.)	39 in / 98 cm
Biceps	Moustafa Ismail (Egypt)	31 in / 78 cm
Foot	Robert Wadlow (U.S.)	18.5 in / 47 cm
Hand	Leonid Stadnyk (Ukraine)	12.2 in / 31 cm
Mouth	Francisco Domingo Joaquim (Angola)	6.7 in / 17 cm
Big Toe	Matthew McGrory (U.S.)	5 in / 12.7 cm
Tongue	Stephen Taylor (U.K.)	3.86 in / 9.8 cm
Nose	Mehmet Ozyurek (Turkey)	3.46 in / 8.8 cm
Eyelash	Stuart Muller (U.S.)	2.75 in / 6.99 cm

➜ Mikel Ruffinelli's hips measure a staggering 100 in (2.5 m) in circumference, giving her the biggest hips in the world and making her so wide that she has to buy two seats to travel by plane and has to go through doorways sideways.

Unable to squeeze into a car, Mikel can only drive a truck. She uses a reinforced chair at her home in Los Angeles, California, and can't close the shower door because her hips get in the way. Although her hips are huge, her waist measures just 40 in (100 cm) in circumference.

Yet the 40-year-old plus-size model was an athletic teenager with no weight problems and in her early twenties weighed a modest 180 lb (82 kg). Then, at 22, she put on 56 lb (25 kg) after giving birth to her first child. After three more children, her weight and hips ballooned further and she now tips the scales at 420 lb (190 kg).

Mikel consumes an average 3,000 calories per day but has no wish to diet. "I don't have health problems," she says, "and anyway men like an hourglass figure. Some people assume I've had surgery to enhance my body shape, but it's all natural. It's the result of having four children—but having large hips also runs in the family.

"Everywhere I go, I get attention for my hips—both good and bad. In the past, I was self-conscious, but as I got older I learned to love my body and now I'm not afraid to show it off. I don't want to get any bigger, but I don't want to lose my curves either. I look great!"

FREAKY LIPS

➜ It looks like an eye, but it's really a mouth! By attaching false eyelashes to her upper lip and using tiny brushes to paint on a lifelike pupil, Sandra Holmbom from Pitea, Sweden, created a third eye on her mouth. She has also decorated her lips with images of roses, apples and even the Northern Lights.

Happy

Hippy

Mikel Ruffinelli's hips measure a staggering 100 in (2.5 m) in circumference, giving her the biggest hips in the world.

100 inches! (2.5 m)

Nail Queen

→ Ayanna Williams has grown her fingernails for more than 20 years, and they now measure more than 18 in (45 cm) long. Seven years ago, she started growing her toenails, too—with the result that the nails on her big toes grew to over 4 in (10 cm) long and those on her little toes extended 2 in (5 cm).

The 56-year-old grandmother from Houston, Texas, devotes several hours a day tending to her nails, and admits she is a perfectionist when it comes to her "ten jewels." The nails are capped (painted on the top and around the edges) to help prevent them from breaking, and Ayanna is a regular at Spathena in Houston, where manicurist Athena Elliot works hard to keep the nails healthy.

When cooking in the kitchen Ayanna needs plenty of room because her fingernails get in the way, and she does not wash dishes by hand because her nails don't fit in the sink. Life can be difficult, but she just takes things at her own pace and eventually gets the job done—and she has plenty of family to help out.

Every morning when she wakes up she asks herself if she should cut them—but it is easier said than done. She once said: "I love them. They are 50 percent of who I am. To cut them would be like losing a limb."

On the phone

Drinking a glass of water

Painting her nails

Applying makeup

Signing a letter

Brushing her teeth

TOENAIL LOSS

Ayanna eventually decided to cut her long toenails. It was not an easy decision, but life wasn't always easy with them. She had to walk slowly on her heels, like a penguin, and when going upstairs she had to walk sideways. She mostly wore flip-flops as she couldn't wear socks or boots in winter, and could only change into tennis shoes if she cut holes in the ends for her toenails to poke through. Despite these challenges, Ayanna did love her long toenails and is currently growing them again.

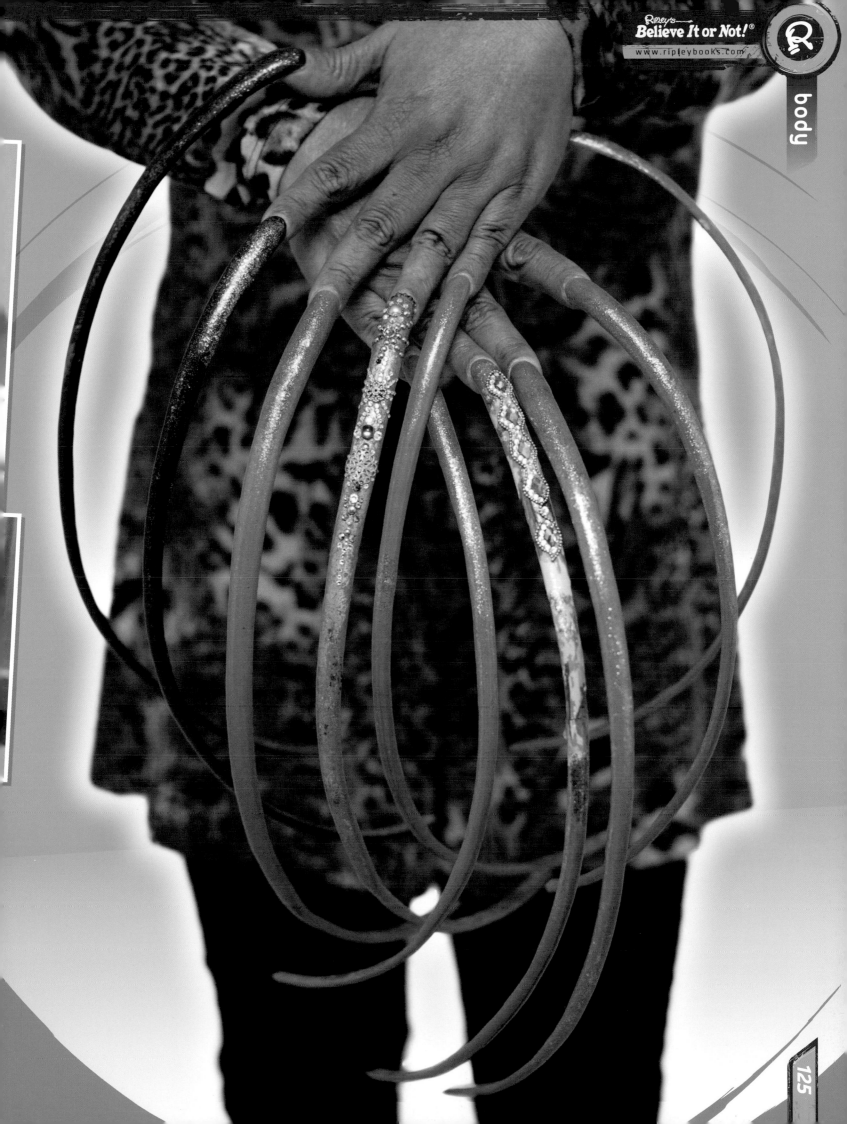

always late Jim Dunbar from Angus, Scotland, suffers from a genuine medical condition called Chronic Lateness Syndrome, which means that his sense of time is warped, making him late for school, work, dates, vacations and funerals. He even arrived 20 minutes late for the medical appointment where he was diagnosed with the disorder.

no joke A person who suffers from laughter-induced syncope can completely lose consciousness just from laughing.

chimp feet A scientific study of visitors to the Boston Museum of Science in Massachusetts has revealed that about one in 13 people have flexible, apelike feet. Visitors to the museum were asked to walk barefoot, but whereas most had very rigid feet, a significant number had floppier feet—similar to the midtarsal break that enables chimpanzees to grip tree branches.

mass hysteria In the fall of 2011, an outbreak of mass hysteria caused a dozen high-school students in LeRoy, New York, to suffer symptoms of painful shaking and verbal outbursts.

pointing the finger When a severed finger landed on the doormat of his home in Padua, Italy, a terrified 64-year-old man thought it was a sinister warning from the Mafia. However, investigations revealed that the finger belonged to an innocent delivery man who, jumping up to reach the pensioner's very high letterbox, got his hand stuck in it and lost a digit.

half brain A jar containing half a brain and another containing two dissected eyeballs were among a collection of carefully preserved human body parts that were found in the garage of a vacant house in Caledonia, Wisconsin, in 2012. Police discovered they had been part of a surgeon's collection dating back to 1901.

DOCTOR RETURNS ARM 47 YEARS AFTER AMPUTATION

■ Dr. Sam Axelrad (left), a urologist from Houston, Texas, arrived in Vietnam in 2013 carrying an unusual item of luggage—the bones of an infected arm that he had amputated in 1966. Dr. Axelrad had kept the skeletal remains in a closet at his home in the U.S.A. for over 40 years to remind him of the North Vietnamese soldier's life he had saved during the Vietnam War. Then, in 2011, he took a fresh look at the bones and began wondering what had happened to their original owner. Eventually, he tracked down the ex-soldier, Nguyen Quang Hung, and flew to Hanoi to hand him back his old arm.

strong girls Teenage sisters Haylee and Hannah Smith of Lebanon, Oregon, lifted a 3,000-lb (1,362-kg) tractor off their father Jeff after it flipped over while he was driving it and pinned him underneath.

boy bonanza Jay and Teri Schwandt from Grand Rapids, Michigan, have 12 children—and they're all boys. Furthermore, Teri's sister, Kate Osberger, who lives in Detroit, has ten children—and they're all boys, too!

snail in knee After four-year-old Paul Franklin from Aliso Viejo, California, fell on some rocks on a beach, a sea snail egg embedded itself in his knee, and hatched and grew there. At first it appeared the fall just left the little boy with an itchy and bruised knee, but three weeks later the wound had turned black and become the size of an orange. When his mother squeezed the wound to drain it, something black emerged. She thought it was a small stone, but when it moved she realized it was a sea snail. The boy must have fallen into a nest in the rock, forcing the egg into his knee.

safe storage Suffering a blow to the head from a fall on a fishing trip to Hell's Canyon, Idaho, Jamie Hilton had part of her skull reattached—after it was stored in her abdomen for more than a month. The fall led to severe brain swelling and to save her life, doctors removed a quarter of her skull and stored it under the skin in her abdomen until her brain had healed. Inside her own body, the skull portion remained sterile and nourished until it was finally reattached 42 days later.

RIPLEY'S RESEARCH

Globe luxation is the forward displacement of the eyeball so that the eyelids close behind it. It occurs most commonly in dogs, but a few humans can do it, either having been born with the condition or subsequently acquiring it as a result of a head trauma. Some people also suffer from spontaneous globe luxation, where their eyeballs pop involuntarily. An alarmed 46-year-old Indian man reported that his eyes had popped out several times over the course of three months.

[YOUR / UPLOADS]

A big Ripley's fan, 17-year-old Denise Salazar from Tracy, California, sent us these amazing pictures of her popping her eyes out of place. Her extreme and rare talent, which she has had since the age of eight, is called globe luxation and means that by pushing her eyelids back, she can squeeze her eyeballs out a long way. It looks spooky, but luckily she can pop them back in again at will.

Human Tail

→ Vang Seo Chung from Hà Giang Province, Vietnam, has lived for over 40 years with a 1.6-ft-long (0.5-m) tail. The hairy appendage grows from his waist at a rate of 4 in (10 cm) a year. A few years ago it was 10 ft (3 m) long and he could wrap it around his stomach, but his wife asked him to trim it back. He straps the tail to his body in a small bag when going on journeys. Vang Seo Chung was born normal except for a strange patch of furry hair on his waist. Once it grew, his tail was said to have brought good luck to his family. Whenever he has had it cut, he has become sick.

sharp shock Doctors in Bialystok, Poland, removed a screwdriver that was lodged 2 in (5 cm) inside the head of a 25-year-old man. The victim had slipped and fallen face first onto the screwdriver, immediately losing consciousness. When eventually he came round, he was unable to remember what had happened, and at first felt only a pain in his hand. When finally he realized that something else was wrong, he looked in a mirror and saw the screwdriver sticking out of his forehead just above his right eye. It took doctors three hours to remove the screwdriver, but the man made a full recovery.

sting addiction A 53-year-old woman from Morningview, Kentucky, stings herself more than 100 times a week with bees and has stung herself more than 50,000 times in total over the course of the past ten years. She began after reading that bee stings help with arthritis, but became so addicted that in a single session she sometimes stings herself up to 20 times in her hip alone. She carries out the painful process by gripping the bee in tweezers and forcing it to sting her, which causes it to die. To ensure she has a constant supply of potential stings, she keeps beehives in her back garden.

air bubble After a tugboat capsized off the coast of Nigeria in May 2013, the ship's cook, Harrison Okene, survived for 2½ days underwater in a small air bubble under the stricken vessel. Trapped in the freezing cold water, he managed to breathe for 60 hours inside a 4-ft-high (1.2-m) bubble of air between the ceiling of the toilet and an adjoining bedroom until finally he heard knocking and saw the torchlight of one of the rescue divers. After he'd been rescued, he had to spend time in a decompression chamber to normalize his body pressure before he could be reunited with his family.

lost years Mother-of-three Sarah Thomson from Exeter, England, woke from a ten-day coma convinced that she was a teenager again, with no recollection of her husband or her children. Sarah was working at her computer when a blood clot burst on her brain and erased 13 years of her life. When she woke up from the coma, she thought the Spice Girls were still together, was "shocked" to hear that Michael Jackson had died, and had never heard of Simon Cowell.

swallowed magnets A 12-month-old boy in Chelyabinsk, Russia, underwent an operation to remove 42 fridge magnets from his digestive system. His mother panicked when she noticed that all of the magnets had gone missing and hospital scans confirmed that her young son had swallowed them.

feather surprise When seven-month-old Mya Whittington from Hutchinson, Kansas, was taken to hospital with a lump the size of a golf ball on her neck, doctors pulled a 2-in-long (5-cm) black feather from it. It is believed she swallowed or inhaled the feather, which then pierced the inside of her cheek or throat before her body forced it out through the swelling.

metal spike Trying to jump over a wall next to a wrought-iron gate, 12-year-old Josh Hassan from London, England, slipped and became impaled on a 12-in (30-cm) metal spike. The spike pierced his chest, but miraculously missed his vital organs by only inches. Once he had been released from hospital, Josh decided to keep the spike as a souvenir.

HAIR COAT

→ British firm Arla commissioned the creation of a coat made entirely from men's chest hair. It took designers 200 hours to weave together about one million strands of hair. The limited-edition coat went on sale for £2,499 ($4,000).

TOPSY-TURVY WORLD → Bojana Danilovic from Užice, Serbia, has an extreme form of spatial orientation phenomenon whereby she sees the entire world upside down. She has to turn books, newspapers, her cell phone and even her TV upside down. At work she uses a special upside-down computer screen and keyboard. Usually the eyes see the world upside-down, and the brain flips the image when processing it, but in Bojana's case this correction doesn't happen.

burns contest To mark the 200th anniversary of the Battle of Lake Erie, 19 men sporting bushy mutton-chop sideburns took part in the Perry Burns contest—a competition staged in Erie, Pennsylvania, to find whose facial hair most looked like that of Oliver Hazard Perry, the commander of the victorious American fleet in the battle against the British in 1813.

sibling symptoms While sitting in the waiting room after driving his brother Bruce to Minnesota's St. Cloud Hospital for emergency gall-bladder surgery, LeRoy Hanson suddenly began experiencing the same symptoms and was told that he would need his gall bladder removed, too. As children, the brothers also had their tonsils removed at the same time.

crash landing Skydiver Liam Dunne from Taupo, New Zealand, cheated death when his main parachute failed and a reserve chute only partially worked after he had jumped from 13,000 ft (4,000 m). He hit the ground at such a speed that he bounced, but his life was saved by landing on soft earth.

selective memory Different types of memories are stored in different parts of the brain, making it possible for a person to suffer amnesia that robs them of all the details of their life, but still allows them to remember how to read and play music.

UNUSUAL BRAIN CONDITIONS

Sleeping Beauty Syndrome causes sufferers to fall asleep regularly for more than 20 hours a day.

Patients with **Alien Hand Syndrome** have an arm that they believe is moving of its own accord and is out of control, sometimes attacking them.

People suffering from **Alice in Wonderland Syndrome** see objects as much smaller or larger than they really are.

The extremely rare brain condition **hyperthymesia** allows a person to remember everything that has happened in their life in minute detail.

Hair Grooming Syncope is a disorder that results in fainting from brushing or cutting hair.

Synesthesia is a condition where people's senses become confused so that, for example, they can "taste" words and "see" sounds.

People with the brain disorder **prosopagnosia**, or "facial blindness," find it impossible to identify people's faces.

Crocodile Tears Syndrome is a rare condition where people start to cry uncontrollably when they eat.

Beard Bowl

→ Isaiah Webb can eat ramen noodles from his beard! The San Francisco, California, beard enthusiast—also known as Mr. Incredibeard—began growing his facial hair long in 2012.

After six months, his wife Angela started molding his beard into weird and wonderful creations. He now boasts over 28 different designs, including one that holds five cups and another that can accommodate a burger, fries and a shake. He shapes his beard with hot curlers, hair spray and a blow-dryer, and posts a new creation online every other Monday.

fluent welsh After suffering a stroke, Englishman Alun Morgan, 81, woke up speaking fluent Welsh and unable to remember any English. He had been evacuated to Wales as a child during World War II and had spoken the language a little during that time, but that was more than 70 years before. Doctors diagnosed him with aphasia, a form of brain damage that causes a shift in the brain's language center, and think that the Welsh he had heard as a boy had sunk in without his knowledge until it was unlocked following the stroke.

beardvertising Kentucky-based advertising agency Cornett-IMS has come up with the idea of Beardvertising, paying men with beards up to $5 a day to wear small adverts clipped on to their facial hair.

LONG TONGUE

Philip Romano, a 21-year-old student from Armonk, New York, sent Ripley's this picture of his supersize tongue. One of the longest in the world, it measures an impressive 3.9 in (10 cm) from its tip to the middle of his closed lip.

bionic hand Having lost his arm in an accident, Nigel Ackland from Cambridgeshire, England, has been fitted with a hi-tech bionic hand that moves like a real limb by responding to his muscle twitches. It is so sensitive he can even use it to peel vegetables and to type on a computer keyboard.

super vision Whereas most people can distinguish about one million different colors, Susan Hogan of Mount Washington, Pennsylvania, can see 100 million! She is a tetrachromat, which means she has a rare genetic condition enabling her to see four distinct ranges of color instead of the three that most of us live with.

surgery gig Brad Carter, a patient at UCLA medical center, sang and played the guitar while on the operating-room table undergoing brain surgery. Doctors were implanting a pacemaker in the brain of the Los Angeles musician to combat the hand tremors caused by Parkinson's disease, which had restricted his playing for nearly seven years—and in order to pinpoint the ideal placement of electrodes they woke him in the middle of the operation and asked him to play his guitar.

perfect match Gordon Henry from Berkshire, England, separated from his girlfriend Jo Macfarlane in 1993, but 20 years later they rekindled their romance after he came forward to give her one of his kidneys. She suffers from a chronic renal condition and was in desperate need of a donor. When her former partner heard about her predicament, he offered his kidney and it proved to be a perfect match.

metal mangler Former New York Giants football player Keith Davis can bend a metal bar 1 in (2.5 cm) thick into the shape of a U, using his arms and teeth. He can also smash stacks of bricks with his hand and roll up metal frying pans into a tight ball.

ancient filling A 6,500-year-old human jaw found by archeologists in a cave wall in northern Slovenia contained a tooth that had been crowned with beeswax.

facial piercings Axel Rosales of Villa Maria, Argentina, has no fewer than 280 piercings on his face. The transformation took him 18 months, which averages out at a new piercing every other day.

face slapping Thai beauticians charge $350 to slap customers' faces—a treatment that is said to give a younger appearance by firming up flabby faces and helping to eliminate wrinkles and frown lines.

THE WILD MEN OF BORNEO

➜ Waino and Plutano were two dwarf brothers who performed as famous sideshow entertainers for P.T. Barnum across the U.S.A. in the late 19th century. They were promoted as the Wild Men of Borneo —a pair of fearsome dwarfs standing just 40 in (1 m) tall who had allegedly been captured on the Malay island of Borneo, a part of the world that was still mysterious and exotic for most of their audience. In 1894, the *New York Times* called the pair "two of the strangest freaks ever exhibited in America." In reality, they were Hiram and Barney Davis, brothers from Ohio with learning difficulties who pretended to be wild "savages" on stage. They became famous when Barnum brought them to New York, where they earned large sums of money performing great feats of strength—it was claimed that they could each lift almost ten times their own weight.

new ear When Sherrie Walter of Bel Air, Maryland, lost an ear to cancer, doctors at John Hopkins University grew a replacement ear on her forearm using her own body tissue. Cartilage was removed from her rib cage to form the new ear, which was then shaped and placed under the skin of her arm near her wrist. It grew there for four months before being surgically attached to her head.

left bias Although only 10 percent of the U.S. population is left-handed, three of the last four U.S. presidents—George Bush Sr., Bill Clinton and Barack Obama—have been left-handed. Before them, Ronald Reagan, too, was naturally left-handed but was forced to switch hands by his schoolteachers and parents.

Tattooed EYES

➔ **Jean Jabril Joseph, a poet from Fort Lauderdale, Florida, has had the sclera, or white part of the eye, tattooed black by means of a series of ink injections.**

Although eyeball inking seems like a new trend, as early as the late 19th century, doctors routinely injected ink into patients' eyes to cover up disfiguring corneal scars.

harpoon horror Fisherman Bruno Barcellos de Souza Coutinho accidentally shot himself in the face with a harpoon and survived even though the spear pierced his left eye and traveled 6 in (15 cm) into his skull before becoming lodged in his brain. He was cleaning the gun in Petrópolis, Brazil, when it went off, firing a 12-in-long (30-cm) spear into his head, but he suffered no brain damage and was even conscious enough to get help.

health benefit Members of a remote community in Ecuador with a rare form of dwarfism called Laron syndrome are almost totally immune to cancer and diabetes.

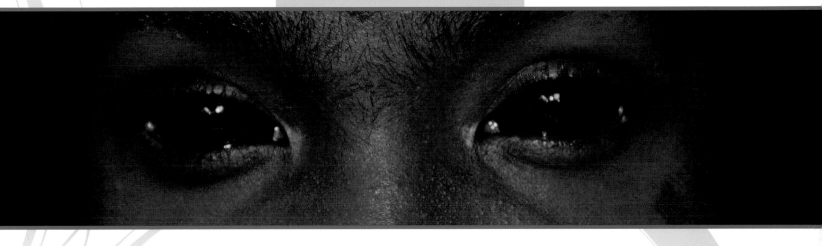

fish finger A human finger found inside a fish in Priest Lake, Idaho, was traced back to a wakeboarder who lost four fingers in an accident 8 mi (13 km) away three months earlier. A fisherman discovered the finger while cleaning a trout he had caught. The sheriff's office helped identify the finger as belonging to Haans Galassi. He turned down the chance of being reunited with his finger and the other three severed digits remain on the missing file.

star student Twelve-year-old Irene Nthambi of Thika, Kenya, who is blind and has no sense of touch in her fingers, is able to join in lessons at her school for the visually impaired by using her tongue to write and her lips to read. She writes by gripping a stylus with her tongue and uses her lips to read a Braille machine. Despite having to adapt, she is always top of her class.

hairy legs To dissuade men from staring at women's legs on Chinese public transport, some women have started wearing hairy stockings—pantyhose covered in a layer of thick, dark hair.

face transplant Fifteen years after Richard Lee Norris was accidentally shot and lost much of his face as a result, he had his jaw, nose and skin all successfully replaced in a 72-hour-long series of transplant surgeries at the University of Maryland.

noisy eyeballs

➔ For seven years every time she turned to look at something, Julie Redfern from Lancashire, England, could hear her eyeballs moving in their sockets. She could also hear the blood coursing through her veins and her brain wobbling in her skull. In fact she could hear every sound her body made—sounds that are normally never heard. Her amplified hearing was the result of a rare inner ear condition—superior canal dehiscence syndrome (SCDS)—and meant that she had to stop eating crunchy foods, such as apples and potato chips, because of the deafening noise in her head as she ate.

framed placenta Artist Amanda Cotton from London, England, makes picture frames out of mothers' placentas so that they can use them to frame photos of their babies. After boiling and cooking the placenta, she grinds it into small pieces. She then puts the dried pieces into a mold and adds resin to create a marble-effect frame.

RIPLEY'S RESEARCH

SCDS is a rare condition of the inner ear caused by small holes forming in the temporal bone that covers part of the ear. It makes the patient over-sensitive to sounds from within the body, such as the noise of fluid moving around and the pounding of the heart. The condition, which was recognized in only 1998, can be caused by slow erosion of the bone or by a blow to the skull.

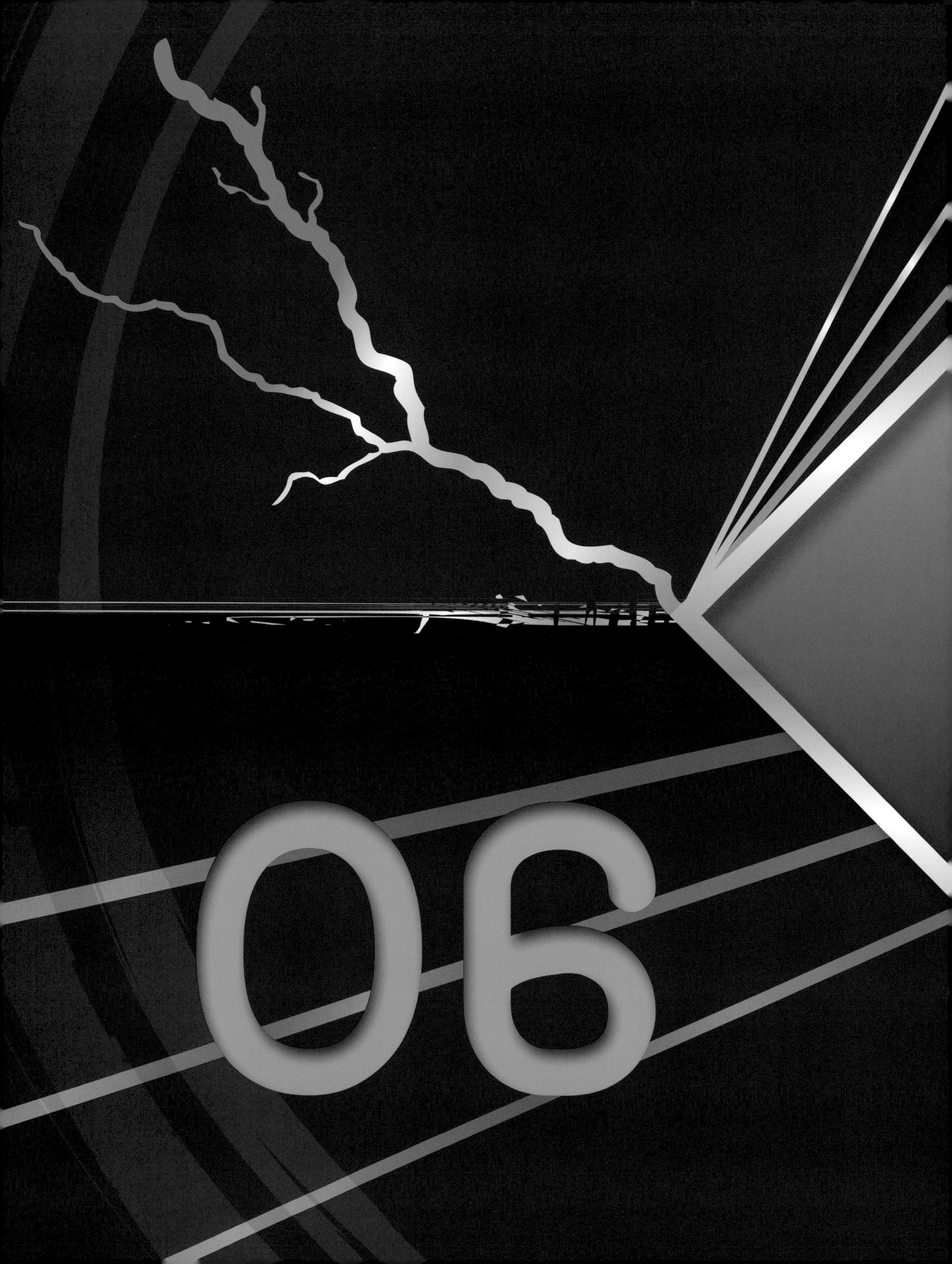
06

POP CULTURE

Margaret Ann Robinson regularly appeared with Singer's Midgets, a troupe founded in 1912 by Austrian Leopold von Singer and his wife Walberga. Recruiting little people wherever they went, Singer's Midgets performed in U.S. vaudeville theaters after World War I, and some of his artists appeared in movies, including *The Terror of Tiny Town* (1938), the world's only musical Western with an all-dwarf cast. Also in 1938, Singer signed a contract with MGM to provide 124 proportionately sized little people to play Munchkins in *The Wizard of Oz*, although Margaret Ann was not among them.

THE MOST MARVELOUS AND ONLY ATTRACTION OF ITS KIND IN THE WORLD
SINGER'S MIDGETS
3 MIDGET ELEPHANTS **30 WONDERFUL MIDGETS** 20 PONIES

To emphasize her diminutive stature, on her 19th birthday, at the California Pacific World's Fair, a waiter carried Margaret Ann on a tray along with her birthday cake.

Margaret Ann with Captain Werner, the "Smallest Man and Smallest Woman in the World", posing inside a traveling bag outside "Midget City" at the Chicago World's Fair in 1934.

The seat of a standard adult chair was too high for Margaret Ann's tiny frame. She lived with other dwarfs in a colony that had specially made tiny furniture and houses.

Who's the little LADY?

➜ Billed in contemporary U.S. sideshows as the "World's Smallest Lady," Margaret Ann Robinson was so tiny she could stand in the palm of your hand.

When she was 19, she stood just 21 in (53 cm) tall and weighed 18 lb (8.1 kg), making her smaller than the average two-year-old. No wonder Shriners' Circus billed her in 1936 as a "Living, Breathing, Walking, Talking Human Doll."

She was born Margaret Ann Meek in Denver, Colorado, in 1916 and weighed a respectable 6 lb 8 oz (2.9 kg) at birth. Both her parents were of normal stature, with her father, a coal miner, standing 5 ft 11 in (1.8 m) tall. When it became apparent that Margaret Ann suffered from dwarfism, she went into show business and, at the 1934 World's Fair in Chicago, she and Captain Werner (far left), "the smallest man in the world," were pictured standing together in a leather carrying case at the gates of "Midget City," a colony of 187 little people living in miniature houses with tiny furniture.

Often traveling with her mother, Margaret Ann went on to perform with circuses for more than 40 years. At the height of her fame, she advertised Johnson's Glo-Coat floor cleaner to show housewives how easy it was to keep their kitchens spotless. By the age of 50, she still wowed audiences billed as "Princess Ann, The Tiny Lady."

21 in (53 cm) tall

IN PERSON

MARGARET ANN ROBINSON

The Smallest Adult Ever Born to Live!

Height 21 ins. - Age 19 yrs. - Weight 18 lbs.

This Living, Breathing, Walking, Talking Human Doll Will Appear Twice Daily At

MELHA TEMPLE A.A.O.N.M.S

SHRINERS' CIRCUS

PRESENTING

The Morton-Hamid Circus

MAY 4TH TO 9TH INCLUSIVE 1936 STATE ARMORY

135

KLINGON WEDDING → 1,063

Star Trek fans dressed up as characters from the show at a convention in London, England, in October 2012. The convention also hosted the wedding of Swedish couple Jossie Sockertopp and Sonnie Gustavsson who got married wearing full Klingon attire. Their service was conducted in the Klingon language.

rare comic Among the old newspapers used to insulate a wall of the house that he had just bought in Elbow Lake, Minnesota, construction worker David Gonzalez found a rare copy of *Action Comics No. 1*, a June 1938 comic book featuring the first appearance of Superman. He later sold the comic at auction for $175,000—more than 17 times the price that he paid for the house.

movie remake Arizona amateur filmmakers Jonason Pauley and Jesse Perrotta spent more than two years creating their own 80-minute, scene-for-scene live action remake of the entire *Toy Story* movie using official merchandise toys and real actors.

hair glasses Two graduates from London's Royal College of Art, Alexander Groves and Azuka Murakami, have designed a collection of fashion glasses with frames made from discarded human hair bound together with bioresin.

dolly's defeat Country singer Dolly Parton once lost a Dolly Parton look-a-like contest in Santa Monica, California—to a man!

U.S. designer Susan Rosen and Steinmetz Diamonds created a **bikini** that used 150 carats of flawless diamonds set in platinum and had no fabric. Tiger Woods was rumored to have bought it in 2010. **Price: $30 million**

British designer Debbie Wingham made a one-of-a-kind black **abaya** (a robe worn by some Muslim women), encrusted with 1,000 rubies and 2,000 diamonds, including a rare large red diamond worth over $7 million alone. **Price: $17.6 million**

Secret Circus created a pair of women's **jeans** with 15 large, high-quality diamonds sewn into the back pockets. **Price: $1.3 million**

Stuart Hughes and Richard Jewels of the U.K. designed a wool and cashmere silk men's **jacket** studded with 480 diamonds, each weighing a whopping 240 carats. **Price: $943,000**

U.S. shoe designer Stuart Weitzman created a pair of ladies' "Diamond Dream" **stilettos** encrusted with 1,420 diamonds. **Price: $500,000**

U.K. department store Selfridges commissioned a **belt** featuring 70 pyramids crafted from 18-carat gold and mounted on white leather. **Price: $32,000** for anyone with a waist under 28 in (71 cm)—each additional inch added $1,300 to the price.

DIAMOND BRA

→ Lingerie-maker Victoria's Secret designed a $2.5-million bra adorned with 5,200 precious gems, including a 20-carat diamond and a huge ruby.

TOP TAGS: LIST OF EXPENSIVE CLOTHES

Roadkill Fashion

children's clown Before he became famous, Hugh Jackman, star of the *X-Men* and *Wolverine* movies, worked as a clown at children's birthday parties in his native Australia for three years, charging $50 per show.

burning topic Nearly one million people tuned in to watch an eight-hour primetime program on Norwegian TV showing nothing but a burning fireplace—and some viewers called in to complain that the wood fuel was stacked facing the wrong way! The show was inspired by Lars Mytting's book about chopping and burning wood, which spent more than a year on the Norwegian best-seller list.

low heels Women require a license to wear shoes with heels more than 2 in (5 cm) high in the Californian town of Carmel-by-the-Sea.

Stephanie Watson from Melbourne, Australia, made her wedding dress from 10,000 plastic bread expiration tags that she had collected over a ten-year period.

bird scarer Workers at Staverton Airport in Gloucestershire, England, keep troublesome birds off the runway by mounting a loudspeaker to the roof of a van and playing Tina Turner songs at full volume.

phone audition English actor Eddie Redmayne did an audition for the role of Marius in the 2013 movie *Les Misérables* on his iPhone. Wearing his cowboy outfit from the movie *Hick* that he was shooting at the time in North Carolina, he filmed himself singing in his trailer on the set and sent it to his agent.

giant tv A giant TV made by Porsche in Austria has a 201-in (510-cm) screen and costs more than $600,000—four times as much as a Porsche 911 sports car. The C SEED 201 is made up of more than 787,000 LEDs, which display 281 trillion colors, and is so big it has to be used outdoors.

➜ Fashion designer Jess Eaton from Brighton, England, created a range of wedding clothes from roadkill, including this bridal cape made from swans' feathers.

She also made a necklace out of human bones after sourcing a ribcage from a university medical department.

soccer dress Karen Bell, a bride from Manchester, England, made her wedding dress by sewing together the groom's collection of Manchester City soccer jerseys, some dating back to the early 1980s.

spider strings Shigeyoshi Osaki of Japan's Nara Medical University makes violin strings from woven spiderweb silk. More than 300 spiders are used to generate the 5,000 individual strands of silk needed to make up each string.

Musical Skateboards

➔ Juhana Nyrhinen from Finland makes $500 electric versions of kanteles and other traditional stringed Finnish folk instruments from ordinary skateboards. Players can hold the instrument on their lap and achieve a distinctive tremolo sound effect by leaning on the wheels.

multitasking Ben Lapps from Mason, Ohio, can play the guitar and basketball at the same time. A YouTube video, which attracted 300,000 views in a single day, shows him maintaining a tune on his guitar while bouncing a basketball and shooting hoops.

in stitches In 2013, Norwegian TV's public broadcasting network announced it was devoting five hours of airtime to live knitting—preceded by a four-hour documentary on how the wool shorn from a sheep's back is turned into a sweater.

girl power The Japanese all-girl pop group AKB48 has 88 members—and because they can't all fit on stage at the same time, before each show they hold a rock-paper-scissors contest to select a limited number of singers to perform.

cool reception In November 2012, English rock guitarist Charlie Simpson, formerly with the band Busted, played a 15-minute outdoor gig in Siberia while enduring temperatures of −22°F (−30°C).

chicken feed The first book published by L. Frank Baum, author of *The Wonderful Wizard of Oz*, was a guide to rearing, mating and managing chickens.

divorce dress Fifteen-year-old art student Demi Barnes from Sussex, England, made a wedding dress from more than 1,500 divorce papers. After constructing a wire bodice frame, it took her ten hours to staple on the genuine—but blank—divorce papers that she had downloaded from the Internet.

ZIP TIE ➔ For men who struggle to fasten their tie, designer Josh Jakus, from Oakland, California, has created an idiotproof, wool felt tie with a zipper sewn down the middle that does up in seconds and eliminates the need for tying knots. Finding that his company, Actual, had a surplus of felt and zippers from manufacturing other products, Josh tried to think of ways of making use of the extra material. He began experimenting with a necklace but ended up with a novel necktie instead.

[YOUR / UPLOADS]

quick change Vanna White has been the hostess on the TV game show *Wheel of Fortune* since 1982, and in that time she has worn over 6,000 dresses, never wearing the same outfit more than once.

CYMBAL OF FAITH

Rocking reverend Mark Temperato from Lakeville, New York, owns a giant drum kit consisting of more than 900 pieces—and he can hit every drum, cymbal or cow bell without moving from his seat, even though some pieces are 8 ft (2.4 m) apart. Temperato, who plays under the stage name RevM and stores the kit in his church, estimates that it takes him an hour to strike each piece in turn. He spent over 20 years building up his collection, which weighs in excess of 5,000 lb (2,270 kg) and requires 17 hours of maintenance per week.

tower drum U.S. composer Joseph Bertolozzi turned Paris's famous Eiffel Tower into a giant drum kit. Using conventional drumsticks, latex mallets and even a large log wrapped in wool, he explored every surface of the 1,062-ft (324-m) tower, hitting its railings, panels and girders with varying intensity to create 2,000 different sounds for a percussion piece titled *Tower Music*. It is not the first monument that Bertolozzi has sampled—in 2007 he composed *Bridge Music* by repeatedly hitting New York State's Mid-Hudson Bridge.

text error A 33-year-old Sussex, New Jersey, man was arrested after sending a text message to a police detective by mistake saying he had drugs to sell and wanted to meet at a pizza parlor.

musical coffin Swedish inventor Fredrik Hjelmquist has created a coffin with a built-in stereo system. It allows people to compile their own personal playlist before they die so that their favorite music can be streamed into their grave. Relatives can even update the songs by using an app and a touchscreen that is built into the headstone.

harp twins Camille and Kennerly Kitt—the world's only known identical twin professional harpists—play rock classics by Metallica, The Rolling Stones, Bon Jovi and AC/DC on harps. They also perform in unusual locations including graveyards, desert tracks and highway slip roads.

dress code Visitors to Chessington World of Adventures safari park in Surrey, England, have been banned from wearing fake leopard-print and tiger-stripe clothes in case they confuse or frighten the animals.

game cure Doctors at McGill University, Montreal, Canada, treat patients with a lazy eye by getting them to play the video game *Tetris* because it trains both eyes to work together.

loud ties Artist Alyce Santoro from Marfa, Texas, makes neckties from stitched cassette tapes—which can still play sounds if a cassette player head is rubbed over the surface of the fabric. Incorporating the music of artists such as Miles Davis, Richie Havens and John Coltrane, as well as the sound of the ocean and birdsong, her sonic fabric is made from 50 percent polyester thread and 50 percent cassette tape and has the consistency of denim.

mom's watching Canadian pop star Justin Bieber has a large tattoo of his mother's eye inked into the crook of his left arm.

avian singer Heavy-metal band Hatebeak from Baltimore, Maryland, who released records in the 2000s, featured an African grey parrot named Waldo on lead vocals.

colonel's suit Masao Watanabe, the President of Kentucky Fried Chicken in Japan, bought the trademark white suit of "Colonel" Harland Sanders for $20,750 in June 2013.

four guitars E.N. Burton from Raleigh, North Carolina, plays four guitars at the same time—lead guitars with each hand and bass guitars with each foot.

TATTOO ROULETTE

→ American singer Ryan Cabrera had to get the face of actor Ryan Gosling inked on his leg after losing a game of tattoo roulette where blindfolded friends get to pick a tattoo for each other.

alien streets Klingon Court and Romulan Court are two streets that meet at an intersection in Sacramento, California. They were named in 1977 by civil engineer and *Star Trek* fan Ted Colbert.

floating cinema For a 2012 film festival, German architect Ole Scheeren designed a floating movie theater in a lagoon on the coast of Thailand. The Archipelago Cinema consisted of a floating screen mounted on wood and foam rafts and a separate floating auditorium, to which filmgoers were transported by boat.

hogwarts model The 50-ft (15-m) model of Hogwarts Castle that was used for every Harry Potter movie contained more than 2,500 fiber-optic lights and was so detailed that if all the hours spent on construction by the 86 artists and crew members were added up, it would total 74 years.

reading pajamas A hi-tech pair of pajamas can be used to read bedtime stories to children. The Smart Pajamas are printed with 47 clusters of dots—each cluster linked to a different story—which act like barcodes when scanned by a smartphone or a tablet.

navajo version Using authentic Native American speakers, *Star Wars* has been dubbed into Navajo to help preserve the language. A team of five Navajo people labored over translating the original script, hampered by the fact that there is no direct translation for famous phrases such as "May the force be with you."

dog leads New York City band Caninus made three records with two pitbull terriers, Budgie and Basil, on lead vocals. Caninus was formed in 2001 by metalcore band Most Precious Blood, who replaced its vocalists with dogs. The band played until 2011 when Basil died.

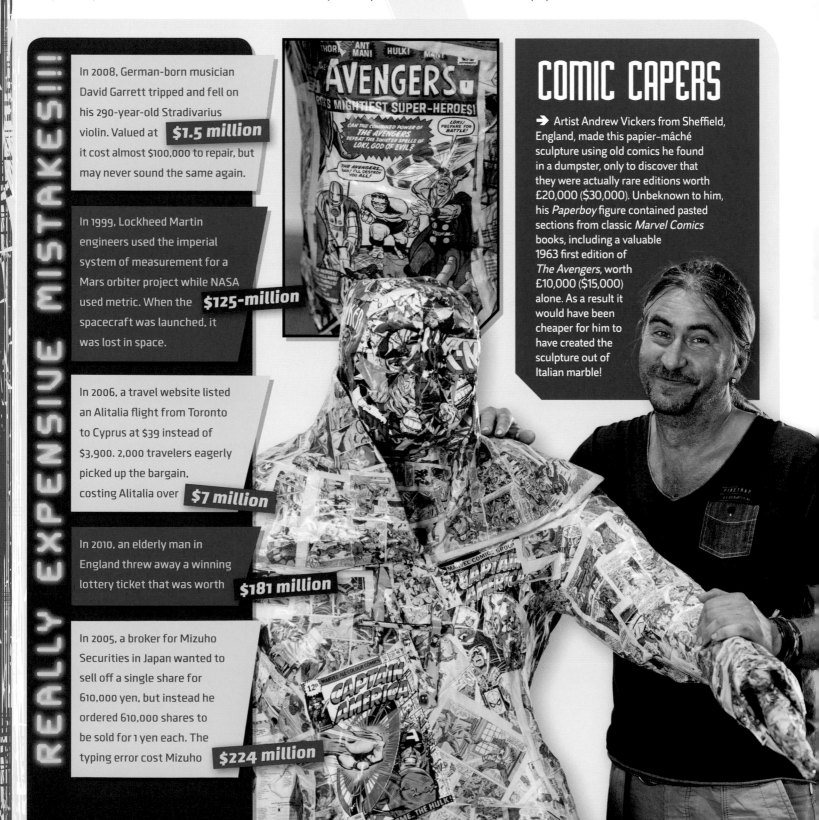

REALLY EXPENSIVE MISTAKES!!!

In 2008, German-born musician David Garrett tripped and fell on his 290-year-old Stradivarius violin. Valued at **$1.5 million** it cost almost $100,000 to repair, but may never sound the same again.

In 1999, Lockheed Martin engineers used the imperial system of measurement for a Mars orbiter project while NASA used metric. When the **$125-million** spacecraft was launched, it was lost in space.

In 2006, a travel website listed an Alitalia flight from Toronto to Cyprus at $39 instead of $3,900. 2,000 travelers eagerly picked up the bargain, costing Alitalia over **$7 million**

In 2010, an elderly man in England threw away a winning lottery ticket that was worth **$181 million**

In 2005, a broker for Mizuho Securities in Japan wanted to sell off a single share for 610,000 yen, but instead he ordered 610,000 shares to be sold for 1 yen each. The typing error cost Mizuho **$224 million**

COMIC CAPERS

➔ Artist Andrew Vickers from Sheffield, England, made this papier-mâché sculpture using old comics he found in a dumpster, only to discover that they were actually rare editions worth £20,000 ($30,000). Unbeknown to him, his *Paperboy* figure contained pasted sections from classic *Marvel Comics* books, including a valuable 1963 first edition of *The Avengers*, worth £10,000 ($15,000) alone. As a result it would have been cheaper for him to have created the sculpture out of Italian marble!

Barbie World

→ **Stanley Colorite of Hudson, Florida, owns 2,000 Barbies and 1,000 Ken dolls.**

His collection is so big it takes up four rooms of his house, including his bathroom. He bought his first doll in 1997 and now buys up to 20 dolls a month, estimating that he spends $30,000 a year on his hobby.

doting husband Paul Brockman from Lomita, California, has bought his wife Margot 55,000 dresses over the past 56 years, and he chose them all himself.

micro book Japanese publisher Toppan Printing has created a book with pages measuring just 0.03 x 0.03 in (0.75 x 0.75 mm). The 22 page book, which contains names and illustrations of flowers, is so small it can be read only with a magnifying glass.

spending spree Five-year-old Danny Kitchen from Bristol, England, ran up a $2,500 bill on his parents' iPad in just 10 minutes after downloading a free game and then ending up in its online store.

spice collection Liz West from West Yorkshire, England, has collected more than 5,000 items of Spice Girls memorabilia, including outfits worn by the group, platinum disks, and books and dolls.

lost for words Actress Jori Phillips from Vancouver, British Columbia, spent months tearing pages out of a thesaurus, then folding and gluing them together to make a strapless paper dress. Lined with fabric and featuring a bodice for support, her recycled dress consists of hundreds of pages of synonyms from A to O.

gaming fan Brett Martin from Denver, Colorado, has over 8,000 items of video game memorabilia, worth an estimated $100,000.

SHIVER ME TIMBERS! → An anonymous multimillionaire has built his own private pirate island in a lake on his estate in Cambridgeshire, England. Featuring wooden buildings in an 18th-century design, Challis Island reflects its owner's love of all things piratical and has its own inn, The Black Dubloon, as well as a guesthouse, beach, waterfall, lagoon and boat dock.

DOCTOR WHO

→ British sci-fi phenomenon *Doctor Who* first aired on television on November 23, 1963, and has now been running for more than 50 years, making it the world's longest-running sci-fi show.

As of December 25, 2013, a total of 800 episodes had been broadcast, and the show is now seen in more than 50 countries every week. Ripley's wanted to celebrate this achievement by introducing some of the world's more unusual "Whovians," as *Doctor Who* fans are known, and their tributes to the show.

- There have been 12 Doctors in total—the First Doctor appeared on November 23, 1963, and the Twelfth Doctor made his first appearance on December 25, 2013.

- The total number of years traveled by all the Doctors is 204,272,560,259,444.

- A total of 52 percent of the Doctor's adventures are set in the future, 22 percent in the past and 16 percent in the present day.

- The Daleks are the most popular adversary in the series, appearing in 22 stories with 9 cameos. The Cybermen come a distant second with 14 stories and 5 cameos.

- Up to 2013, the Daleks said "Exterminate!" 469 times, and killed 210 people on screen.

- The Doctor has appeared in *The Simpsons* TV show four times, but has never spoken a word.

- Tapes containing nine episodes of *Doctor Who* from the 1960s that were thought to be lost to the world were discovered in 2013 in a TV station cupboard in Nigeria.

- The most well-traveled Doctor is the Eleventh, with 70 journeys through time on screen.

- The Doctor speaks five billion languages, including Baby and Horse.

- The longest journey through time was taken by the Tenth Doctor between *Utopia* and *The Sound of Drums*, which was 99.99 trillion years.

- It would take 371 hours 19 minutes 25 seconds to watch every *Doctor Who* episode until the end of 2013.

BAYWHEUX TAPESTRY

Cartoonist Bill Mudron from Portland, Oregon, drew this superb artwork in the style of the Bayeux Tapestry to chronicle *Doctor Who*'s entire adventures over 50 years. The 6-sq-ft (0.5-sq-m) design begins with the First Doctor, William Hartnell, in 1963 and continues through every regeneration up to Matt Smith, the Eleventh Doctor, in 2013.

TARDIS CAKE

Baker and *Doctor Who* fan Lisa Wheatcroft from Carlisle, Cumbria, England, made this amazing 4-ft-tall (1.2-m) Tardis cake. It took her three weeks to make and was constructed from over a dozen blocks of cake held together by a puffed rice and marshmallow mix, chocolate ganache, and icing painted the exact shade of blue.

DALEK COLLECTOR

A fan of *Doctor Who*'s robotic adversaries since the age of seven, Rob Hull from Doncaster, England, has now collected over 1,200 Daleks. It has taken him 25 years to acquire Daleks in every size from tiny miniatures to a life-size model, and they have virtually taken over his family home. Two of his children have also started their own Dalek collections.

keep trying A single scene in the 1982 Jackie Chan movie *Dragon Lord* required 2,900 takes to perfect.

old rapper Jeanne Calment of Arles, France, made a rap album in 1996 when she was 120 years old.

wrong way In the space of three weeks in September 2013, two motorists drove across a runway at Fairbanks International Airport, Alaska, which is used by 737 airplanes, after their smartphone satellite navigation apps gave them wrong directions.

dyslexic type Dutch graphic designer Christian Boer invented a typeface to help dyslexic readers with their reading disability. By varying the size and shape of the letters in Dyslexie so that each is unique, he ensured that all words are recognizable.

mood music A Japanese company has invented a set of mind-reading headphones that play music based on the wearer's mood. The headphones contain a forehead sensor that analyzes brainwaves to detect the person's mood and then connects to an iPhone app that selects the song best suited to that state of mind.

milk jewelry Allicia Mogavero from Wakefield, Rhode Island, makes jewelry from women's breast milk. Mothers from around the world send her their breast milk in sealed bags and she then plasticizes a sample and molds it into miniature shapes—hearts, moons, flowers or tiny hands—which are then set into pendants.

the borrower Louise Brown from Stranraer, Scotland, borrowed more than 25,000 books from local libraries over a period of 63 years.

games sale An eBay user called videogames.museum from Milan, Italy, put up for sale more than 6,850 games, 330 consoles, 220 controllers and 185 accessories at a total price of $550,000. He took more than 10,000 photos in a two-month period to try to illustrate the 30-year collection, which included every Mario, Zelda, Metal Gear and Final Fantasy game ever made.

recruitment boost Following the release of the 1986 Hollywood movie *Top Gun*, starring Tom Cruise, the number of applications by young men wanting to join the U.S. Navy as aviators rocketed by 500 percent.

ghost dating Ghostsingles is a dating website for ghosts wanting to meet other dead people! The site's rules state that living people, the living dead and vampires are all forbidden to access its database of the deceased.

MAIZE MAZE

Farmer and *Doctor Who* fan Tom Pearcy created a 1,000-ft-long (300-m) image of a Dalek that covered an 18-acre (7 ha) field containing more than one million maize plants near York, England. The design takes the form of a giant maze consisting of 6¼ mi (10 km) of pathways.

CYBERMAN GROOM

A Cyberman marries his bride at a mass *Doctor Who* wedding ceremony in London, England, in November 2013 to mark the 50th anniversary of the show. Fifty "Whovian" couples married or renewed their vows in costume before a congregation of Daleks and different incarnations of the Doctor, after which they were given commemorative rings and *Doctor Who* tattoos. Fans flew in from as far afield as Canada and the U.S.A.

WHOSE NAILS?

Nail artist Kayleigh O'Connor from Birmingham, England, has designed a range of beautifully painted fingernails celebrating *Doctor Who*, depicting some of the Doctor's arch enemies as well as the Tardis. She has also created nails portraying characters from Harry Potter and the TV series *Breaking Bad*.

MUSICAL SHELL

➔ This Bolivian musical instrument-maker is working on *charangos*—a traditional South American stringed instrument similar to a lute that is sometimes made from the backs of armadillos.

online backing The 2013 Academy Award-winning *Inocente*, a short documentary about a homeless street artist, was filmed for $52,527—the sum contributed by 294 backers on Kickstarter.

sci-fi shrine Steve Sansweet's Rancho Obi-Wan museum in Petaluma, California, houses his collection of more than 300,000 items of Star Wars memorabilia, including toys, models and life-size exhibits, and includes an entire room of pinball and arcade machines.

marathon game Victor Sandberg from Stockholm, Sweden, played the classic Atari game *Missile Command* for 56 hours straight on a single coin, racking up a score of 81,796,035 points.

trash sounds The child musicians of the Cateura Orchestra from the Cateura slum of Paraguay play instruments—including a violin, cello, flute and drum—which are all made from landfill trash. In such an impoverished area, a real violin costs more than a house.

health app A Facebook app called "Help, I Have the Flu" scans your friends' status updates for words like "sniffles" and "coughing" to suggest which people you should avoid for a couple of weeks.

multi tasking Ukrainian virtuoso Oleksandr Bozhyk can play four violins at once. Using two bows, he rests two violins on his left arm, tucks another under his right arm and a fourth beneath his chin.

mixed messages The sounds made by the brachiosaurs in Steven Spielberg's 1993 movie blockbuster *Jurassic Park* were a combination of whale songs and donkey calls.

witch ancestor A female ancestor of Harry Potter actress Emma Watson was convicted of witchcraft in 16th-century England.

comic temple Chalermchai Kositpipat spent more than a decade building the Wat Rong Khun Buddhist temple near Chiang Rai, Thailand, which is decorated with cultural figures from comics and movies—including Superman, Batman, Neo from *The Matrix* and the aliens from the Predator movies—as well as more traditional religious icons.

beat that! At an extreme drumming event in Nashville, Tennessee, in July 2013, Tom Grosset from Toronto, Ontario, recorded 1,208 single strokes in 60 seconds—more than 20 beats per second.

rolling fine Rolling Stones' guitarist Keith Richards has racked up a library fine of $5,000 (£3,000) after failing to return books he borrowed more than 50 years ago from a public library in Kent, England.

international collaboration *The Owner*, a 2012 movie conceived by Detroit, Michigan, filmmakers Marty Shea and Ian Bonner, was woven together from segments shot across the globe by 25 different directors from 13 countries.

personal superhero In 2012, Marvel Comics specially created a new superhero, Blue Ear, to encourage Anthony Smith, a hearing-impaired four-year-old boy from Salem, New Hampshire, to wear his hearing aid to school. After the young comic-book fan protested that superheroes never wear hearing aids, his mother wrote to Marvel and they responded by inventing a new action figure—named after Anthony's nickname for his aid—who owed his superpowers to his listening device.

fast fail A YouTube video showing a South Korean woman failing her driving test within just seven seconds quickly notched up half a million views. Moments after starting the engine, the woman drove up a bank and overturned the car, while the instructor yelled at her to put her foot on the brake instead of the gas.

FAN POWER ➔ A group of six Star Wars fans, led by Belgian Mark Dermul, traveled to Tunisia in 2012 to save the Lars Homestead—Luke Skywalker's home on the planet Tatooine that was featured in three of the Star Wars movies. They raised $11,700 and worked in 115°F (46°C) heat to restore the igloo-shaped building that had been ravaged by the desert climate and had fallen into disrepair since its last screen appearance in 2005.

LIVING DOLLS

ALTER EGOS

➔ Valeria Lukyanova and Justin Jedlica are a real-life Barbie and Ken.

The slim 28-year-old Ukrainian model is every inch a Barbie doll, enhancing her Barbie looks with clever makeup and colored contact lenses. Justin, 33, from Chicago, has spent over $150,000 on 140 cosmetic procedures to transform himself into Ken, including nose jobs, pectoral, buttock and bicep implants, and facial surgery. He says he treats himself as a human sculpture.

Toby Sheldon, a 33-year-old songwriter from Los Angeles, California, has spent **$100,000** on cosmetic surgery trying to transform himself into his idol **Justin Bieber** including $30,000 to acquire the singer's baby-faced perma-smile. He has also had eyelid surgery, chin reduction and face fillers, and has had his hairline lowered.

Nileen Namita, a mother-of-three from Brighton, England, underwent more than 50 cosmetic surgeries—including eight nose jobs and three facelifts costing a total of **$360,000** to fulfill her dream of looking like the ancient Egyptian queen **Nefertiti**

Herbert Chavez from the Philippines has had **19 surgeries** in 16 years—including skin whitening and a cleft chin—to transform himself into his superhero idol **Superman**

Size 10, 50-year-old redhead Janet Cunliffe spent **$15,000** on surgery to make her look almost identical to her size 4 blonde **daughter Jane** who is 22 years younger than her. They even wear the same clothes.

Mikki Jay from St. Helens, England, spent **$16,000** on having her nose, chin and cheeks remodeled so that she could become a professional **Michael Jackson** impersonator.

Over 20 years, Sarah Burge, a mother from Cambridgeshire, England, has undergone hundreds of cosmetic surgeries and spent more than **$130,000** to turn herself into a real-life **Barbie**

toenail clippings An unnamed woman sold all ten of her toenail clippings—one from each toe—on eBay for $1.

paper app Thousands of Venezuelan people downloaded a smartphone app that helped them find toilet paper—a commodity that was in short supply in the country during much of 2013.

lost tale *The Tallow Candle*, a 700-word fairy tale penned by Danish writer Hans Christian Andersen in the 1820s, remained unknown for nearly 200 years until a copy of the manuscript was discovered at the bottom of a filing box in 2012.

sneaker museum Jordan Michael Geller's ShoeZeum in Las Vegas, Nevada, includes one of every model of Nike Air Jordans ever made and in total houses a collection of more than 2,600 pairs of sneakers. Only a few of the shoes have been worn, but they include a pair that Michael Jordan himself laced as a rookie for the Chicago Bulls basketball team.

heavily edited The total footage shot for Stanley Kubrick's 1968 sci-fi adventure *2001: A Space Odyssey* was around 200 times the final length of the movie.

original members Texas rock band ZZ Top have had the same line-up—Billy Gibbons, Dusty Hill and Frank Beard—since they formed in 1969.

homing shoes U.K. designer Dominic Wilcox has created shoes with computer-linked GPS technology, which send the wearer in the direction of home. The left shoe has a built-in compass and flashing arrows, while the right shoe has a distance gauge. Before setting off, the wearer's home address must be typed into a computer.

tweet panic More than half of stock market trading is done by computers that automatically sift through news, data and even tweets to carry out trades in fractions of a second without any human input. So, on April 23, 2013, when a hoax news agency tweet reported explosions at the White House, the Wall Street computers reacted by unloading $134 billion worth of stocks in just ten minutes.

gold shirt Millionaire Datta Phuge from Pune, India, spent $235,000 on a shirt crafted out of 7 lb (3.2 kg) of 22-carat solid gold. It took a team of 15 goldsmiths two weeks to construct the shirt, which contains 14,000 gold flowerings interwoven with 100,000 gold spangles all sewn into a velvet lining, as well as six Swarovski crystal buttons.

tube song Guitar-playing comedian and singer-songwriter Jay Foreman from London, England, has penned a rhyming song in which he mentions the names of all 270 of London's Underground stations. The song takes just over three minutes to perform.

PAY RAISE → More than 60 employees at New York real estate agency Rapid Realty earned higher commission splits for life by agreeing to get the company's logo tattooed somewhere on their bodies. CEO Anthony Lolli came up with the idea, which can earn agents a pay raise of up to 60 percent, after doing business with a tattoo artist. Employees have had tattoos on their arms, ankles and backs, and one, Robert Trezza, had his done despite working at the company for only a month.

reagan rejection Seventeen years before he became U.S. President in 1981, Ronald Reagan was rejected for the role of a politician in the 1964 movie *The Best Man* because he did not look "presidential."

mouse marriage Wayne Allwine (1947–2009), the voice of Mickey Mouse from 1977 to 2009, was married to Russi Taylor, who has provided the voice of Minnie Mouse since 1986.

CAT BEARDING
→ One of the latest Internet crazes is cat bearding, where pet owners are photographed positioning their cat in front of their face so that it looks as if they have a beard! The craze began on Tumblr when a user uploaded a snap of his fake feline beard and the trick quickly spread across the world.

Dogs too!

Railroad Cinema

→ In 1905, retired Kansas City Fire Chief George C. Hale came up with the idea of making short "phantom ride" travelogues showing film shot from the front of a moving train.

His Hale's Tours films were screened in mock railroad cars, which would rock, vibrate and tilt to simulate real train travel. Sound effects, including steam whistles and thundering wheels, added to the illusion, while painted scenery rolled past the side windows. By 1907, there were 500 Hale's Tours theaters in the U.S., but with the rise of movie theaters and a limited amount of footage, their popularity proved short-lived and most had vanished within four years.

Hale's Tours films were screened in a mock railroad car. Up to 72 passengers sat facing the screen where they saw and felt the movements and heard the sounds that made them believe they were on a real train.

Cameraman Billy Bitzer perched precariously on the front of a moving train while filming the action for a Hale's Tours travelogue.

sky walkers Kung fu movie fans can run through the air or over the water at a martial arts theme park in Kunming, China. The park has the same computerized wire-lifting system that is used on the big screen, allowing visitors to copy the sky-walking stunts seen in movies such as *Crouching Tiger, Hidden Dragon*.

gown trashing The latest trend in bridal photography is called Trash the Dress—and it involves the bride deliberately wrecking her wedding gown straight after the ceremony by getting it wet, dirty, splattered in paint or even partly set on fire!

speedy tweeter On August 3, 2012, Joseph Caswell from Cary, North Carolina, sent 62 tweets in a minute—that's faster than one every second.

smallest library The library in Cardigan, Prince Edward Island, Canada, sits in a building that measures just 11 x 11 ft (3.5 x 3.5 m) and is home to 1,800 books, making it the smallest public library in the world. A lifetime membership costs just $5.

rapid ageing U.S. filmmaker Anthony Cerniello made a video showing a young girl ageing a lifetime in less than five minutes. Attending the girl's family reunion, he and photographer Keith Sirchio took portraits of her female relatives of all ages. These were then morphed slowly before animators brought the pictures to life by adding blinks and mouth movements.

IN 1978, GERMAN FILMMAKER WERNER HERZOG COOKED AND ATE HIS SHOE IN PUBLIC AFTER LOSING A BET.

hot topic The futuristic 1953 novel *Fahrenheit 451* by U.S. author Ray Bradbury (1920–2012) was originally called *The Fireman*, but both he and his publishers thought it was a boring title, so he called his local fire station and asked what temperature paper burned at. The fireman put Bradbury on hold, went away to burn a book and then reported back with the relevant temperature—451°F (233°C).

zombie hoax The regular programming on Montana TV station KRTV was interrupted on February 11, 2013, by dire warnings of a "zombie apocalypse," after hackers infiltrated the system. Alarmed viewers were informed that dead bodies were rising from their graves in several Montana counties and had started attacking the living.

upside down To help cure his writer's block, Dan Brown, the U.S. author of *The Da Vinci Code,* sometimes hangs upside down from gym equipment at his home.

slow burner Published in 1851, Herman Melville's novel *Moby Dick* was initially trashed by reviewers and sold only 3,700 copies in his lifetime. It is now widely regarded as one of the 100 best books of all time and has sold millions of copies worldwide.

name change Jason Sadler of Jacksonville, Florida, agreed to allow a website to become his official last name for $45,500, so that for the whole of 2013 he was legitimately known as Jason HeadsetsDotCom.

screaming sound The "Wilhelm Scream"—a stock sound effect of a man crying out in pain—has been used in over 200 movies and video games since 1951, including the Lord of the Rings' and Star Wars' series.

forever clean U.S. company Wool&Prince has developed an odor-resistant, wrinkle-free wool shirt that can be worn for 100 days straight without being washed.

distinguished composer *It's All in the Game*, a U.S. number one pop single in 1958 for Tommy Edwards, was written in 1911 by Charles G. Dawes, who was later Vice President of the U.S.A. under Calvin Coolidge and a winner of the Nobel Peace Prize.

woody's woes Pixar nearly lost all the animation for *Toy Story 2* after someone mistakenly ran a command that removed every file on the system. Backup files also failed, but just when they thought they would have to spend a year re-creating the erased work, intact copy files were found on the personal computer of technical director Galyn Susman, who had been doing some work on the movie at home while also caring for her new baby.

fast fiddle Violinist Ben Lee from London, England, can play Rimsky-Korsakov's *The Flight of the Bumblebee* in 58 seconds—that's an average of 15 notes per second.

adrenaline rush Watching an adrenaline-charged horror movie can burn more calories than 30 minutes of lifting weights.

real racer Available to just one customer, the video game *Grid 2: Mono Edition* by Codemasters was priced at a cool $190,000— because as well as the racing game itself and a PlayStation 3 console to play it on, the special package included a real 170-mph (275-km/h) BAC Mono supercar, helmet and race suit.

birthday treat Travis Schwend paid $300 to hire the Sun-Ray Cinema in Jacksonville, Florida, for five hours so that his son Jonah could celebrate his 13th birthday by playing video games with his friends on a huge screen, with unlimited pizza, popcorn and soft drinks.

fined himself After his own smartphone went off and disrupted a courtroom hearing at Ionia, Michigan, Judge Raymond Voet held himself in contempt and paid a fine of $25.

HIGH VOICE → SOHO Digital KaraOK Center unveiled a fully functional golden microphone measuring 9 ft (2.8 m) high and 22 in (56 cm) in diameter in Urumqi, China. The microphone is so tall that you need to stand on steps to sing into it.

fishy theory Italian opera singer Enrico Caruso (1873–1921) used to wear anchovies around his neck in the belief that they protected his voice from his heavy smoking habit.

skunk alert Colorado Springs TV station WXRM-TV was knocked off air for 24 hours when a skunk peed on a transmitter. After breaking into the transmitter room on Cheyenne Mountain, the animal burned itself while touching the equipment and responded by spraying the wires, causing a power outage.

ROSE PETAL DRESS

→ Xiao Fan arranged for 9,999 red roses to be made into a flowing gown before making a Valentine's Day proposal to girlfriend Yin Mi at the Guangzhou, China, amusement park where they had first met three years earlier. The gown had a 5-ft-long (1.5-m) train made from individually stitched blooms. The number of roses used to make the dress was also symbolic, as the number nine in Chinese culture represents "forever."

MINI BEAST

pop culture

➜ Believe it or not, this was the King Kong that terrified moviegoers as he climbed the Empire State Building in the final scenes of the iconic 1933 film!

It is a metal armature model standing just 22 in (55 cm) high and consists of a collection of hinges and screws that were covered in cotton and rubber to form muscles, a layer of latex for skin, and then rabbit fur to depict the great ape. The armature, which sold for $200,000 in 2009, has ball-and-socket joints and an aluminum skull molded from a wooden carving. It was brought to life in the movie by technician Willis O'Brien using stop-motion animation.

This small model wasn't the only one used to represent King Kong in the movie. Some close-up scenes featured a huge bust of Kong's head, neck and upper chest, made from wood, cloth, rubber and bearskin. The bust featured 10-in (25-cm) fangs and 12-in (30-cm) eyeballs.

KING KONG FACTS

A scene where King Kong shook four sailors off a bridge, causing them to fall into a ravine where they were eaten alive by giant spiders was cut partly because at the preview screening audience members fainted or ran out of the theater in terror.

The character of movie director Carl Denham was inspired by *King Kong*'s real director, Merian C. Cooper. Actor Robert Armstrong, who played Denham in the 1933 version, and Cooper later died on consecutive days — April 20 and 21, 1973.

The movie originally ran to 13 reels but the superstitious Cooper insisted that another scene be shot to bring the total to 14.

When King Kong was sold to television in 1956, New York's WOR-TV screened it twice every day for a week.

King Kong's roar was a lion's and a tiger's roar combined and run backward.

149

Prize Artist

→ Laura Tyler, who used to work as an artist at the Ripley's Believe It or Not! art department in Orlando, Florida, won the $100,000 first prize in season five of SyFy channel's reality show *Face Off*, where contestants compete for the title of Best Special Effects Make-Up Artist.

Laura made wax figures for Ripley's Odditoriums around the globe and, as you can see here, she displayed her talents to the full on the show, skillfully applying prosthetics and face paint to create imaginative figures such as the Grim Reaper, a face-ripping, blood-soaked Wrath Monster and, in the final, an Italian Renaissance-inspired swan-sorcerer.

OSTRICH PILLOW

→ The Ostrich Pillow is a lightweight cushion hat that lets you take a power nap anytime, anywhere... if you don't mind getting strange looks from passersby. Designed by Key Portilla-Kawamura and Ali Ganjavian, who met at university in London, England, the hat is made from ultra-soft jersey padded out with polystyrene micro-balls so that you can comfortably lean your head against any surface. There are even holes on either side of the helmet so that you can keep your hands warm while dozing.

pet leopard In the 1930s, dancer and singer Josephine Baker (1906–75) walked a pet leopard called Chiquita around Paris, France, on a diamond-studded leash.

pigeons fired Police in the Indian state of Orissa employed a fleet of 1,400 carrier pigeons to deliver messages until 2005, when e-mail and cell phones made the pigeons redundant.

lucky tune In 2010, Louie Sulcer, 71, from Woodstock, Georgia, received a personal phone call from Apple computer creator Steve Jobs and a $10,000 gift card after buying the ten-billionth track downloaded from iTunes.

hard work In a single year (1932), U.S. author Walter Gibson, whose pen name was Maxwell Grant, wrote 28 books using a grand total of 1,680,000 words.

talk show Nepalese talk show host Rabi Lamichhane broadcast for over 62 hours continuously in April 2013, talking for so long that as he neared the end of his third day he had started to grow a beard.

aerial violinist Janice Martin from Racine, Wisconsin, is the world's only aerial violinist, acrobatically playing the instrument upside-down while suspended in midair.

twitter wedding When Cengizhan Celik married Candan Canik in Turkey, they exchanged their wedding vows via Twitter. Mustafa Kara, mayor of Istanbul's Uskudar district, conducted the ceremony by sending tweets to the couple, asking them to respond on their iPads.

golden oldie In September 2013, Fred Stobaugh, a retired truck driver from Peoria, Illinois, had a hit on the Billboard Hot 100— at age 96. *Oh Sweet Lorraine*, a poem set to music about his late wife to whom he had been married for 72 years, entered the list at number 42, ahead of the likes of Bruno Mars and Avril Lavigne. The great-great grandfather also reached number 5 in the U.S. iTunes chart.

TOAD FASHION → Inspired by the fairy-tale idea of a toad transformed into Prince Charming, Paris-based Polish designer Monika Jarosz has turned the whole skins of thousands of real cane toads into top-of-the-range fashion accessories. The toxic toads are a major pest in Australia, so, with the help of a taxidermist, Monika recycles their dyed skins into belts, bags and purses, the largest of which sell for up to $1,600. The toad's skin goes through 14 stages before it becomes high-quality leather. Then, the eyes are replaced with semiprecious stones.

TRASH FASHION

➜ Ripley's staged a "Trashy Fashion Show" in March 2012 with entrants creating imaginative dresses from discarded items such as magazines, bottle caps, grocery bags, paper cups, trading cards, snack wrappers and even an old shower curtain. All three winning designs were acquired for display at its Ripley's Odditorium in St. Augustine, Florida.

Masha Sardari in a formal knee-length gown made from used paint brushes and paper bags.

Analise Barnard and Amani Grant designed this gown and headband made entirely of coffee filters.

KennedyTrugter wore a sleeveless top adorned with newspaper flowers and ruffles, and a triple-tiered skirt made with hundreds of pleated paper sections.

workers' ballet As part of the Ural Industrial Biennial of Contemporary Art, a Russian theater put on an experimental, one-act ballet in a car factory, involving factory employees in their work clothes alongside professional dancers.

fall guys Three friends from Logan, Utah, collected 1,462 trash bags full of leaves to create a pile 17 ft (5.2 m) high and 60 ft (18 m) in circumference. They then filmed themselves jumping onto the pile from a nearby rooftop and posted the video on YouTube.

designer label Jason Hemperly of Dennison, Ohio, created his own suit for his high-school prom from the labels of 120 Mountain Dew soda bottles.

human scarecrow After graduating from university with a music degree, 22-year-old Jamie Fox landed a £250-a-week ($400) job as a human scarecrow on a farm in Norfolk, England, playing the ukulele, accordion and cowbell to scare away troublesome partridges.

light trick A team of scientists at the Massachusetts Institute of Technology have created a camera that can take photos around a corner, using reflected light.

summit conference In May 2013, British explorer Daniel Hughes made the world's first-ever smartphone video call from the summit of Mount Everest—that's from an altitude of 29,029 ft (8,848 m) above sea level.

pants hats For a book signing by *Captain Underpants* author Dav Pilkey at Napierville, Illinois, 270 people—adults and children—wore underpants on their head.

MAN WHO TOOK A PHOTO OF HIMSELF EVERY DAY FOR 12 YEARS

➜ Photographer Noah Kalina from Brooklyn, New York, took a self-portrait every day for over 12 years—making a total of 4,514 photos. He then put them together in a rapid time-lapse video, which soon went viral, and which shows him ageing from 19 to 31 in just seven minutes. What's more, Noah plans to continue taking pictures indefinitely.

START (Photo 1)

FINISH (Photo 4,514)

Just some of Noah's 4,514 selfies taken for his time-lapse YouTube video.

HUMAN SKIN RUG

→ New York City artist Chrissy Conant turned herself into a human skin rug. She made a life-size, flesh-colored, silicone rubber cast of herself to form the Chrissy Skin Rug, which looks like a bear-skin rug—but with *her* as the animal.

To make the controversial piece, which has been exhibited in galleries and museums, Chrissy had to shave her body, cover herself in Vaseline and lie perfectly still for several hours while being coated with buckets full of gelatinous mold-making material.

young programmer Zora Ball from Philadelphia, Pennsylvania, created her own mobile video game—featuring ballerinas, jewels and vampires—at age seven. She used the Bootstrap programming system, which is usually taught to students twice her age.

sheep idol The most popular TV program in Senegal is an *American Idol*-style reality show to find the nation's most beautiful sheep. Khar Bii, or "This Sheep," has been running for over four seasons, airs several times a week, and its Facebook page has nearly 17,000 likes.

reverse video Israel's Messe Kopp filmed himself walking backward while interacting with passersby through the streets of Jerusalem—and then ran the film backward so that he appears to be going in the right direction while everything else, including such things as water spilling back into a bucket, is in reverse.

psy style On April 14, 2013, South Korean singer Psy's single "Gentleman" racked up an incredible 38 million views in 24 hours when the video was first posted on YouTube.

$5-million letter A letter written by English scientist Francis Crick to his 12-year-old son Michael in 1953 about the discovery of DNA sold at a New York City auction for $5.3 million in 2013.

school hobbit In 2012, 70 students aged 8 to 13 from Tower House School, London, England, starred in their own feature-length 90-minute movie version of *The Hobbit*, directed by the school's head of drama.

first year Using more than 1,200 one-second clips recorded on his iPhone, proud father Sam Cornwell, from Portsmouth, England, produced a seven-minute film capturing moments from every single day of his son Indigo's first year of life.

camera happy Kong Kenk from Ho Chi Minh City, Vietnam, has uploaded more than 115,000 photos onto his Facebook page.

atomic hero IBM scientists produced a microscopic stop motion film, *A Boy and His Atom*, that is so small it must be magnified 100 million times to be seen. They used a scanning tunneling microscope to create an animation of a boy hero made of just a few atoms.

TRANSPORT

SINKING FEELING

➜ Sixty-year-old school principal Pamela Knox was driving quietly along a street in Toledo, Ohio, when a 10-ft-deep (3-m) sinkhole suddenly opened up and swallowed her car. Plunged into darkness, she began to fear the worst when water from a burst pipe flooded into the car, but fire crews lowered a ladder into the hole to enable her to climb to safety.

RUBBLE TROUBLE

➜ An entire parking lot in Taiyuan, China, was demolished around a parked solitary vehicle, leaving the car intact but surrounded by a sea of rubble. The builders had waited ten days for the driver to return to the car, but then decided they could not delay the street-widening project any longer.

OUT OF CONTROL

➜ After a 70-year-old man lost control of his Toyota Camry, it accelerated through a parking garage and smashed at high speed into the wall of the Rady Children's Hospital in San Diego, California, ending up hanging over an exterior staircase. It took firefighters 40 minutes to pull the man out through the passenger door.

TIGHT SPACE

➜ Passersby in Kiev, Ukraine, thought they were seeing things when they glanced up and saw a Toyota Yaris parked 60 ft (18 m) above ground on the balcony of a third-floor apartment! How and why the car got there remains a mystery.

IN THE BALANCE

➜ This Chevrolet Epica was left hanging over the edge of a parking lot 50 ft (15 m) above ground in Changsha, China, after the driver reversed too fast and too far, and smashed through the guardrail. Luckily, he and his wife managed to climb out safely.

VEHICLE OVERLOAD

➜ With no safety ropes to hold them in place, two cars were balanced precariously on top of an overloaded truck as it was driven through Zhengzhou, China. The cars had been lowered there by crane in order to avoid paying toll road charges for the separate delivery of the cars.

MAN BUILDS FULL-SIZE TRAIN COACH IN BASEMENT

■ Jason Shron built a full-size replica of a 1980 VIA Rail Canada train coach in the basement of his home in Vaughan, Ontario. It took him more than 2,500 hours and $10,000 to fulfilll his dream, and everything is accurate down to the last detail, including seat numbers, timetable racks, coat hooks and period carpet. He also installed a photographic mural at the end of the coach to make it appear part of an entire train.

YOU BUILT WHAT?

Ken Imhoff spent 17 years building a **replica Lamborghini** in the basement of his home in Eagle, Wisconsin, and had to hire an excavator to smash a hole in the wall to get the car out.

Batman fan Chris Weir built his own $150,000 **Batcave** in the cellar of his home in Middletown, Delaware. Just like in the 1960s *Batman* TV series, the cave is accessed through a hidden door in a bookcase that's opened by a switch on a bust of William Shakespeare.

An unnamed man in Ängelholm, Sweden, was arrested in 2011 for attempting to build a **nuclear reactor** in his kitchen.

Larry Metz took ten years to build a 144-sq-ft (13-sq-m) **scale model of 1950s downtown Los Angeles** in the basement of his home in Coeur d'Alene, Idaho.

Jack Heathcote built a **huge aquarium** containing turtles and stingrays, which measures 7 x 13 x 13 ft (2.1 x 4 x 4 m) and holds 5,400 gal (20,430 l) of water, in the basement of his house in Nottingham, England.

Dan Reeves spent nine years building a **two-seater airplane** in the basement of his home in Lower Allen Township, Pennsylvania.

kiteboarder In July 2013, French kiteboarder Bruno Sroka became the first person to sail the 288 mi (463 km) from France to Ireland—a journey that took him 16 hours 37 minutes.

mower ride Former landscape gardener Phil Voice from England rode a lawn mower 1,250 mi (2,000 km) from Bergerac, France, to John O'Groats, Scotland. It took him 14 days at an average speed of 7.5 mph (12 km/h).

big bike Stunt cyclist Richie Trimble towered over the traffic as he rode through the streets of Los Angeles, California, on a 14½-ft-high (4.4-m) bicycle, with a 32½-ft-long (10-m) chain, called "Stoopid Tall." He needed a wall and two friends to help him climb onto the saddle of the bike, which took him just 12 hours to make.

homemade sub Eighteen-year-old Justin Beckerman from Mendham, New Jersey, built a fully functional, one-man submarine from discarded objects. At a cost of $2,000—a hundredth of the usual price—he constructed its 9-ft (2.7-m) body from drainage pipes, the hatch from a recycled skylight, and its P.A. speakers from a car stereo. He used pressure gauges taken from an old restaurant soda fountain. Powered by a fishing-boat motor, the *Nautilus* is equipped with ballast tanks to maintain depth and equilibrium as well as air vents to bring oxygen down from the surface, and should be able to remain submerged for up to two hours, diving to depths of 30 ft (9 m).

WHALE BOAT

→ Part speedboat and part submarine, Innespace's *Seabreacher Y* not only looks like a killer whale, it can leap out of the water like one, too. With its 260-horsepower engine, the hi-tech two-seater can be launched 16 ft (5 m) into the air when it breaches and is capable of speeds up to 55 mph (88 km/h) on the surface and up to 20 mph (32 km/h) underwater.

Beetle Ball

➔ Sculptor Ichwan Noor from Jakarta, Indonesia, transformed a 1953 Volkswagen Beetle car into a perfect sphere for a 2013 art exhibition in Hong Kong.

He actually used parts from five cars, combined with polyester and aluminum, to create the metallic orb that stands almost 6 ft (1.8 m) tall.

double disaster Four-year-old Markus Koller had amazing escape when he was pulled unscathed from the remains of a car after it had first been rammed by a stag and then crushed by a train. The impact from the deer threw the car onto the tracks at Oberengadin, Switzerland, and into the path of an oncoming train. Markus' mother was trying to get him out of the car when the train hit, throwing her clear. The train derailed on impact but Markus was unhurt.

hop on inn Colin Flitter from Hampshire, England, has turned a red London double-decker bus into a pub. He bought the Routemaster bus, which he has named the Hop On Inn, for £18,500 ($27,000) on eBay and spent a further £14,000 ($21,000) putting in beer pumps and a bar.

futuristic auto Auto designer Mike Vetter from Micco, Florida, transformed an ordinary Chevrolet into a supercharged, 270hp "Extra Terrestrial Vehicle" valued at $100,000. It took him six months to hand-build the futuristic, street legal car, which features front and rear adjustable suspension, a 5-ft-high (1.5-m) windshield, remote-controlled gullwing doors, plasma lights, wireless remote system and three onboard cameras with monitors to help with parking.

good hearing The British Navy's Astute Class nuclear submarine can detect a ship leaving port from more than 3,000 mi (4,800 km) away.

street plane Police officer Jeff Bloch cruises the streets of Kershaw, South Carolina, in a converted airplane. He built the 27-ft-long (8.2-m) *Spirit of LeMons* by combining an abandoned 1956 Cessna 310 aircraft with a Toyota van. He then made the vehicle, which can reach speeds of up to 90 mph (144 km/h), street legal by adding headlights, brake lights and indicators.

ice sprint In February 2013, a Bentley Continental car was driven at a superfast speed of 205.5 mph (330 km/h) across a frozen stretch of the Baltic Sea off the coast of Finland.

sports craft Matthew Riese from San Francisco, California, spent more than four years building an aquatic hovercraft in the shape of a 1981 DeLorean sports car. The body is made out of Styrofoam wrapped in fiberglass and a six-horsepower lawn mower engine in the front powers a 24-in (60-cm) fan that provides the vehicle's lift. The homemade craft can travel at speeds of more than 20 mph (32 km/h).

lifeboat drop A lifeboat was launched from a height of 219 ft (67 m) into the water near Arendal, Norway—and landed upright. The 50-ft-long (15-m) boat was dropped from the top of a crane and fitted with heavy sandbags strapped to each seat. It has a capacity of 70 people and is designed to withstand landing from great heights so that it can be used in conjunction with huge container ships and drilling platforms.

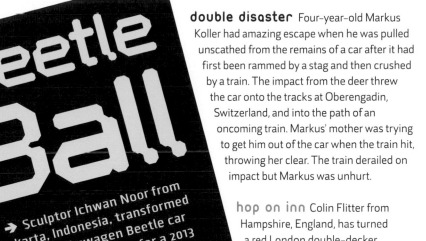

ROCKET BIKE ➔ French cyclist François Gissy hit 163 mph (263 km/h) while riding a self-built mountain bike along an abandoned runway in northeastern France in May 2013. He achieved the astonishing speed by attaching a hydrogen peroxide-powered rocket to the frame of the machine, creating temperatures of 650°F (343°C) and a gas-flow velocity of more than 1,000 meters per second to give the bike its powerful thrust.

BRIGHT IDEA

➔ This mother and son are taking no chances while riding their mobility scooters in Wassenaar, the Netherlands. Both wear high-visibility clothing and have fitted their scooters with an array of bells, sirens, horns and fluorescent stickers. The pair are well known locally. Well, it would be completely impossible to miss them.

vintage car Herman and Candelaria Zapp drove around the world for more than a decade in an 85-year-old car, visiting 44 countries in the process. The couple set off from their home in Argentina in 2000, in their 1920s Graham Paige automobile, and over 13 years traveled some 200,000 mi (320,000 km) and stayed with 2,000 families. They also found time to have four children, all of whom were born in different countries—the U.S.A., Argentina, Canada and Australia. Throughout their world tour they never traveled faster than 40 mph (64 km/h), which is the vintage car's maximum speed.

locked out An Air India flight from Delhi to Bangalore was forced to make an unscheduled landing at Bhopal Airport after the pilot was locked out of the cockpit during a bathroom break. He was unable to re-enter because the door was jammed. The copilot took control and diverted the flight.

cycle tour Glen Burmeister from Leicestershire, England, cycled through 11 countries—Czech Republic, Austria, Slovakia, Hungary, Slovenia, Croatia, Romania, Serbia, Bosnia-Herzegovina, Montenegro and Albania—in just seven days.

traffic zebras As part of a new traffic enforcement initiative in La Paz, Bolivia, volunteers took to the streets dressed in zebra costumes and patrolled pedestrian crossings. They jumped out in front of cars and buses and forced drivers to stop.

monster hog Steve "Doc" Hopkins of Bonduel, Wisconsin, has built a 25-ft-long (7.6-m), four-wheeled motorcycle that seats ten people and has an incredible seven engines. Dubbed "Timeline," the bike incorporates many of the engines that Harley-Davidson has used from 1909 to the present day. The 3,000-lb (1,362-kg) monster hog boasts 40 ft (12 m) of chain and has four wheels—two at the front and two aircraft wheels at the back to aid stability. Amazing as it might seem, the bike is roadworthy and has completed a 900-mi (1,450-km) trip between Wisconsin and South Dakota.

flying bicycle British designers Yannick Read and John Foden have created a flying bicycle that can fly at 25 mph (40 km/h) for up to three hours at a time and reach an altitude of 4,000 ft (1,200 m). Their XploreAir Paravelo consists of a folding bicycle and a trailer, which houses a giant fan, fuel for the engine and a flexible foldaway wing. The machine is light enough to carry into a house or office and is able to take off from any open space.

Play-Doh Car

→ To mark the U.K. launch of the Chevrolet Orlando, eight model makers spent two weeks handcrafting a life-size replica car from Play-Doh modeling clay.

Positioned on a London street, the 15-ft-long (4.6-m) vehicle was made from 1.6 tons—10,000 pots—of the children's putty at a total cost of around $10,000.

CLEAN SWEEP → This man tried to clean the streets of Mohe, China, with his own ingenious, homemade road sweeper—a tractor with 12 large rotating brooms attached. However, people complained that, far from tidying the streets, his whirlwind contraption made them dustier than they had been before.

ketchup crash A truck carrying thousands of bottles of tomato ketchup crashed on Interstate 80 in Reno, Nevada, on February 28, 2013, leaving the highway looking like a blood-soaked disaster even though, luckily, nobody was injured in the crash.

baby driver While his family was asleep, a six-year old Michigan boy took their Ford Taurus station wagon and drove around in it for 3 mi (4.8 km) until he was stopped. When a police patrolman asked him what he was doing, the boy said he was going to a garage to get the car fixed (he had hit a street sign near his house) and was then going to stop off for Chinese food.

desert crash A single-seater RAF Kittyhawk P-40 airplane that crash-landed in the Western Sahara desert in 1942 during World War II was found in almost perfect condition 70 years later. It had remained undiscovered for so long because of its remote location 200 mi (320 km) from the nearest town. It is thought that the British pilot survived the crash, but died while trying to walk out of the desert.

python passenger Passengers on a 2013 flight from Cairns, Australia, to Papua New Guinea were startled to look out of the airplane windows and see a 10-ft-long (3-m) snake on the wing. The amethystine python, thought to have crawled onto the plane in Cairns, was found to be dead on arrival.

little plane "Bumble Bee II," built in 1988 by Robert H. Starr of Phoenix, Arizona, was the world's smallest piloted airplane—with a wingspan of only 5 ft 6 in (1.7 m).

supercar smash Embarrassed car dealer Kurt Schmidt wrote off a $150,000 Lamborghini supercar while he was delivering it to a customer in Böblingen, Germany. He was driving at only 25 mph (40 km/h), but his hand slipped and he accidentally changed gears and smashed into the back of a truck.

bacon stripes To mark International Bacon Day on August 31, 2013, Ford allowed customers to order a new Ford Fiesta wrapped almost entirely in bacon stickers. The vinyl wraps on the car came in four different designs, including bacon strips as racing stripes along the sides.

airplane school A retired Yakovlev 42 airplane has been turned into a unique kindergarten in Georgia. School principal Gari Chapidze bought the old plane from Tbilisi airport and arranged for it to be transported to Rustavi.

jam buster Fed up with spending three hours stuck in traffic jams on his way to work in Zhuzhou, China, Zeng Daxia learned to paraglide. Rising above the busy roads, he now glides to work in just a few minutes. His idea has inspired several other frustrated commuters to copy him. Local flight regulators say the powered paragliders are legal as long as they fly below 3,300 ft (1,000 m).

ninety crossings To celebrate his 90th birthday, John Lawton from Westfield Township, Ohio, made 90 crossings of the U.S.-Canadian border piloting a Cessna 172 airplane in the space of 48 hours.

oldest driver Bob Edwards of Ngataki, New Zealand, was still driving over 50 mi (80 km) a week in 2013—at age 105, making him the oldest driver in the world. He has been driving for 88 years, and first learned to drive in a French car that had a lever instead of a steering wheel. In all that time he has only ever had one accident and has picked up only one solitary speeding ticket.

young pilot Aged 21, James Anthony Tan from Kajang, Malaysia, flew a single-engine Cessna aircraft 23,628 mi (38,025 km) around the world in 48 days.

wrong continent Two U.S. vacationers ended up on the wrong continent after an airline mixed up its airport codes. Sandy Valdivieso and her husband Triet Vo were hoping to fly from Los Angeles, Carolifornia, to Dakar, Senegal, with Turkish Airlines. However, after changing planes in Istanbul, they found themselves ending up in Dhaka, Bangladesh—nearly 7,000 mi (11,265 km) from their intended destination.

$3-million van Covered in gold, a luxury motor home went on sale in Dubai for a cool $3 million. The 40-ft-long (12-m) eleMMent Palazzo comes complete with a huge master bedroom and 40-inch TV, as well as a spa and shower, a pop-up cocktail bar, underfloor heating, marble lighting and even its own rooftop terrace. The state-of-the-art van can reach 100 mph (160 km/h) and also washes itself after a day's driving through the Middle-Eastern desert.

farm machines John Manners keeps 350 old combine harvesters on his farm in Northumberland, England, in a collection so big that it is visible from space.

replica kitt Chris Palmer from Detroit, Michigan, built a fully functional replica of KITT, the *Knight Rider* car, in his garage. It took him 3½ years to build from five Pontiac Trans Ams and using parts bought on eBay.

FULL-SIZE REPLICA MODEL OF ASTON MARTIN

LIFE SIZE!

→ As a tribute to the Aston Martin DBR1 that won the 1959 Le Mans 24-hour Endurance Race, the Evanta Motor Company, from Hertfordshire, England, has produced a life-size model of the famous sports car in the form of an Airfix construction kit. The $38,000 kit measures 21 ft (6.35 m) long and 11 ft (3.4 m) high and consists of the car's body shell, lights, screens, four 16-in (40-cm) wire wheels with race tires, race seats and steering wheel. Also included is a replica of the Le Mans trophy and an Aston Martin cap signed by the two victorious drivers from 1959, Briton Roy Salvadori and American Carroll Shelby.

THE BONEYARD

→ **The Boneyard is a huge aircraft cemetery in Arizona, home to more than 4,400 airplanes on a 2,600-acre area of desert on Davis-Monthan Air Force base. Here, $35 billion worth of old United States Air Force aircraft are kept as spare parts for current models.**

The yard, officially named the 309th Aerospace Maintenance and Regeneration Group, was established after World War II as storage for bombers and transport planes, and now includes 7,000 aircraft engines and even NASA spacecraft. The dry desert environment is ideal for keeping parts in good condition, and the hard soil means that planes can easily be maneuvered without roads and ramps being constructed.

The bizarre appearance of the yard has seen it featured in several Hollywood movies, and its planes have also appeared in films, such as *Top Gun*. However, not all the planes in the cemetery have seen any action. In 2013 a number of brand new military cargo planes were consigned to the Boneyard for financial reasons, in the hope that they may find a home in the future.

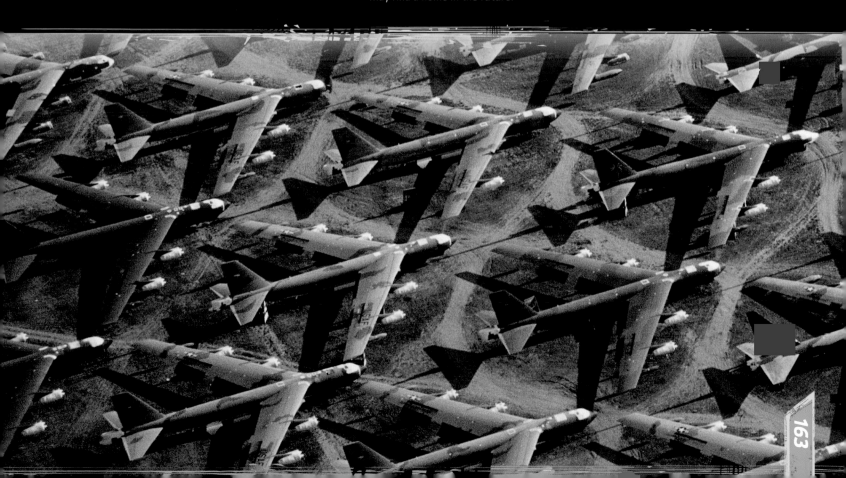

PIPING HOT

→ Tim Burton from London, England, found an unusual way to cook his Christmas turkey—by roasting it in red-hot flames shooting from the exhaust of a £300,000 ($500,000) Lamborghini Aventador. He put the fresh turkey on the end of a pitchfork and stood behind the 700 bhp supercar while the owner revved the engine up to 9,000—and in just ten minutes the bird was cooked to perfection.

auto print Having always wanted an iconic 1961 Aston Martin DB4 sports car, Ivan Sentch from Auckland, New Zealand, set about printing one off in his garage. He used a 3-D printer to print out the car's individual components and then pieced them together to create a mold for the fiberglass body.

airplane hotel Guests at the Hotel Costa Verde in Costa Rica can stay in a 1965 Boeing 727 salvaged from San Jose airport. It cost $28,000 to move and renovate the airplane, which is perched on a 50-ft-high (15-m) pedestal, and has been converted into two bedrooms and a terrace.

veteran driver Margaret Dunning of Plymouth, Michigan, drives a 1930 Packard Roadster that she has owned since 1949. The 103-year-old learned to drive on the family farm at age eight and has been driving ever since—for more than 90 years.

atlantic crossing In March 2013, 50-year-old Charlie Pitcher from Essex, England, finished rowing 2,700 mi (4,320 km) across the Atlantic Ocean from the Canary Islands to Barbados in just 35 days.

plane enthusiasm Volunteers at the San Diego Air and Space Museum, California, spent 12 years and 100,000 man-hours building a 1932 Boeing P-26 fighter airplane from scratch.

teen travels A 13-year-old boy stole his father's Mercedes car in the Italian town of Montebelluna and drove more than 600 mi (960 km) across Europe before he was finally stopped by police in northern Germany.

blind faith Every weekday, Chris Smith of Dedham, Massachusetts, rides his bicycle to and from work—a round trip of 24 mi (38 km)—even though he is legally blind.

perky ride Martin Bacon from County Durham, England, has created a car powered by coffee that can reach 65 mph (104 km/h). To start it, instead of turning an ignition key, he has to load coffee chaff pellets—a by-product of the coffee-roasting process—into the converted Ford pickup truck's charcoal stove until enough hydrogen gas is produced to power the engine.

mini motor Austin Coulson from Phoenix, Arizona, has built a roadworthy car that is just 25 in (63.5 cm) tall, 25¾ in (65 cm) wide and 49¾ in (126 cm) long. It has a tiny windshield, headlights, taillights, turns signals, rear-view mirror, seat belt and functional horn.

green car To cover up a bad paint job, the Australian owner of a 14-year-old Mitsubishi Magna covered the vehicle in 215 sq ft (20 sq m) of AstroTurf to create the ultimate green car.

parking tickets A 1999 Chevy Monte Carlo, abandoned in Chicago, Illinois, was issued with more than $100,000 in parking tickets between 2009 and 2012—yet the car itself is worth just $600.

shopper chopper Cal VanSant of Lancaster, Pennsylvania, spent $15,000 building a 130-mph (208-km/h) oversized supermarket cart to promote his son-in-law's store. The Shopper Chopper is powered by a 5.8-liter V8 Chevrolet engine and can seat six people.

VELVET PORSCHE → This Porsche Panamera is the smoothest car in town after being covered in velvet by British car-wrap company Raccoon. The £2,500 ($3,750) wrap contains special adhesives and durable fibers to withstand severe weather and comes in a range of colors, including orange and fuchsia pink. The material lasts for about three years and can be removed by professionals to restore the car to its original state. It can even be cleaned by hand or with a jet wash, but should definitely not be put through a regular car wash.

coin car Ali Hassan Gharib from Dubai has had his Range Rover covered in $16,000 worth of coins. The 57,412 dirhams amounted to half a ton of spare change. An artist spent weeks polishing the coins and then gluing each one to the vehicle individually by hand.

mail service In 2012, Graham Eccles from Cornwall, England, started his own local postal service delivering mail on a vintage penny farthing bicycle.

jam buster Gridlocked motorists in Wuhan and Jinan, China, can hire someone to sit in the congestion for them. With one call a motorcycle will arrive to pick them up and leave a driver to take the car to its destination.

leather car A wealthy motorist from Moscow, Russia, has had the exterior bodywork of his car completely covered in Canadian wood-bison leather. Inside, the dashboard and seats are covered in leather and fur, while even the engine is draped in treated leather that can withstand high temperatures. The engine and trunk are also inlaid with Swarovski crystals, giving the car a cool price tag of $1,215,000.

golden bike Turkish designer Tarhan Telli has built a golden motorcycle worth more than $1 million. It took him over a year to build the unique bike, which weighs a third of a ton and has a chassis and body shell made of white and yellow gold leaf.

young unicyclist Fourteen-year-old Cameron Peacock makes the 3.5-mi (5.6-km) round journey to school in Stockton, England, each day by unicycle. He owns eight unicycles and has been riding them since he was 11.

IRON BEETLE

→ **Three Croatian craftsmen have created a wrought-iron Volkswagen Beetle.**
Over a period of four months, they removed the car's original sheet metal bodywork and replaced it with wrought-iron sections that had been designed to fit perfectly onto the existing VW frame. As a finishing touch, they added 24-carat gold-leaf embellishments to the car's exterior.

08

FEATS

THE GREAT BLONDIN

➜ **Charles Blondin, born Jean-François Gravelet in France in 1824, was the greatest funambulist—tightrope walker—of the 19th century.**

In 1859, a crowd of several thousand people thronged the shores of the formidable Niagara Gorge to watch him make the first-ever tightrope crossing over the Niagara River, on a 1,300-ft-long (396-m) rope that was just 2 in (5 cm) thick. Blondin never used a harness, or even a net, as he believed that to use safety devices was to tempt fate. As a result, bookmakers took large amounts of money betting against the man who had only a 26-ft-long (8-m) balancing pole to stop him from tumbling nearly 175 ft (53 m) into the waters below. On his first crossing, Blondin terrified onlookers by stopping halfway across to haul up a bottle of wine for refreshment from a tourist boat, before continuing to the other side and returning with a large daguerreotype camera and taking a snapshot of the watching crowds!

During subsequent Niagara crossings, merely walking along the rope wasn't enough, and he went on to perform increasingly outlandish stunts such as walking backward, turning somersaults, walking blindfolded, standing on his head, being locked in chains, and standing on stilts.

Blondin became a sensation and performed in China, Australia, India and the U.K., where he later settled, altogether clocking up an estimated 10,000 mi (16,000 km) of tightrope walking. By the end of his slip-free career, he had crossed Niagara Falls no less than 300 times. He died at the age of 72.

Blondin on his first-ever tightrope walk across the Niagara Gorge in 1859.

—AT—

NIAGARA FALLS,

NEW AND DARING FEATS BY THE INTREPID

BLONDIN.

EXTRAORDINARY FEATS

OF

BALANCING.

—ON—

Wednesday, Aug. 1st, at 4 P. M.

Blondin's manager posted newspaper adverts to drum up spectators for his client's daring feats of balance. People would pay up to 50 cents to watch the daredevil perform.

On more than one occasion, Blondin wheeled a stove across his tightrope and stopped to cook on it midway. He once did this while crossing Niagara and lowered food down to passengers who were waiting in a boat in the waters below.

Blondin once stopped midway and sat at a table —which he'd been carrying— to eat an omelet and drink a glass of wine.

Blondin could cross the tightrope by balance alone—here he has a sack placed over his head, so that every footfall relies upon his agility, skill and instinct.

Not content with getting only himself across the tightrope, Blondin showed his strength as well as his agility by carrying someone on his back.

Performing a headstand midway along the tightrope was another trick Blondin would perform to amaze his audiences.

Blondin successfully carried his manager, Harry Colcord, on his back across Niagara Falls on more than one occasion.

STUNT TEAM

➜ Members of a stunt group called Bir Khalsa ("The Brave Pure") perform daring feats for villagers in the Punjab region of India. They chew glass tube lights, play with fire, fight with swords and spiked maces, and allow themselves to be run over by cars. The 450 members, whose ages range from young children to men in their thirties, practice the ancient Sikh martial art of *ghatka*. The group's founder, Kamaljeet Singh Khalsa, says that children are initially trained to perform *ghatka* using wooden swords, but when they reach the age of six they graduate to iron ritual daggers—but always under adult supervision.

A man uses a baseball bat to smash a coconut placed on a fellow Bir Khalsa member's forehead. The group recently broke 59 coconuts in one minute in this way.

Bir Khalsa's Inderjeet Singh performs a breathtaking stunt where he is run over by a car while lying on broken glass.

steely climb French rock climber Jean-Michel Casanova scaled the 564-ft-high (172-m) Bailong Elevator, built on a cliff in Zhangjiajie, China, with no safety equipment apart from a pair of sticky sneakers. A climber since the age of five, Casanova ascended the huge steel tower in a mere 68 minutes 26 seconds.

marathon hike Matt "The Walker" Livermanne from Salt Lake City, Utah, walked 10,000 mi (16,000 km) around the U.S.A.— including the old Route 66 from Los Angeles, California, to Chicago, Illinois, a mammoth 2,400-mi (3,862-km) hike—in just 19 months. He clocked up more than 20 million steps.

electrifying stunt Illusionist David Blaine spent three days and three nights standing in the middle of a million volts of electrical currents on a podium 20 ft (6 m) above the ground at New York City's Pier 54. He wore a 27-lb (12.2-kg) chainmail bodysuit as a barrier between himself and the currents, which were emitted by Tesla coils. The hardest parts were staying awake and avoiding any instinctive movements. For example, if he had absentmindedly touched his face, he would have received an electrical shock equivalent to shocks from 20 Tasers.

world walk Masahito Yoshida from Tottori, Japan, walked 25,000 mi (40,000 km) around the world in 4½ years. He set off from Shanghai, China, at the start of 2009 with a two-wheeled cart carrying 110 lb (50 kg) of luggage and walked across Asia and Europe to Portugal. He then flew to the east coast of the U.S.A. before walking from Atlantic City, New Jersey, to Vancouver, Canada. After hiking across Australia, he ended his epic trek walking from the southern tip of Asia back home.

human flag A total of 26,904 residents of Vladivostok gathered on the city's Zolotoy Bridge and held aloft red, white and blue flags to create a living image of the Russian flag.

giant snowball The Silver Star Mountain Resort at Vernon, British Columbia, made a snowball that was nearly 12 ft (3.6 m) tall and weighed 40,000 lb (18,000 kg).

cow costumes A total of 470 people turned up for a restaurant-sponsored event in Fairfax, Virginia, dressed as cows, wearing one- or two-piece black-and-white costumes complete with heads and matching shoes.

strong teeth Former circus strongman Mike Greenstein of Queens, New York, can still pull cars with his teeth at the age of 92.

DEFYING DEATH

A Ukrainian daredevil who calls himself Mustang Wanted hangs hundreds of feet in the air from a skyscraper in Moscow, Russia, just by the fingertips of one hand.

The 26-year-old gave up his desk job as a legal advisor to become a skywalker, balancing without a safety harness on the edge of tall buildings and cranes, knowing that the slightest slip would mean certain death. His exploits as a real-life Spider-Man have brought him thousands of followers on social network sites. Although he has performed push-ups on a metal girder 300 ft (90 m) above the ground, he says his greatest fear is being caught by the police.

FULL HAND

➜ Philip Osenton, a U.K. wine consultant based in Beijing, China, can hold 51 wine glasses in one hand at the same time. He learned his skill while working as a wine steward at top London hotels.

disney days Southern Californians Tonya Mickesh and Jeff Reitz visited Disneyland every day during 2012—a total of 366 trips. They each walked up to 4 mi (6.4 km) per visit, meaning that between them they clocked up a total of nearly 3,000 mi (4,830 km) in the course of the year. They also posted more than 2,000 photos of their adventure on Instagram.

surfboard balance Doug McManaman of Nova Scotia, Canada, balanced a 9-ft-long (2.7-m), 20-lb (9-kg) surfboard on his chin for 51.47 seconds.

stroller push Dougal Thorburn from Dunedin, New Zealand, ran 10,000 meters in 32 minutes 26 seconds—while pushing a stroller containing his 2½-year-old daughter Audrey. His time was only six minutes slower than the world 10,000-meters record for athletes not pushing a stroller!

twin peaks Twenty-nine-year-old Nepalese mountaineer Chhurim climbed Mount Everest twice in a week in May 2012—the first woman to climb the world's highest mountain twice in a season. She made her first ascent on May 12, then returned to base camp for a couple of days' rest before scaling the peak again on May 19.

domino cascade In July 2013, a team from Sinners Domino Entertainment toppled more than 270,000 dominoes in one go in a sports hall in Büdingen, Germany.

head over heels U.S. Army soldier Jalyessa Walker performed 49 consecutive backflips in the University of Texas, El Paso, football stadium in November 2012.

wine buff Alain Laliberte from Toronto, Ontario, has a collection of about 160,000 wine labels from around the world, stored in more than 120 shoeboxes. His oldest label comes from Germany and dates back to 1859. His fascination with wine does not stop at the labels—he samples an average of 5,000 wines a year.

balloon crossing Matt Silver-Vallance became the first person to float from Robben Island to Cape Town, South Africa, using only helium balloons. Attached to 160 balloons, he took about an hour to make the 3.7-mi (5.9-km) crossing above the shark-infested waters of the Atlantic. He carried bags filled with water that could be jettisoned to increase his altitude and an air gun and a makeshift spear to pop the balloons to hasten his descent.

NARAYAN TIMALSINA FROM PALPA, NEPAL, IS ABLE TO HOLD 24 TENNIS BALLS IN ONE HAND FOR 90 SECONDS.

polar swap Mike Comberiate, a retired NASA engineer and polar traveler, has poured water from the North Pole onto the South Pole, and water from the South Pole onto the North Pole. He has also traveled around the world 17 times, including making more than ten trips to the Poles. As a legacy of his days on the University of Maryland gymnastics team in the mid-1960s, he performs a handstand at every landmark that he visits.

FRIDGE WALK
➜ Tony Phoenix-Morrison from Tyneside, England, ran the length of Great Britain from John O'Groats, Scotland, to Land's End, Cornwall, while carrying an 88-lb (40-kg) fridge on his back. He completed his 1,000-mile (1,609-km) run for charity in just 40 days.

bubble pop On January 28, 2013, 336 pupils at Hawthorne High School, New Jersey, popped over 8,000 sq ft (743 sq m) of bubble wrap in two minutes. The event celebrated Bubble Wrap Appreciation Day—Marc Chavannes and Al Fielding invented bubble wrap in Hawthorne in 1960.

dove hunt Olney, Texas, is home to an annual one-arm dove hunt in which hand and arm amputees gather for competitions such as billiards, golf, cow-chip throwing and skeet shooting in addition to dove hunting. The hunt started out as a joke in 1972 by local residents Jack Northrup and Jack Bishop ("the one-armed Jacks"), both of whom had a limb amputated at the shoulder.

pogo flips In Montpellier, France, Dmitry Arsenyev from St. Petersburg, Russia, performed 15 consecutive backflips on a pogo stick.

flipping cool! In February 2013, Frenchman Guerlain Chicherit, driving a modified Mini Countryman, performed the first-ever 360-degree car backflip. He had trained for the stunt for four years, driving up the 25-ft-high (7.6-m) ramp at precisely 37 mph (60 km/h) before soaring 75 ft (23 m) into the air and landing on all four wheels.

brains and brawn Michael Kotch of Upper Milford Township, Pennsylvania, solved a Rubik's Cube puzzle with one hand in just 25 seconds while simultaneously doing push-ups with the other arm.

FIRE JUMPERS

→ Since the 1970s, members of the Findon Skid Kids Display Team from Adelaide, Australia, have been fearlessly jumping through walls of fire.

Teenage boys and girls ride their speedway bicycles, which have no brakes or multiple gears, through a cardboard frame that has been doused in fuel to send flames shooting high into the sky.

mouth juggler In June 2013, entertainer Mark Angelo from Hudson, Ohio, juggled two ping-pong balls using nothing but his mouth for a total of 212 spits and catches in 2 minutes 8 seconds. Mark, who first discovered his unusual talent by tossing popcorn in the air and catching it in his mouth, can also juggle with his eyes closed and can balance a golf club vertically on his chin with a golf ball on top if it and another club spinning on top of the ball!

ice wheelie Using special studs on his tires, Ryan Suchanek performed a motorbike wheelie on ice at an incredible speed of 108.5 mph (174.6 km/h). He rode on one wheel for more than 660 ft (200 m) on frozen Lake Koshkonong, Wisconsin.

173

BURNING RUBBER

➔ At the wheel of a specially modified replica 1937 Ford Sedan hot rod with a 1,250cc motorcycle engine, U.K. stunt driver Terry Grant spun his car 360 degrees (a donut) a total of 39 times in 100 seconds at a show in Devon, England. He averaged a time of 2.5 seconds per donut.

super sled Students at Lakeland College in Vermilion, Alberta, built a toboggan that was big enough to accommodate three Smart cars. Over 40 people rode on the toboggan, which measured 36 ft (11 m) long and 9.3 ft (2.8 m) wide.

eiger leap Wearing wingsuits, three members of the British Armed Forces—former Warrant Officer Spencer Hogg, Sgt. Deane Smith and Major Alastair Macartney—leaped in arrowhead formation off the notorious north ridge of the Eiger, a Swiss mountain more than 10,000 ft (3,048 m) above sea level. After free-falling through the Swiss Alps at 130 mph (209 km/h), they opened their parachutes for a safe descent.

phone throw In March 2013 at Wellington, New Zealand, 20-year-old Massey University student and javelin champion Ben Langton Burnell threw a cell phone a world record distance of 396 ft (120.6 m).

young wing-walkers Reaching speeds of up to 100 mph (160 km/h) and flying only yards apart, schoolgirls Rose Powell and Flame Brewer performed wing-walking stunts in formation—at age nine. When they took to the skies over Gloucestershire, England, the cousins, from London, became the third generation of their families to wing walk on two of their grandfather's vintage biplanes.

23 tongues Seventeen-year-old Timothy Doner from New York City has taught himself to speak 23 languages, including Hebrew, Arabic, Swahili, Chinese, Japanese, Italian, Turkish, Indonesian, Farsi, Russian, Dutch, Croatian and German.

crutch stilts In April 2013, circus performer Tameru Zegeye of Ethiopia walked for 249 ft (76 m) upside down on crutches.

SPIN MASTER ➔ Eighteen-year-old Michael Kopp from Germany is able to spin a basketball on a toothbrush held in his mouth.

sword pull In January 2013, "El Lurchio," from the Isle of Wight, U.K., pulled a 3,750-lb (1,702-kg) van for 20 ft (6 m) by the handle of a sword swallowed in his throat.

cold comfort In February 2013, six competitors—four men and two women—perched for 48 hours on 8.25-ft-high (2.5-m) blocks of ice in temperatures that dipped to below −18°F (−28°C) to become joint winners of a national ice pole-sitting contest that takes place in Vilhelmina, Sweden.

29 degrees At the age of 72, Michael Nicholson of Kalamazoo, Michigan, had received a total of 29 college degrees—in such diverse subjects as home economics, library science and health education.

happy hopper After rupturing his Achilles tendon during an indoor soccer game in 2009, truck driver Joseph Scavone Jr. from Hamburg, New Jersey, started hopping as a form of rehabilitation—and three years later he hopped into the record books by completing the fastest mile on one foot in 23 minutes 15 seconds.

tape ball A ball built from various tapes—including masking, electrical and duct—by the Portland Promise Center in Louisville, Kentucky, weighed 2,000 lb (908 kg) and had a circumference of 12¾ ft (3.9 m)—more than five times the size of a standard basketball.

birthday jump Dorothy Custer of Twin Falls, Idaho, celebrated her 102nd birthday by BASE jumping off the state's 486-ft-high (148-m) Perrine Bridge. The previous year, she had celebrated her 101st birthday by zip-lining Idaho's Snake River Canyon.

vietnam tribute Between 1982 and 2013, Mike Bowen from Flushing, Michigan, ran a whopping 58,282 mi (93,796 km)—one mile for every American who did not return from the Vietnam War. During that time he competed in more than 50 marathons and 26 road races in addition to regular runs through his local park.

delayed diploma More than 80 years after dropping out of high school despite needing only one credit to graduate, Audrey Crabtree of Cedar Falls, Iowa, finally received an honorary diploma—at age 99. She had left Waterloo East High School in 1932 following an accident that caused her to miss some school and because she also had to care for her sick grandmother.

blind shot Firing shots just half a second apart, gunslinger Jim Miekka from Homosassa, Florida, hits about 80 percent of his targets— even though he is completely blind.

special delivery Morris Wilkinson was still delivering mail to homes in Birmingham, Alabama, at age 93. When he finally retired in November 2012, he had served as a mailman for 65 years despite being hit by a car in 2009 and undergoing knee-replacement surgery when he was 80.

hot lips Fire-eater Carissa Hendrix of Calgary, Alberta, can hold a flaming torch in her mouth for more than two minutes.

Lonnie leaps from a 1,150-ft-high (350-m) bridge in Hunan, China.

WHEELCHAIR JUMPER

→ Canadian BASE jumper Lonnie Bissonnette throws himself off 1,000-ft-high (330-m) bridges in his wheelchair.

He has been paralyzed from the waist down since a 2004 BASE-jumping accident. Doctors told him he would never jump again, but within 12 months he was back traveling the world fulfilling his passion. He is unable to walk, but has enough strength in his right arm to be able to pull the parachute chord for a safe descent and landing. He is the first and only paraplegic BASE jumper to jump off all four BASE objects—Buildings, Antennae, Span (bridge) and Earth (cliff).

veteran climber On May 23, 2013, Japanese mountaineer Yuichiro Miura reached the summit of Mount Everest at the admirable age of 80 years 223 days.

big push U.S. Marine Sgt. Enrique Treviño from Dallas, Texas, completed one million push-ups in 2012—that's an average of nearly 2,740 per day.

river cleaner Since 1997, Chad Pregracke from East Moline, Illinois, has helped remove 7 million lb (3.2 million kg) of debris from U.S. waterways, including 67,000 tires, 1,000 refrigerators and four pianos. He has also found 64 messages in bottles, all of which he has kept as a collection.

high wire Chinese tightrope walker Aisikaier Wubulikasimu traversed a 60-ft-long (18-m), 2-in-wide (5-cm) steel beam linking two hot-air balloons flying 108 ft (33 m) above the ground—in just 38.35 seconds.

same route Ninety-three-year-old Newt Wallace has walked the same paper route in Winters, California, every week since 1947 to deliver the *Winters Express*. In total he has been delivering newspapers for more than 80 years.

mickey fan Janet Esteves of Celebration, Florida, has collected more than 6,200 items of Mickey Mouse memorabilia, including key chains, figurines, snow globes and plush dolls.

big bubble Canadian bubble artist Fan Yang encapsulated no fewer than 181 people in a single bubble that measured 164-ft-long (50-m) and 13-ft-high (4-m) in Vancouver, British Columbia.

card frenzy In 1989, when he was nine years old, Craig Shergold from Surrey, England, was diagnosed with a brain tumor. In the 24 years since, he has received over 350 million "Get Well" cards and business slips. His initial round-robin letter requesting cards produced replies from the likes of Bill Clinton, Kylie Minogue, Madonna, Arnold Schwarzenegger and Ripley's Believe It or Not!, and although Craig begged people to stop sending them in 1997 when the total reached 140 million, the cards kept coming despite the fact he is now healthy and moved house over 18 years ago.

cathedral crossing In May 2013, Austrian tightrope walker Christian Waldner became the first man to walk a 164-ft (50-m) slackline between the two towers of Vienna's famous St. Stephen's Cathedral. He made the perilous crossing, some 200 ft (60 m) above ground, not just once, but four times.

10,000-mile run Since 2008, super-fit 70-year-old Charles Wilson, of St. Augustine, Florida, has missed only a handful of days of completing his daily 8-mi (12.8-km) barefoot run along the beach. In that time he has clocked up well over 10,000 mi (16,000 km).

head smash Scott Damerow, a student at the Georgia Institute of Technology, U.S.A., cracked 142 eggs in one minute, using only his forehead.

letter openers William L. Brown of Gainesville, Florida, has collected more than 5,000 letter openers. He bought his first letter opener in Rome, Italy, in the late 1950s and became hooked.

canyon crossing

→ In June 2013, Nik Wallenda tightrope walked across the Little Colorado River Gorge near the Grand Canyon, defying high winds 1,500 ft (457 m) above the Little Colorado River and without a tether or safety net. He took 22 minutes 54 seconds to walk the 1,400 ft (427 m) on a steel cable just 2 in (5 cm) wide. As well as the wind, Nik, who has been high-wire walking since he was two and comes from seven generations of aerialists, had to contend with desert dust that impaired his vision by getting into his contact lenses and also settled on the cable, making it slippery underfoot. Twice he had to stop and crouch down—first when a gust of wind made him unsteady and the second time when he spat on his hands and rubbed his saliva on the sole of his shoe to obtain a better grip on the cable. "My arms are aching like you wouldn't believe," he said afterward, "but it was a dream come true. This is what my family has done for 200 years, so it's part of my legacy." In 2012, he became the first person in over 100 years to complete a high-wire walk over the Niagara Falls.

blood donor Edward Kisslack of Waynesboro, Pennsylvania, has donated 30 gal (114 l) of blood in the last 50 years—enough to replace the blood in his own body 20 times.

butter knife Schoolteacher Claes Blixt from Skene, Sweden, made a giant wooden butter knife that measures 97 ⅝ in long (248 cm) and weighs 62 lb 13 oz (28.5 kg).

massive mural Amanda Warrington spent more than 1,000 hours solving a 24,000-piece jigsaw puzzle. When she had finished, she glued the 14 x 5 ft (4.3 x 1.5 m) montage to a wall of her home in Gloucestershire, England.

long service Loyal employee Rose Syracuse Richardone, aged 92, worked at Macy's New York City department store for 73 years, from 1939 to 2012.

extreme pogo On July 27, 2013, in New York City, extreme pogoist Tone Staubs from Danville, Ohio, made 266 pogo stick bounces in one minute.

strong beard Kapil Gehlot of Jodhpur, India, can pull a 2,300-lb (1046-kg) car with his beard while wearing roller skates.

daring doris Great-great-grandmother Doris Long from Hampshire, England, celebrated her 99th birthday in May 2013 by bravely rappeling down the side of a 110-ft-high (34-m) building.

open wide Dinesh Shivnath Upadhyaya from Mumbai, India, can fit 800 drinking straws in his mouth at the same time.

fast hands Bryan Bednarek, from Chicago, Illinois, can clap his hands together more than 800 times in a minute—that's an incredible 13 times a second.

bike climb Without his feet ever touching the ground, Italian Vittorio Brumotti cycled up 3,700 steps to the top of the tallest building in the world—the 2,715-ft-high (828-m) Burj Khalifa in Dubai. He jumped his way up the 160 floors in 2 hours 20 minutes.

homemade shoes Since 1971, George Walter from Pittsburgh, Pennsylvania, has traveled the world on foot, visiting more than 40 countries and wearing sandals he makes himself from tire treads, nails and nylon straps.

can castle The Toyohashi Junior Chamber from Japan re-created a corner tower of Yoshida Castle from 104,840 aluminum cans. The cans, which were held together by glue, formed a tower measuring 16 ft (5 m) high, 21.6 ft (6.6 m) wide and 18 ft (5.5 m) long.

frog lady Thayer Cueter (aka The Frog Lady) of Edmonds, Washington State, has built up a collection of over 10,000 items of frog-related memorabilia, including 400 Kermit the Frog toys, 490 plush frog toys and 20 different pairs of frog pajamas.

In 1924, Al Wilson became probably the first man to drive a golf ball from the wings of a plane.

Barnstormers

➜ **The Barnstormers were daredevil pilots and stuntmen who performed outrageous airplane stunts for traveling air shows, flying circuses and Hollywood movies in the U.S.A. in the 1920s.**

Named after entertainers that performed in rural New York barns in the early 19th century, many Barnstormers caught the flying bug from when they were pilots in World War I, and they often flew ex-Air Force Curtiss biplanes. Barnstormers were famous for their death-defying wing-walks, where stuntmen and women would climb from the cockpit and perform stunts on the wings, usually completely unsecured, at flying speeds of up to 90 mph (145 km/h). The moves didn't just look dangerous, they could be genuinely deadly, and many Barnstormers lost their lives in the pursuit of ever-more imaginative stunts to thrill crowds on the ground or while shooting Hollywood movies.

By the late 1920s, the Barnstormers' casualty rate was so high that the Government stepped in and made it illegal for stunt aircraft to fly within 300 ft (90 m) of each other.

Al Wilson made a dangerous leap onto a plane from a car traveling at 80 mph (129 km/h) in 1927.

Legendary pilot Charles Lindbergh, the first man to fly solo nonstop across the Atlantic in 1927, was a Barnstormer early in his aviation career.

MORE...

177

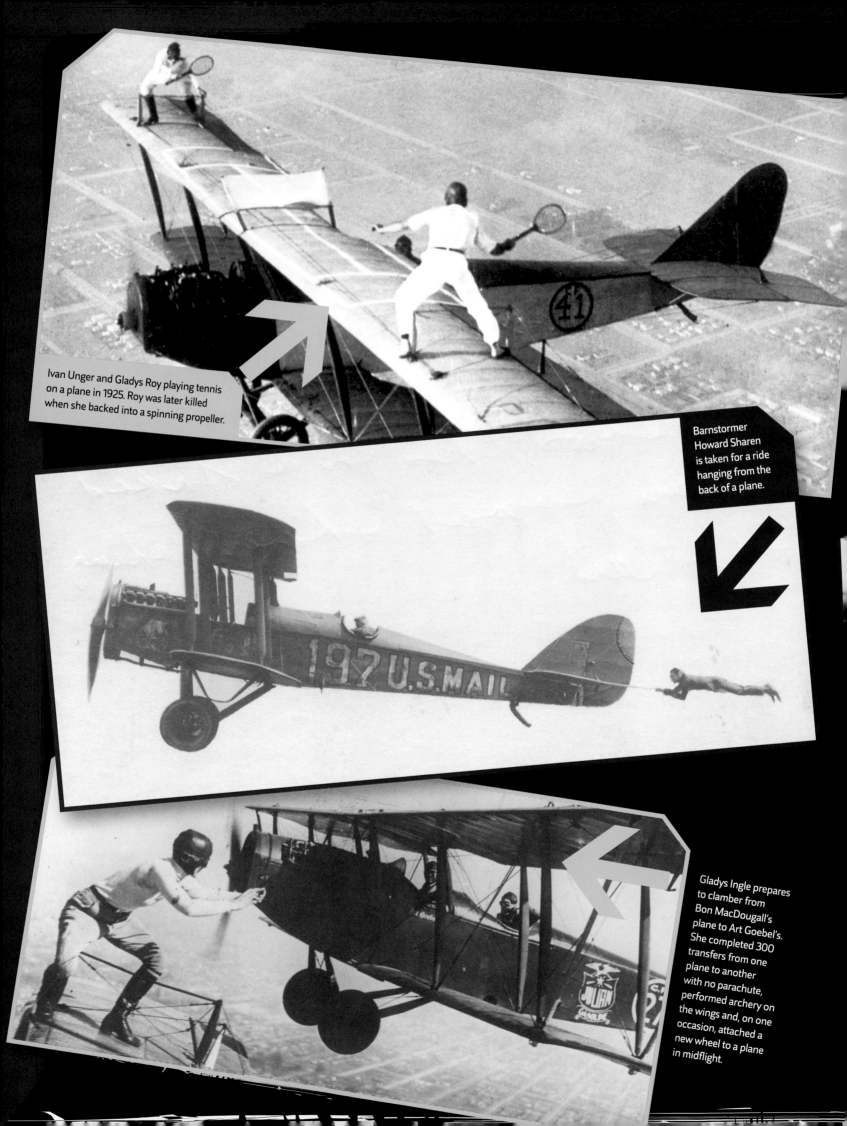

Ivan Unger and Gladys Roy playing tennis on a plane in 1925. Roy was later killed when she backed into a spinning propeller.

Barnstormer Howard Sharen is taken for a ride hanging from the back of a plane.

Gladys Ingle prepares to clamber from Bon MacDougall's plane to Art Goebel's. She completed 300 transfers from one plane to another with no parachute, performed archery on the wings and, on one occasion, attached a new wheel to a plane in midflight.

"WE'LL DO ANYTHING!" —THE 13 BLACK CATS

➜ A man tied to a speeding plane by only his hair, a woman climbing from one plane to another midflight, a pilot crashing a plane on purpose, the 13 Black Cats were a troop of Hollywood stuntmen and women specializing in madcap airplane and automobile exploits in the 1920s. They flew on barnstorming tours when not shooting movies, and proudly kept to the motto on their calling card—"We'll do anything!" The Cats, led by risk-loving Bon MacDougall, included the most famous pilots and stunt performers in the country. In 1928 MacDougall told a journalist that he had seen 50 of his flying companions fall to their deaths, but "I never had an airplane smash-up, unless it was an intentional one." While MacDougall rode his luck in the air, colleagues were not so fortunate, and five founding members died in action with the Black Cats.

A Black Cat group photo—there were never actually 13 of them, the unlucky number and black-cat symbol were chosen because the team literally flew in the face of bad luck and superstition.

The 13 Flying Black Cats
WILL DO ANYTHING
AIRPLANE · MOTORCYCLE · AUTOMOBILE
STUNTS
Parachute Jumps, Ship Changes
Upside Down Flying
Delayed Opening Jumps, Ocean Landings
Rope Ladder and Wing Walking
Fast Racing Automobiles, Powerful Airplanes
Experienced Camera and Stunt Men
ART GOEBEL   BON MacDOUGALL
HERRD McCLELLAN
CROSS AERIAL PHOTO SERVICE
IF A BLACK CAT CAN'T DO IT - IT CAN'T BE DONE

The Cats' calling card.

13 BLACK CATS PRICE LIST

The Cats provided a price list for Hollywood movie producers looking to hire their services.

General stunt rate per hour — **$35**	A plane crash into an automobile — **$250**
Fire on plane — **$50**	Upside-down plane-to-plane transfer — **$500**
Plane-to-plane transfer — **$100**	A plane crash into a house or trees — **$1,200**
A loop with man standing on wing — **$150**	Explode a plane midflight — **$1,500**

Chief White Eagle would hang from planes at 5,000 ft (1,525 m) attached by only his hair, a stunt that would later kill him when the pilot attempted a loop-the-loop and his locks came loose.

"Spider" Matlock, Al Johnson and "Fronty" Nichols strike a pose on a plane piloted by Bon MacDougall. Nichols would die in a parachute accident and Matlock was killed in a motor race.

tough teeth Hungarian strongman Zsolt Sinka pulled a 55-ton Airbus A320 airplane nearly 130 ft (40 m), using just his teeth. Sinka, who has previously used his teeth to pull fire engines and trains, achieved his latest feat in just 52 seconds at Liszt Ferenc Airport in Budapest.

oldest family In 2012, nine brothers and sisters of the Melis family from Ogliastra, Sardinia, boasted a combined age of 818—this works out to an average age of 91 and makes them the world's oldest living family. The siblings, who ranged in age from 78 to 105, attribute their longevity to minestrone soup.

tight fit New Zealand contortionist Skye Broberg crammed her body into a box measuring 20 x 18 x 18 in (52 x 45 x 45 cm) in just 4.78 seconds.

elephant diving Karin Sinniger, a Swiss, U.S. and British citizen who lives in Angola, has SCUBA-dived in more than 122 countries, logging more than 1,000 dives in total. She has dived under ice, in volcano craters and with an elephant off the Andaman Islands!

capital knowledge At just 18 months old, Aanav Jayakar from Cleveland, Ohio, could correctly identify 21 countries on a map of the world, and recite 61 capital cities.

EXTREME THERAPY → People in Russia stand on a bed of razor-sharp nails as a way of confronting their biggest fears head on. The tortuous trial is part of a two-day course called "Life Without Fear" that helps participants overcome their phobias by undertaking a series of extreme activities. These include stopping falling knives with their bare stomach, walking on hot coals, breaking wooden poles with their neck, sitting on broken glass, allowing giant bugs to crawl over their face, walking on knife blades, eating pieces of burning cotton, swimming in freezing water and being buried alive.

coconut cracker Keshab Swain of Odisha, India, can crack open 85 green coconuts with his elbow in just 60 seconds. He can also smash 18 coconuts in one minute with his forehead.

34-hour speech In June 2013, professional speaker Alex Cequea, editor-in-chief of *iPhone Life* magazine, gave a 34-hour speech in Fairfield, Iowa, mostly about his own life and his family's journey from Venezuela to the U.S.A.

3-ton impact Strongman Mike Gillette of Des Moines, Iowa, survived having a 14-lb (6.4-kg) bowling ball dropped on his stomach from 8.5 ft (2.5 m) in the air, while lying on a bed of broken glass! A china plate was placed on top of his stomach to act as a target and when this shattered on impact, it created a layer of shards above his abdomen in addition to the shards he was lying on. The dropped ball reached a speed of over 15 mph (24 km/h), so that it impacted his body with a staggering 6,000 lb (3 tons) of force.

deadly waters On September 2, 2013, 64-year-old American endurance swimmer Diana Nyad became the first person to swim the treacherous waters from Cuba to Florida without a shark cage. She swam without a wetsuit or flippers, but wore a silicone mask to protect her face from the jellyfish stings that had foiled two of her four previous attempts. Diana completed the 110-mi (176-km) crossing in just under 53 hours. She had first attempted the swim 35 years earlier, in 1978.

island swim In 2013, Anna Wardley from Hampshire, England, became the first person in nearly 30 years to swim nonstop around the Isle of Wight. She completed the 60-mi (97-km) challenge in just over 26½ hours, making some 87,500 strokes in the process.

REDHEAD FESTIVAL

→ More than 5,000 redheads from 80 countries gathered in Breda, Netherlands, for the 2013 Redhead Days Festival—with Ronald McDonald, one of the world's most celebrated red-headed icons, at the center of the red sea. To accentuate their distinctive hair coloring, all attendees were asked to wear blue clothing. Some arrived on a special "redhead-only" flight from Inverness, Scotland, where auburn-haired pilots and cabin crew served red-haired passengers ginger beer.

Man in a Bag Swims Lake

Bulgarian Jane Petkov swam $1\frac{1}{4}$ mi (2 km) across Lake Ohrid in Macedonia while tied up in a bag. With his arms and legs strapped to his body, the 59-year-old swam on his back "like a dolphin" for nearly three hours, averaging $2/5$ mph (0.7 km/h).

sharp practice Sword-swallower Aerial Manx from Melbourne, Australia, can turn cartwheels with a sword in his throat.

martial arts On June 9, 2012, 10,000 students of kung fu gathered in Henan, China, to put on a martial arts display for the country's Cultural Heritage Day.

heavy burden Jim "The Shark" Dreyer from Grand Rapids, Michigan, swam 22 mi (35 km) in 51 hours across Lake St. Clair, near the U.S.–Canada border, hauling a ton of bricks.

stiff upper lip Saddi Muhammad pulled a 1.9-ton truck that was attached to his mustache for 200 ft (60 m) in his hometown of Lahore, Pakistan, in October 2012.

pier pressure Jay and Hazel Preller from Somerset, England, traveled 7,000 mi (11,265 km) over the course of two years visiting all 60 seaside piers in the U.K.—and kissed on the end of each one. They first met on Weston-super-Mare's Grand Pier and got married on Brighton Pier.

marathon bounce Phoebe Asquith, aged 24, from Yorkshire, England, bounced 4.1 mi (6.6 km) on a Hippity Hop (Space Hopper) toy. The journey took her 4½ hours at an average speed of just under 1 mph (1.6 km/h).

park walk Since 1990, Herbert Langerman of Wilmington, Delaware, has walked more than 25,000 mi (40,000 km)—equal to once around the world. However, he achieved this feat on only a half-mile track in the city's Bonsall Park.

fancy dress In June 2013, David Smith from Derbyshire, England, ran an incredible 69 mi (110 km) along Hadrian's Wall in the north of England in 14 hours 24 minutes—wearing a full Roman centurion costume. He had previously competed in marathons wearing such diverse outfits as handcuffs, a straitjacket, flip-flops and a gingerbread-man costume.

memorial parade In 2013, at age 99, former U.S. Navy sailor John Casey from Connecticut marched in his 67th consecutive Shelton–Derby Memorial Day Parade.

ferris ride In May 2013, Clinton Shepherd spent over 48 hours riding the Ferris wheel at Navy Pier, Chicago, Illinois. He stayed awake for the two days by playing video games and watching James Bond and Batman movies.

Ripley's Believe It or Not!® www.ripleybooks.com

battery power As part of a recycling enterprise, the region of Durham, Ontario, Canada, collected 11,288 lb (5,120 kg) of batteries in just 24 hours.

giant envelope Using card sheets joined by glue, student Garima Angel from Uttar Pradesh, India, spent more than a month making an enormous envelope measuring 48 x 32 ft (14.5 x 9.8 m) and weighing 110 lb (50 kg)—that's over half the size of a tennis court.

animal skulls Alan Dudley from Coventry, England, has a collection of more than 2,000 animal skulls in his house. He collected his first skull—a fox—in 1975, and now acquires skulls from all over the world, ranging from rats to hippos, giraffes and crocodiles. Among his most unusual items is a two-headed cow. His hobby is not to everyone's taste—his former wife threatened to destroy his entire collection because of the awful smell of a rotting iguana.

kitty crazy Asako Kanda, a 40-year-old receptionist from Japan, has a collection of over 4,500 "Hello Kitty" items, including pillows, curtains, hats, a toaster, an electric fan and a frying pan. When she got married in 2000, she asked her mother to make a Hello Kitty toy bride and groom for the wedding reception.

cross country *Star Wars* fan Jacob French raised more than $100,000 for charity by walking 3,100 mi (4,960 km) from Perth to Sydney, Australia, dressed in a stormtrooper costume. The walk took him nine months, during which time he lost over 26 lb (12 kg) in weight and wore out seven pairs of shoes.

memory man

→ Aurelien Hayman, a 21-year-old student from Cardiff, Wales, can remember what he had to eat, what he did, what he wore, what was in the news and even what the weather was like on any given day dating back over a decade. He is one of about 20 people in the world with hyperthymesia, or highly superior autobiographical memory.

℞ RIPLEY'S RESEARCH

The average person retrieves information such as dates from their long-term memory in the right frontal lobe of the brain. Aurelien does the same, but his condition means he is also able to use the left frontal lobe and occipital areas at the back of the brain, thereby greatly increasing his long-term memory capacity.

matchstick marker Shourabh Modi of Madhya Pradesh, India, wrote the name of Madhya Pradesh chief minister Shivraj Singh Chauhan 11,111 times on 2,778 matchsticks—four times per match—in 30 days.

juggling genius Ravi Fernando, a math undergrad at Stanford University, California, can solve a Rubik's Cube puzzle in 1½ minutes while juggling it and two small balls.

cardboard fort A team of nearly 400 students and staff from Duke University built a 16-ft-tall (5-m) fort from 3,500 recycled cardboard boxes on the university campus at Durham, North Carolina.

dual writer Chinese translator Chen Siyuan can not only write with both hands at the same time, she can do it in different languages—Chinese with one hand and English with the other. She discovered her incredible talent by chance while trying to save time on large amounts of English homework at high school.

duck call Father and son Mark and Damen Hillery from Danville, Illinois, built a wooden duck call that measures a staggering 56 in (1.4 m) long. When blown into, its barrel makes a deep quack that sounds like a giant duck.

sky lights More than 15,000 sky lanterns were flown simultaneously in the sky over Iloilo City, Philippines, on May 24, 2013. Made of rice paper with bamboo frames, each of the lanterns was 60 in (150 cm) tall and had a diameter of 20 in (50 cm).

snowball fight A total of 5,834 people took part in a mass snowball fight in Seattle, Washington State, on January 12, 2013, to mark the city's Snow Day. More than 30 truckloads of snow were brought in for the event.

crossword compiler Roger Squires, from Shropshire, England, has been creating crossword puzzles for national newspapers for more than 50 years. By the age of 81, he had compiled nearly 75,000 crosswords—more than 2.25 million clues!

BOOK CHAIN

→ Seattle Public Library in Washington State kicked off its Summer Reading Program for 2013 by toppling 2,131 discarded and donated books in a domino-like chain.

STAR TREK HOUSE

➔ **Steve Nighteagle Doman spent four years turning the front room of his home in Guffey, Colorado, into a *Star Trek*-themed Federation Room.**

Driven by 14 computers, his starship was created for $25,000 by recycling ordinary household objects, including parts of old printers, pieces of cutlery, hair dryers, air filters from trucks, plumbing and drainage pipes, bottle caps, Christmas lights, old cassette players, curling irons and vacuum cleaner hoses. Now the sci-fi fan and carpenter plans to give the rest of his house a 23rd-century makeover.

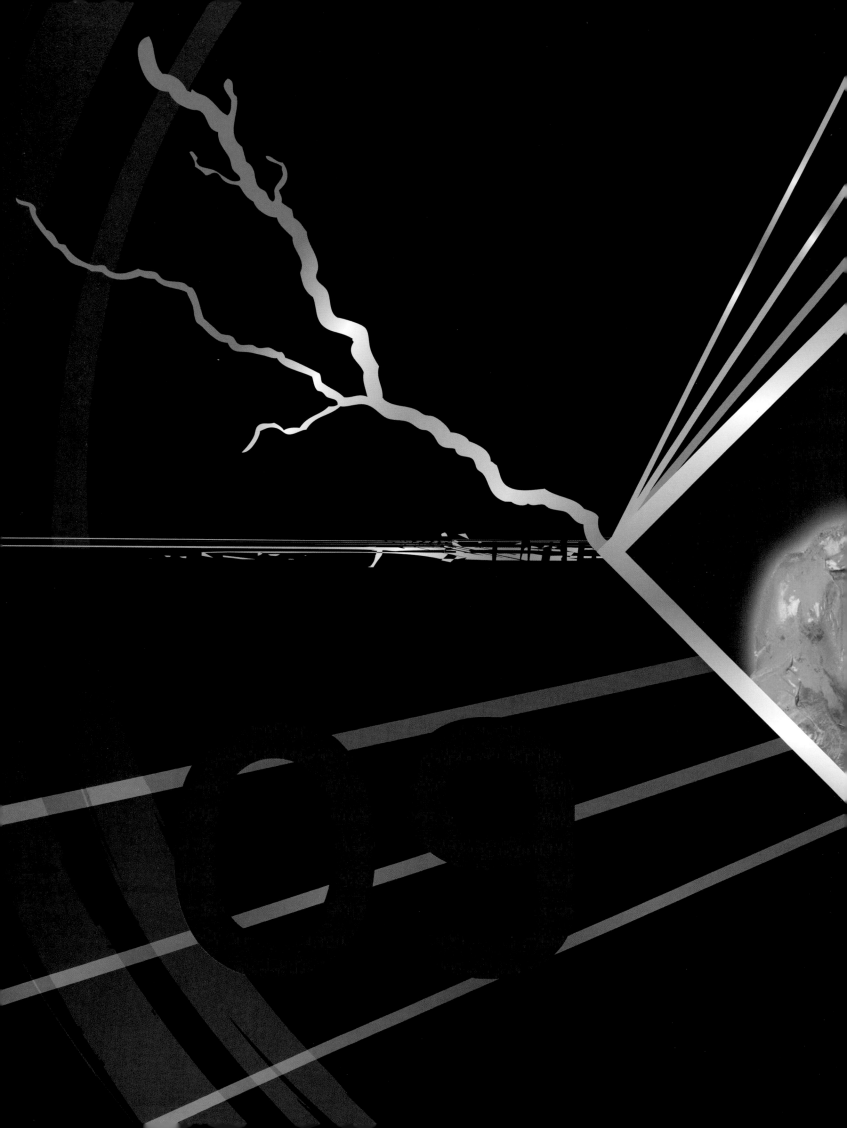

ART

Graffiti
BLOCK

→ For just one month before it was demolished in early 2014, an unremarkable derelict Paris apartment block was transformed into an incredible ten-story art installation by 100 of the world's finest street artists.

The artists were invited by gallery owner Mehdi Ben Cheikh to create whatever they wanted on every available surface of Tour 13, which stands close to the River Seine in the French capital's 13th district. The result was a rich mosaic of faces, animals, mythical creatures, patterns and scriptures—some warm and welcoming, others more serious and thought-provoking—that decorated all 36 apartments as well as the stairwells and the exterior brickwork.

Some artists brought their own props to extend the fantasy, while others created clever optical illusions featuring boxes that appeared to float and walls that seemed to bend.

THIGH Doodles

→ Jody Steel, a student from Boston, Massachusetts, draws incredible portraits of people and animals on her thighs—and they are so striking that people mistake them for tattoos.

She began doodling on her legs during lectures, but when her lecturer reprimanded her for not paying attention, he was so impressed by her drawings that he offered her a job illustrating a novel.

www. JODYSTEEL.com

PRECISE V5

ivory ships A fifth-generation carver, David Warther II of Sugarcreek, Ohio, has painstakingly carved more than 80 ships from antique ivory, depicting the history of the ship from 3000 BC to the present day. He started carving ships when he was just six years old and his work is so precise that the vessels' ivory rigging is handworked to a diameter of 0.007 in (0.18 mm).

bread city Food artist Lennie Payne from London, England, sculpted models of the city's landmarks—including Tower Bridge, St. Paul's Cathedral and Big Ben—out of bread. He also used muffins, crumpets and sandwiches to form a complete 3-D city skyline.

bouncy chair Preston Moeller from Cleveland, North Carolina, made what must be the world's bounciest office chair—out of 65,000 rubber bands. The chair weighs 35 lb (15.8 kg) and it took him 300 hours to loop the bands together to make the chair.

mirror writing Leonardo da Vinci's personal notes were always written starting from the right side of the page and moving to the left, a technique known as "mirror writing," because anyone who wanted to read his private notebooks had to use a mirror. He wrote in the standard manner from left to right only if he intended for others to read what he had written down.

It looks as if Jody's leg has been ripped open to expose the bone, but happily it is just another of her imaginative doodles.

Jody first used her flesh as a canvas because there was no paper handy, but in any case she says her skin is so pale it offers the same qualities as paper, as can be seen in this lifelike drawing of an elephant.

ARTY BOOTHS

→ To deter graffiti sprayers and vandals, 100 artists transformed 100 street-side public phone booths in São Paulo, Brazil, into creative and colorful works of art. For *Call Parade*, a project sponsored by telecommunications firm Vivo, one booth creepily took on the appearance of a human brain, while another became a workman's helmet with a pencil through it.

mouse stuffing Taxidermist Shannon Marie Harmon from London, England, runs a class teaching people how to stuff dead mice and to dress and pose them in unusual positions, all in the name of art. Each student leaves the four-hour session with their own stuffed and embalmed mouse.

missing island Is Land, a $13,000, 23-ft-wide (7-m), helium-filled sculpture of a desert island, floated away from a 2011 music festival in Cambridgeshire, England, after vandals cut its tether ropes. Although its creators, Sarah Cockings and Laurence Symonds, launched a worldwide search for the giant inflatable and sightings were reported in Canada and Switzerland, the island has never been found.

underwater wheelchair At a swimming pool in Weymouth, England, disabled artist Sue Austin performed an exhibition of acrobatics in the world's first self-propelled underwater wheelchair. Her art project *Creating the Spectacle!* featured a series of stunning underwater SCUBA routines in her modified wheelchair that is fitted with swimming floats, fins and two foot-controlled propulsion drives.

straw dalek To mark the 50th anniversary of *Doctor Who*, staff at an ice-cream parlor in Cheshire, England, built a 35-ft-tall (10.6-m) Dalek (the Doctor's arch enemy) from 6 tons of straw and 5 tons of steel.

tea-bag collage Armenian artist Armén Rotch arranges hundreds of used tea bags into intricate patterns to create huge pixelated collages. By selecting bags that have been left to steep for different lengths of time, he is able to use different shades of gold and brown.

prolific picasso Spanish artist Pablo Picasso (1881–1973) was the most prolific artist who ever lived. In his 75-year career, he produced around 150,000 works—an average of 2,000 a year. These included an estimated 13,500 paintings and designs, 100,000 prints and engravings, 34,000 book illustrations, and 300 sculptures and ceramics. His works have been valued at $788 million. Every year, some 3,000 Picasso works are sold and bought, amounting to about $200 million of business.

healthy profit A 1,000-year-old Chinese bowl, bought for $3 at a yard sale, sold for $2.2 million at auction in 2013.

human bones During the Napoleonic Wars, French prisoners-of-war built model warships out of human bones.

DOOR DRAWINGS → Artist Charlie Layton from Philadelphia, Pennsylvania, has created a series of pen and ink drawings—including Darth Vader, Godzilla and a skeleton—on the door of his fridge freezer. After discovering that the door was made from the same material as a dry-erase board and could therefore work as an artistic surface, he did a new drawing every Friday, each one taking him about half an hour.

189

Toy
Soldiers

➔ Artist Joe Black from London, England, made this incredible portrait of former Chinese leader Mao Tse-tung from more than 15,000 hand-painted, plastic toy soldiers.

Joe, who specializes in mosaics using everyday objects such as ball bearings and button pins, has also created a portrait of President Obama using 11,000 black-and-white toy soldiers, a sculpture of former Soviet dictator Joseph Stalin from 10,000 chess pawn pieces and one of former British Prime Minister Margaret Thatcher from iron bolts.

SCRAP SCULPTURES

➜ French artist Edouard Martinet creates delicate metal sculptures of insects, fish, animals and birds from old pieces of scrap, including bicycle parts, kitchen utensils and typewriter keys. As with this wasp, the individual pieces are screwed rather than welded together, and each artwork can take him anything from a month to 17 years to complete as he scours flea markets and garage sales for the perfect parts.

everest debris A group of 15 Nepalese artists collected several tons of garbage that had been left behind on Mount Everest and turned it into more than 70 different sculptures. The artworks incorporated discarded oxygen cylinders, cans, bottles and climbing tools, and even the remains of a helicopter that had crashed into the mountain in the 1970s.

unfinished picture U.S. President Franklin D. Roosevelt was posing for a portrait when he collapsed and died in 1945. The painting has never been completed.

reflected beauty Simon Hennessey from Birmingham, England, creates stunningly realistic paintings of famous world landmarks—including Tower Bridge, the Eiffel Tower and the New York City skyline—reflected in the lenses of tourists' sunglasses. Each picture can take him several months and will cost a buyer over £22,000 ($36,000).

dutch master A painting that had been branded worthless for over a century was revealed to be the work of Dutch master Vincent van Gogh and is now valued at around $50 million. *Sunset at Montmajour* had been painted by Van Gogh in 1888 but was pronounced a fake, dumped in an attic and hidden from public view until it was finally declared genuine in 2013—the first full-size new Van Gogh to emerge in 85 years.

artistic field Dario Gambarin used a plow as his paintbrush to create a 328-ft (100-m) portrait of Pope Francis in a field on his parents' farm near Verona, Italy. The scale of his tractor pictures, which have also included Barack Obama and Edvard Munch's *The Scream*, means they can be viewed only from the air and he always removes them after a few days so that the field can be cultivated.

driftwood sculptures Sculptor Jeffro Uitto from Tokeland, Washington, combs the coastline for abandoned driftwood and turns it into items of furniture and giant wooden creatures such as a rearing horse or a swooping eagle. His pieces can take years to create while he searches for the right pieces of driftwood.

backyard landmark Ken Larry Richardson from Mulvane, Kansas, spent 11 years and nearly $5,000 building a 150-ft-long (46-m) replica of San Francisco's Golden Gate Bridge to cross a small creek on his farm. He built it using 98 tons of concrete and lots of recycled materials, including cables from an oil rig and suspender cables salvaged from an old Boeing aircraft.

radioactive chandeliers Ken and Julia Yonetani from Sydney, Australia, produce vintage chandeliers made from radioactive uranium glass. They replace the crystals with uranium glass beads and add ultraviolet light to make them glow a beautiful green. They use a Geiger counter to check that their chandeliers emit safe levels of radiation.

domino tower Tom Holmes, a graduate engineer from Bristol, England, spent a staggering 7½ hours and used 2,688 dominos to build a freestanding tower that was more than 17 ft (5.2 m) tall.

heavy work Beth Johnson of LaRue, Ohio, built an enormous wooden yo-yo that measured 12 ft (3.6 m) in diameter and weighed 4,620 lb (2,096 kg)—and bounced it up and down using a crane.

gargoyle honor Nora Sly, a worshiper at St. Mary's church in the village of Cowley in Gloucester, England, for more than 60 years, has had her smiling face carved into a stone gargoyle mounted on the church roof.

lint figures Cheryl Capezzuti from Pittsburgh, Pennsylvania, sculpts dryer lint into animals, angels and life-size human figures. She gets lint sent to her by people from all over the world and mixes it with glue to form her fluffy sculptures.

TOILET TUBES ➜ Whereas most people simply throw old toilet paper tubes away, French artist Anastassia Elias has transformed more than 75 of them into imaginative miniature scenes. Using a scalpel and manicure scissors and the same paper color as the tubes, she spends hours patiently cutting out tiny shapes of everything from construction workers and dinosaurs and circus performers to carefully fitting ballerinas before the used toilet rolls them inside with a pair of tweezers.

Body Writing

➔ Beauty really is skin deep for Ariana Page Russell. She has a medical condition called dermatographia, meaning that when she lightly scratches her skin it quickly puffs up into a red imprint. Yet, instead of trying to hide her condition, she embraces it by transforming her body into a magical canvas, using a blunt knitting needle to write elegant text or to create intricate patterns on her legs, arms and torso.

When the 34-year-old artist, based in Brooklyn, New York, scratches her hypersensitive flesh, the welts that appear usually last for about 30 minutes before fading. This allows her enough time to photograph the results. Sometimes she incorporates the freckles on her body into her designs. Although the marks look painful, she says they don't hurt and produce only a "warm" sensation.

Ariana's amazing "body art" photographs have been exhibited all over the U.S.A. and as far afield as Ireland, Bolivia and Australia. She also makes wallpaper, collage and temporary tattoos using the pictures of her skin cut into decorative designs.

Ariana only learned a decade ago that she had dermatographia (which literally means "writing on the skin") but, by then, she had already become interested in using her skin as art.

To help others with the condition to become similarly empowered, she has started a blog, Skin Tome, where people can celebrate their exceptional skin. Ariana says that even if there was a cure, she wouldn't want one. She says "I think it's fun to be able to draw on myself. I like it."

For *Index*, Ariana wrote a description of one of her dreams on her legs with a knitting needle, and then photographed the resulting text.

Ariana's photograph entitled *!!!!!* shows a mass of exclamation marks covering her back, shoulders and arms.

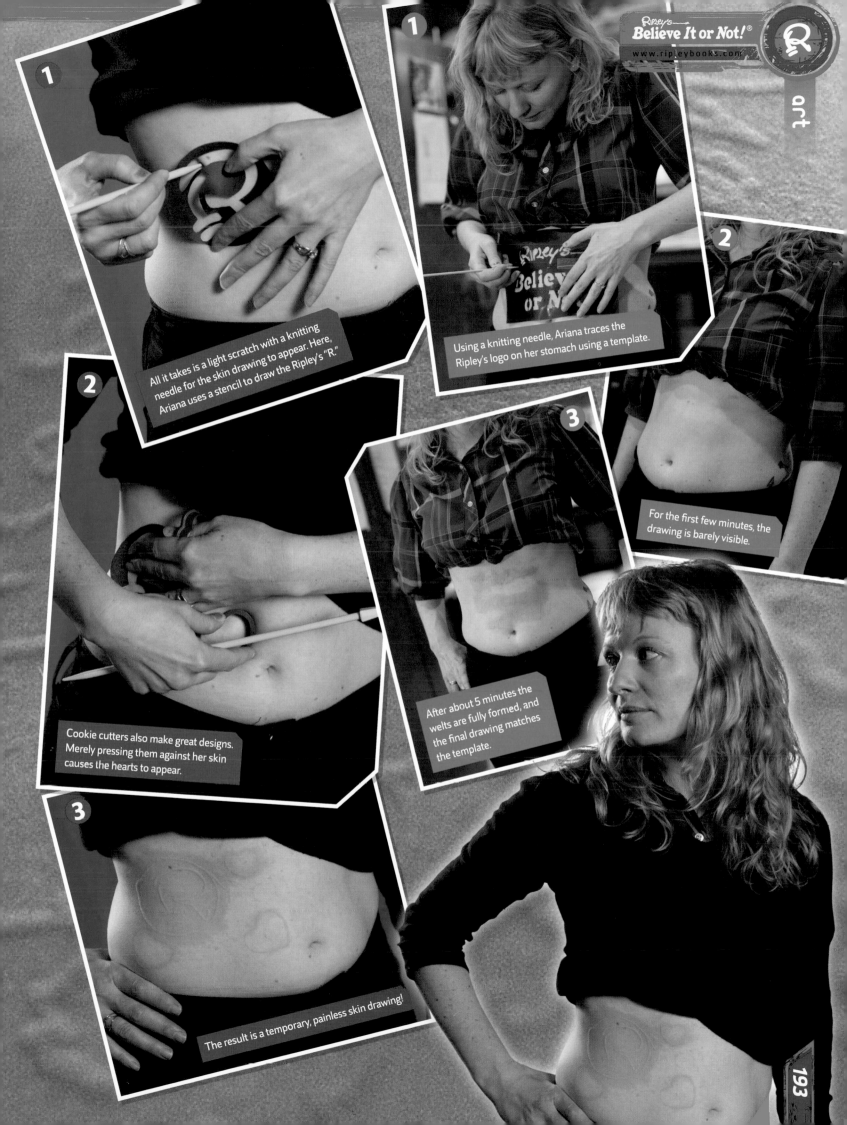

Ripley's
Believe It or Not!®
www.ripleybooks.com

1 All it takes is a light scratch with a knitting needle for the skin drawing to appear. Here, Ariana uses a stencil to draw the Ripley's "R."

1 Using a knitting needle, Ariana traces the Ripley's logo on her stomach using a template.

2 Cookie cutters also make great designs. Merely pressing them against her skin causes the hearts to appear.

2

3 For the first few minutes, the drawing is barely visible.

3 After about 5 minutes the welts are fully formed, and the final drawing matches the template.

3 The result is a temporary, painless skin drawing!

Tree Trunk

→ Chinese artist Zheng Chunhui spent four years carving an intricate 40-ft-long (12-m) artwork from a single tree trunk.

The carving, which is 10 ft (3 m) tall at its highest point and 7¾ ft (2.4 m) wide, is a copy of the famous 12th-century Chinese painting and features boats, bridges, animals, buildings and 550 individually crafted people.

titanic model Working 12 hours a day for ten days, Vivek Kumar of Uttar Pradesh, India, made a 6-ft-long (1.8-m), 3-ft-tall (0.9-m) model of the *Titanic* from 8,000 ice cream sticks.

crochet timelords For a unique Christmas gift, Allison Hoffman from Austin, Texas, made mini crocheted dolls of the first 11 Doctor Whos from the popular TV series.

wooden wonders Arizona State professor Tom Eckert produces sculptures that look as if they are made of silk, glass, paper, stone, plastic, metal or fruit—even though they are really made entirely of wood. Working mainly with basswood, linden and limewood, he carves, turns, whittles, bends and laminates the wood. Then he applies fine layers of waterborne lacquer paint with spray guns and brushes to incorporate subtle wrinkles and reflections into his pieces, making them almost impossible to distinguish from the real thing.

single hair

Mukesh Thapa from Himachal Pradesh, India, painted a self-portrait in oils using a single hair from his own beard. It took him a year to finish the picture with his unique, ultra-thin brush.

milk magic

French artist Vivi Mac creates celebrity portraits from foodstuffs, including crème brûlée and milk. She uses a straw to guide the liquid carefully around the plastic trays that serve as her canvases.

leather etchings

Welsh artist Mark Evans uses leather as his canvas and a knife as his brush. He carefully cuts through the surface of animal hides to create amazing etchings that sell for up to £450,000 ($700,000) each.

dot mosaics

Lacy Knudson from San Diego, California, creates beautiful mosaics from thousands of tiny balls of Play-Doh. She paints the image first and then arranges the Play-Doh balls on the canvas over the corresponding colors. One piece took her six months to make and used 152 jars of Play-Doh rolled into 12,000 individual dots.

word art

Artist Michael Volpicelli from Stillwater, Oklahoma, makes portraits of famous people using only written words relating to their life. Using pen and ink, he draws inspirational figures such as Pope John Paul II and Malala Yousafzai, the 16-year-old Pakistani girl shot by the Taliban for going to school, from hundreds of words linked to their lives.

complex corkscrew

Mechanical sculptor Rob Higgs from Cornwall, England, has built the world's biggest and most complex corkscrew—a 5ft-3-in-tall (1.6-m) brass contraption that weighs more than three-quarters of a ton and has 382 moving parts, including gears, pulleys, levers and springs.

bean portrait

Malcolm West from Surrey, England, used more than 5,000 jellybeans in 20 different flavors to create a 4-ft-high (1.2 m) portrait of the Duchess of Cambridge. He used licorice and chocolate-pudding flavors for her hair and candy floss and pink grapefruit for her complexion, painstakingly gluing each bean into place on a canvas.

CHIRPY CHIP CHIP

→ These beautiful life-sized sculptures may look like fluffy animals and birds, but instead of fur and feather they are really made of small slivers and chips of wood. Russian artist Sergey Bobkov uses 3-in-long (7.5-cm) sticks from Siberian cedar trees, which he cuts into around 150 thin slices. He prevents the strips from falling apart by soaking them in water for several days before carving them into shape with great precision.

boxing clever

Giles Oldershaw from Oxford, England, takes old pieces of corrugated cardboard and, using nothing more than tweezers, scalpels and scissors, turns them into stunning portraits of movie stars such as Marilyn Monroe, Marlon Brando and Bette Davis. He does not incorporate any ink, paint or charcoal in his works, using only the cardboard's layers to highlight the subject's facial features.

colorful cords

Founded by Keith and Stephanie Duffy from Salt Lake City, Utah, Little Cord Art creates custom-made artworks from newborn babies' umbilical cords. The customer sends a sample of the baby's cord to the artists, who put it on a microscope slide and cut it so that its cellular details become visible. The cross-section is then stained, magnified 400 times, photographed and framed to create a colorful digital picture of the baby's unique cord cells.

wooden puzzle

Dave Evans of Dorset, England, spent 35 days hand-cutting a 40,000-piece wooden jigsaw puzzle featuring 33 images of Queen Elizabeth II's Diamond Jubilee. However, as he was making final adjustments to the 21 x 8 ft (6.45 x 2.41 m) jigsaw on its sloped board mounting, the whole thing collapsed and it took him another four days to reassemble.

WOODEN BIKE

→ Istvan Puskas from Tizaors, Hungary, spent two years crafting a fully working motorbike from wood. He built the machine from weather-resistant black locust wood, embellishing it with deer antler decorations and adding handlebars and exhaust pipes made from cow horns. Even the gas tank is a small wooden barrel and fuels a small Fiat car engine, enabling the bike to reach a top speed of 17.5 mph (28 km/h).

PAPER BONES

➜ Canadian artist Maskull Lasserre intricately carved a human spine and ribcage into a compressed stack of ordinary daily newspapers. To maintain the required level of concentration, he worked in short bursts of no longer than an hour at a time. He says: "Paper is a very difficult medium to carve because of its grain and the fact the pages are not connected to each other laterally." Aside from newspapers, Maskull also works with different media such as books, tree branches and coat hangers.

spooky sculptures Sculptor Brandon Vickerd from Toronto, Ontario, created a series of taxidermy statues—human bodies dressed in hooded tops but with stuffed animal heads in place of their faces. He put his sculptures, which featured the heads of raccoons, skunks, squirrels and a bunch of ducklings, in busy areas of major cities to observe public reaction.

beaver bowls Artist Butch Anthony's Museum of Wonder at Seale, Alabama, includes such oddities as a chandelier made from cow bones and a range of bowls woven from sticks chewed by beavers. Even the bathroom windows in his house are made from gnawed beaver sticks.

clip art Every year for the past decade, Mike Drake from New York has collected hundreds of nail clippings and made a paperweight from them.

painting by jet Instead of traditional brushes, artist Princess Tarinan von Anhalt from Aventura, Florida, paints with $10-million airplane jet engines. She creates abstract artworks by hurling paints into the airflow of a Learjet engine, which splatters the colors onto a large 8 x 8 ft (2.4 x 2.4 m) canvas about 30 ft (9 m) away with a force many times stronger than a hurricane. The technique was pioneered by her late husband, Prinz Jurgen von Anhalt, 30 years ago and became so popular that her clients will pay $50,000 just to watch her work!

medical jars Artist Tamsin van Essen of London, England, has created a series of ceramic jars containing deliberate faults and blemishes to represent different illnesses and diseases. Inspired by apothecary jars of the 17th and 18th centuries, her "Medical Heirlooms" range includes acne, osteoporosis, psoriasis and scars, and, as family heirlooms, her jars can be passed down through generations like hereditary medical conditions.

miniature world Nichola Battilana from Brighton, Ontario, makes miniature landscapes in thimbles. She sculpts tiny houses with paper clay, uses tufts of moss to represent a garden and then carefully positions them in the thimble.

paper windows Eric Standley, an associate professor of art at Virginia Tech, creates 3-D images of beautiful Gothic stained-glass windows from hundreds of pieces of colored paper. With mathematical precision, he spends up to 80 hours laser-cutting the paper and he then stacks the cut pieces together into layers, often more than 100 deep, before binding the sheets together.

mini marxes To celebrate the 195th anniversary of Karl Marx's birth, artist Ottmar Hörl placed 500 miniature statues of him throughout the philosopher's hometown of Trier, Germany. The little Marx men were all the same size and shape, but were cast in different shades of red.

styrofoam ship In Jeddah, Saudi Arabia, a group of artists built a giant Styrofoam ship that measured 45 ft (13.6 m) high, 60 ft (18.4 m) long and 15 ft (4.5 m) wide.

passport picture Instead of a photograph on his passport, Swedish artist Fredrik Säker has a painted self-portrait. As government regulations stipulated that he had to submit a photo, he decided to photograph the brilliantly lifelike self-portrait that he had taken 100 hours to paint—and it was accepted without question.

heavy painting *The Rose*, a 1966 painting by San Francisco artist Jay DeFeo, used so much oil paint that it took eight years to complete and weighs more than 2,000 lb (908 kg).

smooth sculptures Artist Vipular Athukorale from Leicester, England, makes highly detailed sculptures—including a vintage Rolls-Royce and a scene from *Little Red Riding Hood*—out of margarine. First, he creates a wire frame and then he covers it in margarine, which he molds with tiny scalpels. His sculptures are up to 2 ft (60 cm) long and each one takes months but, as long as they are kept cold, they can last for years.

TREE HOLE PAINTINGS ➜ Art student Wang Yue uses tree trunks as her canvas to brighten up the streets of Shijiazhuang, China, a city with one of the worst levels of air pollution in the world. Once she has found a suitable hole, she composes a digital drawing before painting the image onto the exposed bark. Wang Yue has already created more than a dozen images, including pictures of raccoons, pandas, birds and botanic landscapes.

Human Frog

➜ Body-painter Johannes Stoetter from South Tyrol, Italy, produced this amazing image of a tropical tree frog resting on a leaf by using five cunningly camouflaged painted women to re-create the creature's torso, legs, arms and head.

He takes up to five months to plan each project, working out the coloring and the precise positioning of his human models. He then spends eight hours applying special breathable paint to their bodies to turn them into animals, fruit and landscapes that play unbelievable tricks on the viewer's eye.

He started body-painting in 2000 and has become so successful that in 2012 he became the world champion. He says: "Body-painting is special because the artwork is alive and can move. While a canvas painting lasts forever, a body-painting exists only for a few hours."

Wrapper's Delight

→ Artist Laura Benjamin from East Hampton, New York, used dozens of torn and cut candy wrappers to make this multi-layered collage of Miss Piggy, part of her Wrapper's Delight collection.

matchstick models Djordje Balac from Gospic, Croatia, has made a fully functional model of the world's largest crane—a Liebherr LTM 11200—from 175,518 matchsticks, 44 lb (20 kg) of glue and 17.6 lb (8 kg) of varnish. Working every day from 8 a.m. till midnight, it took him three months to make the crane, which, just like the real thing, has an extending arm. He has also made detailed matchstick models of trucks, complete with detachable cabins.

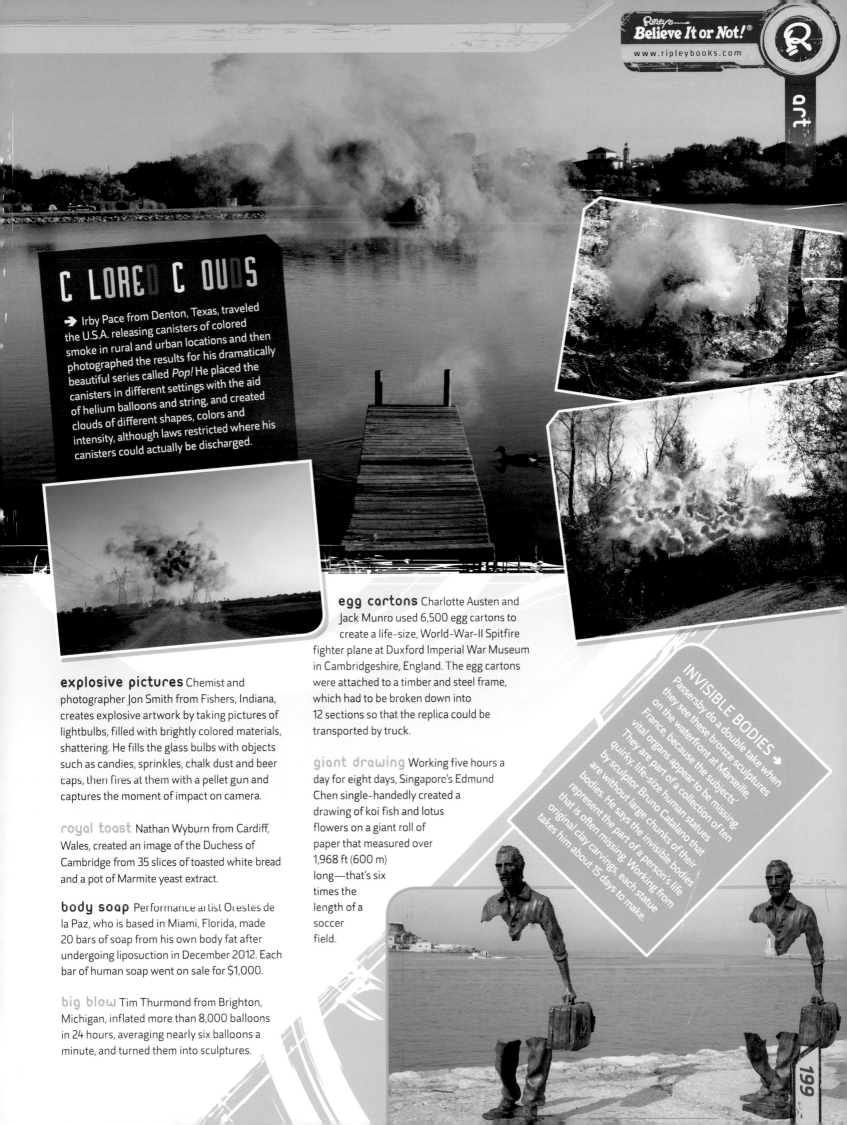

C LORED C OUDS

→ Irby Pace from Denton, Texas, traveled the U.S.A. releasing canisters of colored smoke in rural and urban locations and then photographed the results for his dramatically beautiful series called *Pop!* He placed the canisters in different settings with the aid of helium balloons and string, and created clouds of different shapes, colors and intensity, although laws restricted where his canisters could actually be discharged.

explosive pictures Chemist and photographer Jon Smith from Fishers, Indiana, creates explosive artwork by taking pictures of lightbulbs, filled with brightly colored materials, shattering. He fills the glass bulbs with objects such as candies, sprinkles, chalk dust and beer caps, then fires at them with a pellet gun and captures the moment of impact on camera.

royal toast Nathan Wyburn from Cardiff, Wales, created an image of the Duchess of Cambridge from 35 slices of toasted white bread and a pot of Marmite yeast extract.

body soap Performance artist Orestes de la Paz, who is based in Miami, Florida, made 20 bars of soap from his own body fat after undergoing liposuction in December 2012. Each bar of human soap went on sale for $1,000.

big blow Tim Thurmond from Brighton, Michigan, inflated more than 8,000 balloons in 24 hours, averaging nearly six balloons a minute, and turned them into sculptures.

egg cartons Charlotte Austen and Jack Munro used 6,500 egg cartons to create a life-size, World-War-II Spitfire fighter plane at Duxford Imperial War Museum in Cambridgeshire, England. The egg cartons were attached to a timber and steel frame, which had to be broken down into 12 sections so that the replica could be transported by truck.

giant drawing Working five hours a day for eight days, Singapore's Edmund Chen single-handedly created a drawing of koi fish and lotus flowers on a giant roll of paper that measured over 1,968 ft (600 m) long—that's six times the length of a soccer field.

INVISIBLE BODIES

→ Passersby do a double take when they see these bronze sculptures on the waterfront at Marseille, France, because the subjects' vital organs appear to be missing. They are part of a collection of ten quirky, life-size human statues by sculptor Bruno Catalano that are without large chunks of their bodies. He says the invisible bodies represent the part of a person's life that is often missing. Working from original clay carvings, each statue takes him about 15 days to make.

FEATHER ART → Chris Maynard from Olympia, Washington, creates beautiful images of flocks of birds by cutting into real feathers. He sources the feathers from private aviaries and zoos, waiting patiently for the right shape and coloration to become available. The feathers he uses come from a range of birds, including parrots, pigeons, crows, pheasants and turkeys. He strengthens the feathers with backing to stop them curling, and then working with magnifying glasses, tiny surgery scissors, scalpels and forceps, he carefully cuts and carves them before mounting them onto frames known as shadowboxes to create a 3-D effect.

beach debris Ukrainian artist Svetlana Ivanchenko creates intricate artworks from beach debris—sand, seashells, pebbles, tree roots and bark. Although it takes her eight hours to sift through and sort just 2 oz (50 g) of material, she has produced over 80 works in 12 years, including a lion emerging from undergrowth and a sleeping cherub. She uses no coloring and painstakingly arranges each item by hand.

art of regurgitation Los Angeles, California, artist John Knuth feeds ordinary houseflies water and sugar mixed with watercolor pigments and lets them paint by regurgitation. He harvests hundreds of thousands of flies from maggots he orders online and, after feeding them the mixture, he simply allows nature to take its course. Sure enough, within a few weeks his entire canvas is covered with millions of tiny colorful specks of fly vomit.

extreme exhibitions Australian artist Edgy has exhibited his paintings in the Qatar Desert at temperatures of more than 122°F (50°C) and at Mount Everest Base Camp at an altitude of 17,598 ft (5,365 m).

soapy pictures Amateur photographer Jane Thomas from Kilmarnock, Scotland, takes close-up pictures of soapy water and turns them into works of art that look like psychedelic paintings from the 1960s. She was inspired by seeing "the strange and fantastic patterns in soap" while she was washing dishes.

fingernail scenes Photographer and artist Alice Bartlett from London, England, creates miniature park scenes on her own fingernails. She coats her nails in textured green flocking to look like grass and then places tiny figures on them so that they appear to be enjoying a picnic or going for a stroll.

ticklish subject Instead of using oils or watercolors, artist Dinh Thong from Hoi An, Vietnam, creates imaginative pictures from chicken feathers. He gets his material from poultry markets, storing the feathers in plastic bags and spending hours sorting through them deciding which to use. After sketching an outline of his picture on paper, he glues the feathers over it, choosing different shades of brown and incorporating hundreds of feathers into his larger works.

PLAYING WITH FIRE

→ San Francisco, California, photographer Rob Prideaux literally plays with fire to achieve these pictures. Using a propane torch and a spray bottle, he sets fire to tiny amounts of gasoline in the loading bay of his studio and, with a wave sensor that reacts to the sound of the explosion to trigger the camera, he is able to capture that split second when flame erupts. He also creates patterns from smoke by burning incense in the dark and photographing it as it drifts through the air.

tiny ship Micro-artist Willard Wigan from Birmingham, England, has created a luxury watch featuring a model of a ship that is half the size of the period at the end of this sentence. He spent 672 hours crafting the watch, which is valued at $1.5 million because the ship and sails are made from 24-carat gold.

snot shots

→ Photographer Ulf Lundin invited models to his studio for an unusual and unflattering photo and video session—he asked them to sneeze into his camera and captured each nose explosion in graphic detail for a project named *Bless You*.

The Swedish artist was inspired by the drama and loss of control that everybody displays when they sneeze.

auto robot French artist Guillaume Reymond created an art installation called *Transformers* from more than a dozen real vehicles—cars, vans and trucks. He carefully positioned each vehicle so that when viewed from above, the arrangement looked like a giant Transformer robot.

perfect pictures Using just pencils, oil paints and charcoal, Zimbabwe-born artist Craig Wylie creates huge portraits that are so accurate they are often mistaken for photographs. Working from images on his laptop screen, which enables him to zoom in on the tiniest facial detail, he spends up to three months on each piece, his largest to date measuring 6½ x 9¾ ft (2 x 3m).

chewed gum Ukrainian artist Anna-Sofiya Matveeva creates portraits of celebrities such as Elton John and the late Steve Jobs from hundreds of pieces of gum chewed by her friends. After separating the gum into different colors and shades, she warms it up in a microwave. Each finished artwork can weigh up to 11 lb (5 kg).

chain quilt Artist and cyclist John Lefelhocz of Athens, Ohio, created a quilt made entirely out of hundreds of individually hand-painted bicycle chains.

CRUSHED MAN

➜ It looks like this homeless man has been crushed under the corner of a falling apartment block in Prague, Czech Republic—but it is really a wacky urban artwork by Italian artist Fra Biancoshock whose "pop up" installations have been appearing unannounced in streets all over Europe.

MANA LISA ➜ Established in 1994 by antique dealer Scott Wilson and his friend Jerry Reilly, the Museum of Bad Art in Boston, Massachusetts, proudly collects, celebrates and exhibits over 600 pieces of art that are so bad they are good! Thousands of visitors flock to the museum every year to see original works such as the *Mana Lisa*, an anonymously painted, cross-gender version of Leonardo da Vinci's masterpiece.

mini lisa Scientists at Georgia Institute of Technology created a copy of Leonardo da Vinci's *Mona Lisa* that is just one-third of the width of a human hair in size. They used an atomic force microscope and heat-based nanotechnology to make the tiny painting. By varying the amount of heat applied at each pixel, they were able to control the picture's shades to accurately replicate the original.

boxed in Artist Tyler Ramsey, based in Los Angeles, California, spent a week living in a storefront window of a shoe store in Venice Beach. Between eating, sleeping and chatting to passersby, he customized newly bought shoes at the store by painting them with his fingers.

body-painting A team of artists body-painted 316 people in just five hours at Cork, Ireland. The models removed all their clothes apart from their underwear before paint was applied to every exposed part of their bodies except for the soles of their feet.

LEONARDO DA VINCI COULD WRITE WITH ONE HAND AND PAINT WITH THE OTHER SIMULTANEOUSLY.

graffiti revenge A worker was sent to remove graffiti from a wall in London, England, just eight hours after stencil artist DS had finished creating it. Frustrated, DS secretly photographed the man as he worked and painted an image of him on the same wall a few hours later!

rock gods French photographer Léo Caillard gave iconic statues of ancient Greek gods a hip makeover by dressing them in Ray Bans, rolled up chinos and check shirts. Unable to dress the actual statues from the Louvre art gallery in Paris, France, he instead sought people with the same body shape as the gods. After photographing the statues, he took pictures of his models in hipster clothing and in identical poses to the gods before mixing the two images in post-production using Photoshop.

empty frames The Gardner Museum in Boston, Massachusetts, has 13 empty picture frames where $500-million-worth of paintings stolen in 1990 once hung.

nutty celebs Steve Casino from Fort Thomas, Kentucky, turns peanut shells into $500 mini statues of celebrities including Elton John, Sean Connery and Joey Ramone. Having found a shell the right shape for his subject, he removes the nuts, glues the shell back together and sands down the surface. Using a tiny brush, he then applies acrylic paint before creating arms, legs and any props from wood, bamboo or dense foam.

genetic likeness New York City student Heather Dewey-Hagborg creates portrait sculptures from DNA she finds on discarded chewing gum, hairs and cigarette butts. She extracts the genetic material in a laboratory and then uses a computer program to build up an idea of the person's physical features before turning the information into sculptures for her *Stranger Visions* project.

egg-straordinary Vietnamese Ben Tre uses a tiny electrical dentist's drill to carve detailed portraits and landscapes onto eggshells. Each artwork takes a day and because the shells are not chemically hardened, they are extremely fragile, so he offers customers the option of having them encased in a glass globe for protection.

paper towels To give his artworks extra depth, artist Ken Delmar from Stamford, Connecticut, uses absorbent kitchen paper towels as his canvas—and sells his oil paintings on them for up to $10,000. He discovered his unlikely medium by accident. One evening he was cleaning his paintbrushes with paper towels and noticed that the colors on the towels were more vibrant than on the actual painting.

water colors Wearing full diving gear, Ukrainian artist Alexander Belozor paints underwater landscapes—at depths of up to 85 ft (26 m). His canvases are covered in a waterproof coating to prevent the colors running.

ROCKY IMAGE

→ This might be Sylvester Stallone like he has never been seen before, but, believe it or not, there is a real person underneath.

It is the work of artist Marie-Lou Desmeules from Quebec, who uses layers of paint, hair and plastic to turn her human models into exaggerated sculptures of iconic figures such as Michael Jackson, Pamela Anderson, Barbie and Sly.

Ripley's ask

What gave you the idea for your human sculptures? *Sitting in my workshop in Berlin in 2008, I decided to mold my boyfriend so that he blended into the wall behind him. I evolved the techniques I used that day to the more aesthetic techniques I use for my sculptures now. I began making the celebrity sculptures in 2012.*

Why did you choose celebrities as your subjects? *I wanted to challenge stereotypes—the judgments we make without knowing the person. The series* Celebrities *was inspired by society's obsession with plastic surgery—with image, identity and consumerism.*

Why did you choose Rambo as one of your subjects? *Rambo is a very complex and controversial character. I think his muscular body represents a shell that actually hides a sad interior. My next subject is going to be David Bowie.*

How long does each sculpture take? *I research each subject, then collect ideas and materials. This process may take one day—or one lifetime! The creation (or "surgery" as I call it) takes three hours including the time for the transformation, the lighting and the photographing. The model wears the sculpture for about 15 minutes before we take the photograph.*

What materials do you use? *I use mostly acrylic paint, sheets of plastic, lengths of hair, duct tape, clothes, paper and anything else useful that comes my way.*

Finally, if you were a human sculpture, who would you be? *I would like to sculpt myself into the Invisible Man.*

CANDY murals

➔ **Artist Kristen Cumings from Martinez, California, makes amazing pictures from thousands of colorful jellybeans.**

As well as recreating iconic artworks, such as Van Gogh's *Starry Night*, Kristen has immortalized her son (below, left) and her young neighbor (below) in Jelly Belly Bean Art portraits. Starting from a photo of the subject, she paints an acrylic version onto a blank canvas. When it has dried, she applies the beans, matching the colors to the original as closely as possible and using spray adhesive to make sure the beans stick.

mini monet By the age of ten, talented landscape artist Kieron Williamson from Norfolk, England, had made more than £1.4 million ($2.2 million) from the sales of his paintings. His artworks are so sought-after that a 2013 sale of 23 of his paintings raised more than £230,000 ($360,000) in just 20 minutes.

gum metropolis Inspired by houses of cards and matchstick constructions, artist Jeremy Laffon from Marseille, France, took nearly three months to build a 6.6-ft-tall (2-m), 10-ft-long (3-m) city skyline from 4,000 pieces of chewing gum. The sticks of gum were stacked, carefully balanced and assembled into towers, held upright initially with just his saliva before he eventually had to use glue. Finally, he melted a few pieces of gum so that the skyline would gradually crumble to the ground, replicating a city that had turned to rubble.

SCREW HEADS

→ Believe it or not, this lifelike crumpled shirt was created from around 6,500 metal screw heads. It is the work of Andrew Myers from Laguna Beach, California, who draws his outlines on wood before drilling in thousands of screws at various depths to create an amazing 3-D effect. He then paints each screw individually by hand to form a finished piece that is a drawing, sculpture and painting all in one.

shoe animals Kenya's Ocean Sole company has made more than 100 different sculptures from old flip-flops that have been discarded on the country's beaches, including elephants, warthogs and an 18-ft-tall (5.5-m) rubber giraffe.

cork rhino Californians Jim and Mary Lambert from Carmichael, and Bob and Di Nelson from Fair Oaks, spent three years making a life-sized, 12-ft-long (3.6-m) rhinoceros sculpture out of plywood, foam and 12,000 wine-bottle corks. Jim has been collecting corks for 20 years and named the sculpture *Rhinocirrhosis* after the liver disease often caused by heavy drinking.

rubber duck Since 2007, several giant yellow PVC rubber ducks created by Dutch artist Florentijn Hofman have made a big splash in cities all over the world, appearing in harbors in Japan, Australia, New Zealand, Brazil, the Netherlands and China.

rice statue New York City–based artist Saeri Kiritani created a 5-ft-tall (1.5-m), life-sized sculpture of herself by gluing together one million grains of rice. Even the statue's hair was made from rice noodles.

gnome invasion More than 2,300 paintings of gnomes—with little red hats, white beards and brown shoes—suddenly started appearing on telephone poles all over Oakland, California, in 2012. The hand-painted portraits on 6-in (15-cm) blocks of wood proved so popular that the Pacific Gas & Electric Co. decided to leave them in place.

space fillers Swedish artist Michael Johansson creates large Tetris-like installations filled precisely with diverse everyday objects including wardrobes, filing cabinets, household appliances, suitcases and even cars, caravans and tractors. His colorful, compartmentalized artworks have occupied spaces in abandoned storefronts, between buildings and between stacked shipping containers.

bargain buy Russian artist Ilya Bolotowsky's painting *Vertical Diamond* sold at an auction for $34,375—five months after Beth Feeback from Concord, North Carolina, had bought it at a Goodwill store for $10.

corn mural Murals made from 275,000 ears of corn of different colors, including blue, orange and black, decorate the exterior and interior of the Corn Palace building in Mitchell, South Dakota. The corn murals are changed annually and have portrayed such iconic American images as Mount Rushmore and cowboys riding horses.

egg shell Manjit Kumar Shah from Assam, India, used a black gel pen to draw 1,615 portraits of Mahatma Gandhi onto a single eggshell.

bidding frenzy British artist Francis Bacon's studies of his friend Lucian Freud sold for $142.4 million at auction in New York City in 2013—after just six minutes of bidding, with the price going up at $395,500 a second.

petroleum portraits Belarusian artist Ludmila Zhizhenko paints with petroleum. She needs only ⅓ oz (10 g) of petroleum for one of her typical oil paintings, which resemble vintage, yellowed photos. However, because of the dangerous fumes, she usually has to paint outdoors and has to keep the finished paintings away from fire.

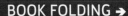

BOOK FOLDING →
Through painstaking hand cutting and origami folding, Isaac G. Salazar from Artesia, New Mexico, gives new life to old books by turning their paper pages into works of art that spell out words such as "Read," "Dream," "Faith" and "Love." A full-time accountant who has never been to art class, Isaac works on art in his spare time. Each piece can take him anything from two days to two weeks.

PUMPKIN ART

→ **For its month-long 2013 Halloween Fest, Ocean Park theme park in Hong Kong exhibited the world's largest collection of pickled pumpkin sculptures—more than 400 spooky designs created by master carvers Ray Villafane and Andy Bergholtz.**

The centerpiece was a grotesque gremlin carved from a giant pumpkin (right) weighing more than 1,000 lb (454 kg), which had been specially handpicked by Ray in the U.S.A. Using just spoons and scalpels, Ray and his team spent hours on each sculpture before the finished pumpkins were immersed in vinegar to preserve them for visitors to enjoy.

When looking for a good pumpkin to carve, Ray selects the meatiest. "I also like a pumpkin with character—one with knobbly ridges is good so that I can utilize that in the carving process, like sculpting noses." However, because the process is unpredictable, he can never be sure whether the texture or flesh color will be ideal for sculpting until he actually starts carving.

His previous lifelike pumpkin sculptures have included gorillas, clowns, birds and actor Johnny Depp. He began carving pumpkins one day to entertain his art students at a school when he lived in Bellaire, Michigan. "Sculpting has always been my passion," he says, "but most importantly the kids at school absolutely loved them. For days after that there would be a dozen pumpkins sitting on my desk waiting for me to carve them."

The finished designs are dipped in vinegar to preserve them.

Ray uses the natural textures in the pumpkin flesh to work on his design's features.

Andy cuts away the skin of the pumpkin before setting to work, using just a scalpel and a spoon.

CHOCOLATE ONIONS
For a real sweet-and-sour taste, Chocolate by Mueller sells onions covered in white or milk chocolate at its store in Reading Terminal Market, Philadelphia, Pennsylvania. The idea originated back in 1981 when a TV comedy show asked Mueller to make something crazy for Valentine's Day. As well as the $5 chocolate onions, Mueller sells chocolates in the form of life-sized, anatomically correct hearts, lungs, kidneys, ears and teeth.

hot pizza Using ghost chili enhanced with a special chili paste, Paul Brayshaw of East Sussex, England, has created the Saltdean Sizzler, a pizza that is three times hotter than police pepper spray.

lab burger At a cost of $325,000, Dr. Mark Post of Maastricht University in the Netherlands has grown a beef burger in a laboratory from the stem cells of a cow.

fruit cake Three hundred children in Managua, Nicaragua, baked a giant fruitcake that stretched 1,640 ft (500 m)—the length of four city blocks—and weighed 31,865 lb (14,454 kg). The cake included more than 60,000 eggs.

spicy sauces Vic Clinco from Phoenix, Arizona, has a collection of more than 6,000 bottles of hot chili sauces. He has been collecting for nearly 20 years and his most expensive bottle is worth around $1,500.

sweating mushroom The "sweating mushroom" of Europe and North America causes uncontrollable sweating and crying if ingested.

heavy cup In 2012, In London, England, kitchen appliance manufacturer De'Longhi made a coffee cup that was 9½ ft (2.9 m) high and 8½ ft (2.6 m) wide and held 3,434 gal (13,000 l) of coffee. When full it weighed nearly 14 tons—the same as a double-decker bus laden with passengers.

Scary Cake

David and Natalie were watching a horror movie when she came up with the idea for a severed head wedding cake.

➜ For her marriage to a horror movie fan, cake artist Natalie Sideserf designed a gruesome wedding cake in the shape of their severed heads.

Topped with buttercream frosting and modeling chocolate, the cake showed Natalie and husband David with blank eyes, matted hair and blood seeping out of their necks. After their Halloween season wedding in Austin, Texas, Natalie admitted that her grandma was not too keen on the gory cake but had appreciated the detail and realism of the heads.

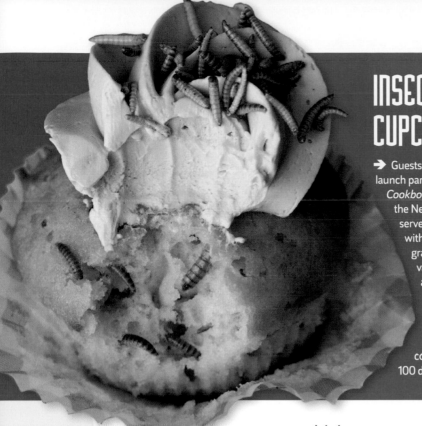

INSECT CUPCAKES

➔ Guests attending the launch party for *The Insect Cookbook* in Wageningen, the Netherlands, were served cupcakes topped with maggots or glazed grasshoppers. Henk van Gurp, who co-authored the book, which promotes the eating of protein-rich insects, also cooked a giant pie containing more than 100 dead grasshoppers.

silent supper Eat restaurant in Brooklyn, New York City, runs special events where customers have to eat their meals in complete silence. It's the idea of head chef Nicholas Nauman, and if customers make so much as a sound, they have to finish their food outside on a bench.

chinese fan Since 1955, Los Angeles attorney David Chan has eaten at more than 6,300 Chinese restaurants—and he has kept a spreadsheet documenting his experiences at every single one.

oldest diner Franks Diner in Kenosha, Wisconsin, claims to be the oldest continuously operating lunch car in the United States. Old-timers recall it being pulled to its 58th Street location in 1926 by six horses.

worm soup Earthworm soup is a popular dish in the Guandong Province of China and is thought to cure fevers.

dumpster diet To raise awareness about the amount of food wasted in the U.S., Rob Greenfield from San Diego, California, ate only out of dumpsters for a week—and managed to fill his fridge with fresh fruit, vegetables and bagels worth $200.

chocolate sausage Chefs in Cavalese, Italy, used chocolate, eggs, butter and cookies to make a 250-ft-long (76-m) chocolate sausage on a row of tables that stretched through the town center.

sun baked People in Villaseca, Chile, use only the sun to cook their food—and have found that their solar-powered ovens can generate temperatures of 356°F (180°C). The region has over 300 days of sunshine a year and turned to solar-powered cooking after wood, which had previously fueled ovens, became scarce.

armpit cheese U.S. scientist Christina Agapakis and Norwegian scent expert Sissel Tolaas have made a range of 11 cheeses from skin bacteria found in human feet, belly buttons and armpits. Each cheese was created from starter cultures sampled from human skin and taken from volunteers by means of sterile cotton swabs.

dream diet To celebrate the German beer festival Oktoberfest, Evo Terro from Arizona drinks up to six beers a day and eats only sausages for the whole of October—a total of about 15,000 calories a week. Amazingly, his diet results in him losing up to 14 lb (6 kg) in weight and his cholesterol dropping by a third.

rich honey Elvish honey is extracted from caves, not hives, and at $6,800 per kilo it is as expensive as a small car. The mineral-rich, natural honey is prized because it can only be found lining the walls of a 5,900-ft-deep (1,800-m) cave in Turkey's Saricayir Valley.

fruit feast To celebrate the start of the 2013–14 academic year, 500 students and staff from the University of Massachusetts created a 15,000-lb (6,800-kg) fruit salad that was so big it had to be mixed in a swimming pool. The salad contained 150 different varieties of fruit, including 20 varieties of apple and 19 varieties of melon.

PRINCELY PIZZA ➔ Restaurant owner Domenico Crolla from Glasgow, Scotland, created a pizza decorated to show the Duke and Duchess of Cambridge holding their newborn baby, Prince George. He used a scalpel to sculpt the cheese and tomato and coated the finished artwork in resin to preserve it. He has also made pizza portraits of Barack Obama, Marilyn Monroe and Marlon Brando.

lord of the rings At the first Riders 4 Relief National Onion Ring Eating Championship, held in Coshocton, Ohio, in May 2013, Jamie "The Bear" McDonald of Granby, Connecticut, ate 6.73 lb (3.1 kg) of onion rings in only eight minutes.

monster cheesecake At the 9th Annual Cream Cheese Festival in Lowville, New York, Philadelphia Cream Cheese unveiled a 6,900-lb (3,130-kg) cheesecake that was big enough to serve 24,533 people! It was prepared in a pan that measured 90 in (2.25 m) in diameter and was 30 in (0.75 m) deep.

wedding reception After a string of burger-joint dates, Steven and Emily Asher held their wedding reception at a McDonald's in Bristol, England. They arrived by stretch limo and paid £150 ($225) to feed 33 guests with milkshakes and McNuggets.

champion chopper Using just a sharp knife, Orlando, Florida, grocery store manager Matt Jones can slice and dice an entire watermelon in 21 seconds.

banana binge After Damu Gupta was arrested for stealing and swallowing a train passenger's gold chain on a journey from Mumbai to Gondia, Indian police forced him to eat 96 bananas over a three-day period so that they could retrieve the jewelry in his poop.

milk boost Dairy cows fitted with dentures can chew for longer than cows with regular teeth, enabling them to produce more milk.

steel cubes To cater for people who like their drinks on the rocks, but do not want extra water from melting ice, Dave Laituri from Wayland, Massachusetts, has designed ice cubes made from stainless steel. He was inspired by 20th-century French designer Raymond Loewy, who used to drink scotch chilled with ball bearings.

raw blood Tiet Canh, a soup made with raw ducks' blood, infused with herbs and nuts and served cold, is a popular dish in Vietnam.

special melons The Japanese Yubari melon is the most expensive fruit in the world. In 2008, one pair sold for more than $30,000.

radioactive rum As an alternative to the lengthy process of maturing cachaça —a rum-like spirit—in barrels, Brazilian researchers have tried zapping the drink with gamma radiation for a few minutes. They say, not only is it much quicker than the barrel method, it is also safe to drink immediately after being irradiated.

pumpkin worship Residents of Bokaro, India, began worshiping and leaving offerings to a huge oval 190-lb (86-kg) pumpkin in March 2013, believing it to be a reincarnation of the Hindu god Shiva. The pumpkin bore a resemblance to a shivalinga—a symbolic object used for worship in Hindu temples.

clean bowls The Hachikyo seafood restaurant in Sapporo, Japan, issues fines to customers who don't finish one of the restaurant's signature meals—right down to the last grain of rice.

recycled pee NASA scientists have designed special bags for astronauts to urinate in, which then turns their urine into a safe, pleasant-tasting, sugary drink.

TUNA EYEBALLS

→ If you don't mind your food looking back at you, tuna eyeballs can be found staring at you in most Japanese stores for $1. The eyeball is surrounded by fish fat and severed muscles that, when cooked and seasoned, are said to taste like squid.

ACTUAL SIZE!

watermelon Brain

→ Qian Weicheng, a student from Beijing, China, created this lifelike replica of a human brain by carving into a watermelon with a spoon.

He has carved more than 40 designs from watermelon flesh, including an elegant rose, a skeleton hand and a miniature Eiffel Tower. Each sculpture takes him up to an hour to complete and, after photographing it, he promptly eats it.

sausage charge Bradley Davidson of Perth, Scotland, was cleared in 2012 on a charge of behaving aggressively with a blood sausage.

coconut curse Police seized an inscribed coconut from a polling station on Guraidhoo—an island in the Maldives—for fear that it had black magic powers and was being used to influence voters in the country's 2013 presidential election.

beer room Market research company PAR Research has an 11,000-sq-ft (1,020-sq-m) test room at its headquarters in Evansville, Indiana, which is full of more than 17,300 unique beer bottles and nearly 12,000 different brands of beer from around the world.

extra dry Pakistan's 153-year-old Murree Brewery produces millions of barrels of beer a year—in a country in which it is illegal for 97 percent of the population to drink it.

mighty dog Big Hot Dog in Chicago, Illinois, makes a hot dog that weighs 7 lb (3.1 kg), measures 16 in (40 in) long and 4 in (10 cm) thick and can serve 40 people.

canned meal British student Chris Godfrey has created a 12-course meal in a can. With 12 different layers of food, the "All In One" includes French onion soup, ravioli, halibut, shiitake mushroom, pork belly, rib-eye steak, crack pie and ice cream, and pastry and coffee.

holy veg After Praful Visram, a caterer from Leicester, England, spotted an eggplant that resembled Ganesh, the Hindu elephant god, he placed it in the firm's temple, where people come to pray to the holy vegetable. Once rotten, the eggplant was given a Hindu funeral.

short stay The 1,500-seater McDonald's restaurant, the largest in the world, at the London 2012 Olympic Park was open for only six weeks.

chicken feet Packets of fried chicken feet are sold in Chinese supermarkets as a snack, often seasoned with rice vinegar and chili.

choc loco Chocolate artist Andrew Farrugia of Malta spent more than 700 hours creating a chocolate sculpture of a train measuring 112 ft (34 m) long and weighing 2,755 lb (1,250 kg).

bacon sandwich Paul Philips, a café owner from Cheltenham, England, has created a £150 ($237) bacon sandwich made from seven slices of bacon from a rare-breed pig, truffle spread, a free-range egg, sliced truffles, saffron and edible gold dust. It is cooked in truffle oil.

caffeine shot For coffee lovers, a popular toothpaste company has devised a special toothbrush that releases a shot of caffeine directly into your mouth while you are brushing your teeth.

birthday cake Competitive eater Matt Stonie from San José, California, consumed 5½ lb (2.5 kg) of birthday cake in just under nine minutes at his 21st-birthday party on May 26, 2013.

exploding chutney A jar of exploding rhubarb chutney blew the door off the fridge in Margaret Goodwin's retirement apartment in Oxfordshire, England, flinging it across the kitchen and causing widespread damage to the walls and ceiling. The chutney, a gift from a friend, exploded after gas had fermented and built up inside the jar.

poppadom pile Tipu Rahman, a chef from an Indian restaurant in Northampton, England, spent two hours creating a 5-ft-8-in (1.7-m) stack of 1,280 poppadoms.

snake sausage Speciality Meats & Gourmet of Hudson, Wisconsin, sells sausages made from equal part rattlesnake and rabbit meat, flavored with jalapenos.

SHELL CHICKEN → Designer Kyle Bean, based in London, England, made this ingenious chicken sculpture titled *What Came First?* by patiently gluing together dozens of eggshells of varying colors that he had collected from his local bakery.

final burger When fast-food fan David Kime Jr. died on January 20, 2013, at age 88, the funeral procession stopped at his favorite restaurant, a branch of Burger King in York, Pennsylvania, where each mourner got a burger for the road. Kime had one last burger, too—it was placed atop his coffin at the cemetery.

resignation cake When Chris Holmes, a part-time baker from Cambridgeshire, England, decided to quit his day job as an immigration officer at Stansted Airport, he baked a cake for his bosses and wrote his resignation on it piped in frosting.

ROTTEN EGG

→ Century egg is a Chinese dish where an egg is preserved for several months in a mixture of clay, ash and lime. This turns the egg yolk dark green and gives it a putrid stench of sulfur.

lime pie At Key West, Florida, in July 2013, bakers prepared an 8¼-ft-wide (2.5-m) key-lime pie. Containing 5,760 key limes, 200 lb (91 kg) of graham crackers and 55 gal (208 l) of condensed milk, the pie was big enough to feed 1,000 people.

monthly bill U.S. presidents must pay for all of their food in the White House. They receive a food bill every month.

the big pitcher Staff at Ceviche Tapas Bar & Restaurant in Tampa, Florida, served 270 gal (1,022 l) of Sangria—made from 200 gal (758 l) of red wine, 17 gal (63 l) of brandy, 17 gal (63 l) of triple sec, 28 gal (126 l) of syrup and 505 lb (229 kg) of fruit—in a huge, 9-ft-tall (2.7-m) pitcher.

long fry Kim Medford of Waynesville, North Carolina, was eating a meal in an Arby's fast-food restaurant when she found a curly fry that measured 38 in (95 cm) long.

chocolate castle A 10-ft-high (3-m) castle made out of 90,000 sugar-coated chocolate pebbles was built on the beach at Brighton, England. The colorful chocolates were stuck to a mainframe with the help of a quarter of a ton of fondant icing and 44 lb (20 kg) of icing sugar.

table for two A restaurant in Vacone, Italy, seats only two people. The Solo Per Due (Italian for "just for two") is so exclusive that it has just one table and a set price of $335 per person (not including wine and champagne)!

swallowed toe In a display of bravado, a U.S. worker swallowed a pickled human toe at the Downtown Hotel in Dawson City, Yukon, in 2013. The preserved toe is the focal point of the Sourtoe cocktail, a 40-year-old ritual, which requires customers merely to touch the toe with their lips while downing their drink. However, this customer swished the toe into his mouth, washed it down with a beer chaser and then slapped $500 onto the bar—the hotel's fine for toe-swallowing. The tradition began in 1973 after the frostbitten toe of a former proprietor was found in a nearby cabin. Since that event more than 60,000 people have downed the unique cocktail.

dinosaur cake Asked by her son Logan to bake him a dinosaur cake for his eighth birthday party, Maria Young from Portsmouth, England, created a 4½-ft (1.4-m) model of a triceratops. Even though she had only ever baked three cakes in her life, she spent five days beating 130 eggs to make the body and used up 12 boxes of puffed rice to shape the legs and head.

ZOMBIE CAKE

➜ We've all seen cakes that look too beautiful to eat...
well, this zombie cake looks too terrifying to eat.

It was made by Elizabeth Marek from Portland, Oregon, who began her
monstrous creation by layering cake over an internal structure that was used
to keep the torso, head and arm upright. She then used Rice Krispie Treats to
build up the ribcage and hideous facial features. She made the single eye and
ripped shirt from fondant before painting the eyeball with food coloring. She
also added melted marshmallows to make it look as if the face had simply
rotted away. The entire zombie cake took three days to make.

The zombie's brain
was made from
strawberry jello.

The spine and
skin were textured
using a sculpting
tool and then
colored with
oil-based food
coloring, modeling
chocolate and
petal dust.

feces wine A traditional South Korean health drink is made from human or animal feces. *Ttongsul*, or feces wine, is made by pouring distilled grain alcohol into a pit filled with chicken, dog or human feces and leaving it to ferment for three months. Extra ingredients are added to the mix, including herbs, ash trees and cat bones! The liquid is then extracted from the pit and drunk straight.

hot egg India Dining, a restaurant in Surrey, England, has created a spicy chocolate Easter egg that is as hot as 400 bottles of Tabasco sauce. The "Not for Bunnies" egg, made from fiery ghost chili, Scotch bonnet and habanero chilies and Belgian chocolate, is so hot that it can only be served to over 18s—and even then they must sign a disclaimer and wear protective gloves before they take a bite.

garlic shrine The Stinking Rose restaurant in San Francisco, California, serves more than 3,000 lb (1,360 kg) of garlic every month and is home to dozens of items of garlic-related memorabilia, including a braid composed of 2,635 garlic bulbs.

busy restaurant The Varsity in Atlanta, Georgia, is the largest drive-in restaurant in the world, serving up to 40,000 people every day.

elephant dung Coffee made from beans plucked from elephant dung sells for $50 a cup at the Anantara Hotel in Golden Triangle, Thailand.

frog tubes A popular Chinese dessert called *hasma* is made from the fallopian tubes of the Asiatic grass frog. It is sold in dried form, but when soaked in water it expands to form a gelatinous mass. Sweetened with rock sugar, *hasma* is often served with milk as a tapioca-like dessert or as an ice-cream topping. It is said to promote healthy skin and fertility.

squid bottles In Japan's Fukui Prefecture, the dried bodies of whole squid are traditionally used as liquor bottles.

big bag Planet Organic, a tea company from Queensland, Australia, made a tea bag that was 10 ft (3 m) high, weighed 332 lb (151 kg) and was big enough to brew a staggering 100,000 cups of tea.

live bomb While gutting a squid caught off Guangdong Province, China, fishmonger Mr. Huang hit an 8-in (20-cm) live bomb with his knife. The bomb, which the squid had mistaken for part of its usual diet, was safely detonated at another location.

super sundae An ice-cream sundae made from 212 gal (803 l) of ice cream stretched out on tables over a distance of 1,101 ft (335 m) at White Bear Lake, Minnesota—covering three blocks of the city.

baker's error When 22-year-old Laura Gambrel from Zionsville, Indiana, graduated from university, her proud mother Carol ordered a graduation cake with a cap drawn on it. However, the baker misheard her instruction and when the cake was delivered it had a drawing of a cat perched on top of her daughter's head instead!

← MOON CAKES →

→ These cheeky butt-shaped moon cakes—complete with confectionery thong and hand—were baked by a Hong Kong firm for the Singapore Full Moon Festival in reference to the eighth lunar month, which in Cantonese is a slang word for "buttocks."

sandwich riot A 45-minute riot involving 60 inmates of New York's Rikers Island prison was started by an argument over a grilled cheese sandwich. Eleven prisoners were injured in the battle—some with stab wounds—after members of the Dominican Trinitarians were apparently upset when a rival gang refused to let them cook the snack on a kitchen hot plate.

fork lift A British company has invented a dumbbell cutlery set that includes a 2.2-lb (1-kg) fork and a 4.4-lb (2-kg) dessertspoon, so you can get fit while you eat.

banana bonanza The Cabot Creamery Co-Operative created a 400-gal (1,515-l) smoothie in New York City—made from more than 3,200 bananas, one ton of ice and nearly 1,000 lb (454 kg) of yogurt.

scorpion addict Scorpion farmer Ismail Jasim Mohammed of Samarra, Iraq, has been eating potentially deadly live scorpions daily for over 15 years. He says getting stung a few times has made him immune to the venom.

big steak The Duck Inn in Redditch, England, has a £110 ($177), 150-oz (4.2-kg) steak on the menu that is free to anyone who finishes it in under an hour. Heavier than most newborn babies, the steak is typically 12 in (30 cm) long, 12 in (30 cm) wide and 4 in (10 cm) thick, and it needs two hours to cook it medium rare.

chocolate stamps The Belgian Post Office released a grand total of 538,000 chocolate-flavored stamps for Easter 2013. The stamps had pictures of chocolate on the front and essence of cacao oil impregnated in the glue at the back to give them a chocolate taste when licked. The ink with which they were printed was also infused with cacao oil so that the stamps smelled of chocolate.

burger king Dennis Rosinlof from Salt Lake City, Utah, has eaten 12,000 Big Macs over the past 30 years, consuming at least ten a week. The only day he takes a break is Sunday, when his wife Lauri cooks him a meal. In spite of his fast-food diet, the 64-year-old salesman is fit and healthy at 6 ft (1.8 m) tall, weighing 165 lb (75 kg) and with a good cholesterol level.

Live Octopus

→ **This man at a food festival in Seoul, South Korea, is eating an octopus that is still very much alive.**

Festival-goers can pull the wriggling creatures out of a bucket and then force the tentacles into their mouth—no mean feat when the suction pads on the eight arms automatically cling on to fingers, lips, cheeks and even the inside of the mouth. Novices are strongly advised to chew thoroughly before swallowing because they might choke to death if the octopus tries to climb back up their throat.

SOME CREATURES THAT HUMANS EAT ALIVE

For the Japanese dish *ikizukuri*, **fish** are filleted without being killed and are served while their hearts are still beating and their mouths are gasping.

In China, live **shrimps** are often doused in strong liquor, not only for taste, but also because it makes them drunk and therefore less likely to struggle when swallowed.

In some Vietnamese restaurants, people eat live **cobra** —the snake is decapitated at the table, the venom and the blood are drained into a bottle ready to be drunk and then its still-beating heart is placed on a saucer to be eaten by the bravest diner.

Live **scorpion** is a Chinese delicacy, and although diners occasionally get stung in the mouth as they swallow, apparently the swelling soon goes down and is a small price to pay for the delicious taste.

The Japanese dish, frog sashimi, is often served alongside a freshly killed dead **frog** while the creature's heart is still beating.

spit drink Masato, a traditional drink in Amazonian Peru, is full of human saliva. It is home-brewed from the root of the cassava plant, chunks of which are chewed by local women before the liquid part is spat back into a vat. Proteins in the spit spark fermentation and produce a cloudy white drink with a sweet and sour taste.

prison food Visitors to the Prison Cafeteria at Japan's Abashirishi Prison are served the same food that the inmates eat on a daily basis.

dried grub A 22-year-old man who flew from Burkina Faso to England in 2013 and was stopped at London's Gatwick Airport with 207 lb (94 kg) of dried caterpillars in his luggage told customs officers that the insects were intended as food for his personal consumption.

hornet vodka A rare type of Japanese vodka is made from fermented giant hornets—venomous insects with quarter-inch stingers that cause over 40 human deaths every year. The hornets are left to ferment in alcohol for three years, producing a muddy-brown liquor that smells like rotting flesh and has a salty aftertaste from the insects' poison.

chocolate mosaic In the town of Bendigo in Victoria, Australia, in March 2013, more than 1,000 chocolate bars were arranged to form a mosaic measuring 233 sq ft (21.6 sq m) and spelling "Happy Easter."

chili champ Tim "Eater X" Janus of New York City ate 2 gal (8 l) of chili in just six minutes to win Ben's Chili Bowl's World Chili Eating Championship in October 2012.

$1,000 pizza Nino's Bellissima Pizzeria in Manhattan, New York City, sells a 12-in (30-cm) pizza that costs $1,000—share it between eight for $125 a slice! The luxury pizza features six different types of caviar and has pieces of Maine lobster sprinkled on top.

fiery pepper The Trinidad Moruga Scorpion, the world's hottest pepper, is 800 times hotter than a jalapeno and as potent as weapons-grade pepper spray.

turned green A 24-year-old man was hospitalized in Guizhou Province, China, after turning green because he ate too many snails. The man had been feasting daily on river snails. However, parasitic worms that live in the snails had entered his body and caused an infection in his liver, which made his skin go green.

Death Row
DINNERS

➜ **Since 2000, Oregon artist Julie Green has painted images of the final meals of almost 600 death row inmates onto plates.**

Her project, *The Last Supper*, began after she moved to Norman, Oklahoma. The state has the highest number of executions per capita in the U.S.A. and each week the local newspaper printed several notices of execution, which included the inmate's last food request. These ranged from ice cream to cigarettes, but mostly consisted of burgers and KFC. Green creates her poignant artworks by applying cobalt-blue mineral paint to second-hand ceramic plates, which are then kiln-fired by her technical advisor Toni Acock. She plans to add 50 plates a year to her collection until capital punishment is finally abolished in every U.S. state.

INDIANA, 14 MARCH 2001
A dish of German ravioli and chicken dumplings was prepared as an inmate's final meal by his mother and prison dietary staff.

TEXAS, 21 SEPTEMBER 2011
An inmate requested two chicken-fried steaks, a triple-patty bacon cheeseburger, 1 lb (450 g) of barbecued meat, a meat-lover's pizza, three fajitas, an omelet, a bowl of okra, a pint of Blue Bell ice cream, some peanut butter fudge and three root beers, but ate none of it. As a result, Texas banned the option of allowing prisoners to request final meals.

fish supper Five chefs cooked a giant portion of fish and chips at Poole, England, comprising 65 lb (30 kg) of halibut and 130 lb (59 kg) of fries—making enough to feed 180 people.

hard graft Paul Barnett of West Sussex, England, grows 250 different varieties of apple—on one tree. Every winter for the past 25 years he has grafted new varieties onto his single 20-ft-tall (6-m) tree to produce a range of cooking, eating and cider apples.

he never had a birthday cake so we ordered a birth-day cake for him.

pizza

MONTANA, 16 FEBRUARY 1917
On the eve of an execution almost 100 years ago, a death row inmate requested an apple because he had a bad taste in his mouth.

INDIANA, 5 MAY 2007
An inmate who had spent 22 years on death row had never had a birthday cake in his life, so one was ordered specially for his final meal.

TEXAS, 22 OCTOBER 2001
A prisoner with a sweet tooth requested a bag of assorted Jolly Rancher sweets.

massive mousse At the 2013 Chocolate Festival, the Aventura Mall in Florida invited chefs to create a gigantic chocolate mousse weighing 496 lb (225 kg)—2½ times the weight of an average man. It included 108 lb (49 kg) of chocolate, 66 lb (30 kg) of butter, 24 lb (11 kg) of egg yolk, 20 lb (9 kg) of sugar, 50 quarts (47 l) of heavy cream and 5 gal (19 l) of milk, and took five hours to make.

cake figures Baker Lara Clarke from Walsall, England, has created a life-size cake replica of Jack Sparrow, Johnny Depp's character from *Pirates of the Caribbean*. The 5-ft-5-in-tall (1.7-m) model was made from chocolate, marshmallows, rice krispies, icing and food coloring, all built around an internal structure of stainless steel, PVC pipes, and wood. It took Lara 20 hours to plan the sponge extravaganza and another 70 hours to make it. She has also made a 4-ft-high (1.2-m) Grinch cake, which was big enough to feed a staggering 500 people.

owl eateries In some Japanese cafés, customers can have coffee with real owls watching over them. People have to queue patiently outside for admission to the owl-themed cafés because too many inside at one time might spook the birds.

noodle diet After suffering food poisoning as a child, Georgi Readman, from the Isle of Wight, England, has eaten virtually nothing but noodles for more than ten years. She goes through about 30 mi (48 km) of noodles every year, and even eats them dry and uncooked.

waiting list There is a five-year waiting list to eat at Damon Baehrel's restaurant, Damon Baehrel, in the basement of his home in Earlton, New York. It has 12 tables and has attracted visitors from nearly 50 countries.

brain curry Spicy cow-brain coconut curry is a popular dish among the Minangkabau people of Indonesia.

deadly dish Several people have died while eating *sannakji*, a Korean dish of live, wriggling octopus. Usually the chef prepares the dish by dismembering a small octopus, but it can also be eaten whole. If the octopus's suckers stick to the customer's tongue and mouth, they can cause fatal choking.

sweet tooth After breaking into a house in Birmingham, England, a burglar was caught by police because he could not resist helping himself to some chocolate cookies. He was sentenced to 7½ years in prison after forensic experts found his middle finger imprint on the cookie box.

cupcake tower At the 75th birthday party for the City of Myrtle Beach, South Carolina, in 2013, a 21-ft-5-in (6.5-m) tower was built in two hours from 7,860 cupcakes.

fried salamander A restaurant in Osaka, Japan, serves deep-fried axolotl salamander on a bed of noodles with red and green peppers. Coated in thin batter so that its eyes are visible, it looks like a miniature fried dragon, but is said to taste like chicken.

exotic ices Snow King, an ice cream shop in Taipei, Taiwan, sells more than 70 exotic flavors of ice cream, including sesame-oil chicken, pig knuckle, beer, and curry.

polite cafe La Petite Syrah Café in Nice, France, charges customers less if they say "hello" and "please" when ordering. Manager Fabrice Pepino charges 7 euros if a customer just asks for "a coffee," but only 1 euro 40 cents if they say, "Hello, a coffee, please."

sweat martini A new martini cocktail was created in 2013 using 70-year-old moisture extracted from the walls of Winston Churchill's World-War-II bunker. The dirt, stress and sweat from the Cabinet War Rooms, located 10 ft (3 m) beneath London's Whitehall, were bottled to make bitters, which were used to make the "War Rooms Martini."

christmas cookie Leslie Canady, of Wichita, Kansas, keeps a 28-year-old Christmas cookie in a blue velvet jewelry box. The cookie, which still looks as good as new, was made for her by her mother when Leslie was five months old.

cocktail king Erik Mora, a bartender in Las Vegas, Nevada, can make and pour 1,559 different cocktails in one hour.

super nugget To celebrate the company's 75th anniversary, Empire Kosher Poultry made a giant chicken nugget weighing 51.1 lb (23 kg) and measuring 3.25 ft (1 m) long and 2 ft (0.6 m) wide at Secaucus, New Jersey. The gigantic nugget was coated in more than 2¼ lb (1 kg) of breadcrumbs. It took six people more than three hours to make the nugget, which was larger than 720 regular-sized nuggets combined.

Lizard Lunch

→ The *Uromastyx* lizard is a popular meal in the Arabian Peninsula. Also known as "fish of the desert," the reptile can grow to 3 ft (0.9 m) in length. It may be grilled as part of a traditional kabsa rice dish or eaten raw, as some believe its blood can treat diseases. The lizards, which live in sand burrows, are caught in the spring by hunters using sniffer dogs.

GOURMET GATOR
→ Chicago restaurant Frontier, which serves whole smoked animals, has one creature on the menu that might not appeal to everybody. Smoked alligator, served whole, and big enough to feed 12 hungry people is available for around $600. The gators are sourced from Louisiana, then prepared by stuffing them with whole chickens, and smoking them for six hours. Chef Brian Jupiter describes the meat as having a "delicious, tender taste, similar to that of frog legs," and recommends beer to wash down the snappy supper.

seahorse wine Chinese consumers eat 250 tons of dried seahorses each year—that's tens of millions of seahorses. In China, seahorse wine is a traditional health tonic.

prize pumpkin Tim Mathison of Napa Valley, California, grew a pumpkin that tipped the scales at 2,032 lb (922 kg)—almost the weight of a small car—during a weigh-off at Morgan Hill in October 2013. The colossal pumpkin, which had been growing for 105 days in a backyard, earned him more than $15,000.

luxury pudding Chef Martin Chiffers of London, England, created a luxury Christmas pudding that went on sale in 2013 for £23,000 ($38,000). It contained expensive cognac, limited-edition liquors, extremely rare almonds from Iran and a 15th-century Henry VI Salut d'Or gold coin that alone is worth £11,000 ($12,500).

chili churn More than 170 volunteers served 2,420 lb (1,098 kg) of chili con carne—enough to feed around 4,000 people—from a 348-gal (1,317-l) milk container in Minto, North Dakota.

schnitzel choice Micha Hentschel, owner of the Haus Falkenstein Restaurant in Lougheed, Alberta, has 347 different varieties of pan-fried schnitzel on his menu—that's nearly twice as many as any restaurant in Germany. Hentschel's favorite fare from his extensive menu is the green peppercorn cream schnitzel.

heavy drinker The owner of Britain's smallest pub—the 15 x 7 ft (4.5 x 2.1 m) Nutshell in Bury St. Edmunds, Suffolk—banned Adam Thurkettle from visiting the establishment during peak hours because, once he had ducked his head to get through the doorway, he took up too much room while standing at the bar. At 6 ft 7 in (2 m) and 294 lb (133-kg), the tree surgeon's presence on a busy night meant landlord Jack Burton had to turn away at least four normal-sized drinkers.

BLOODSUCKER
→ The creations of Chris Verraes look disgusting yet taste great. From his base in London, England, he specializes in candies that confuse the taste buds. He created this leech feasting on a wound by sculpting a clay shape to make a silicone mold for the chocolate. Colored cocoa butter completes the illusion.

Blood Lust

➜ For Halloween, young people in China get the chance to act like vampires by drinking blood. It is not real blood, however, but a red beverage served in plastic bags that look just like hospital blood packs.

HALLOWEEN TREATS

Larvets Real larva snacks that are dried and coated with different flavors, including barbecue sauce, cheddar cheese and Mexican spices.

Eyes of Terror Gruesome, blood-shot human eyeball candies complete with red veins and spots to make them look frighteningly lifelike.

Scorpion Lollipops Real dead scorpions encased in hard candy flavored with apple, banana, strawberry and blueberry. When you have chewed through the candy, you can munch the crunchy scorpion.

Sour Toilet Flush Candy A plastic toilet filled with candy powder that comes with two lollipop plungers. You lick the plunger, then stick it into the toilet to get it coated with the deliciously tasty candy powder.

Harry Potter Cockroach Cluster Candy

Based on the Cockroach Clusters sold at Honeydukes Sweetshop in the Harry Potter books, this snack looks alarmingly like a genuine giant cockroach, but is really a gummy candy with a crunchy shell.

Zit Poppers Candy

Plump, ripe and ready to pop, this candy is designed with liquid inside to look like a bloody pimple, which bursts when you bite into it.

career switch Ben Cohen and Jerry Greenfield, the founders of Ben & Jerry's, originally intended to make and sell bagels, but when the equipment proved too expensive, they instead paid $5 for a correspondence course at Penn State University on how to make ice cream.

canned bugs Sold online, the Edible Bug Gift Pack features seven cans of flavored and cooked bugs—barbecue bamboo worms, bacon and cheese grasshoppers, nori seaweed armor-tailed scorpions, salted queen weaver ants, sour cream and onion dung beetles, wasabi house crickets and giant waterbug chili paste.

no tomatoes Although ketchup is an iconic American product, the sauce actually originated in 17th-century China, where it was made with pickled fish and spices and did not contain tomatoes.

sidewalk grill As cities in southern China baked in temperatures of over 108°F (42°C) in the summer of 2013, people were able to fry eggs and brown pork ribs just by placing them on the hot ground.

flying tray Customers at Japanese restaurant chain YO! Sushi can have their meal delivered to them on a flying tray traveling at 25 mph (40 km/h). The lightweight, carbon fiber tray has a range of 160 ft (50 m) and is guided through the air by waiters using an iPad app.

menu collection The Cornell University Library in Ithaca, New York, maintains a collection of more than 10,000 menus from restaurants and banquets, dating from the modern day back to the 1850s.

blood sausage Chefs in Burgos, Spain, made a blood sausage—or *morcilla*—that measured 614 ft (187.2 m) long—that's as long as the city's cathedral towers are tall. The sausage's main ingredients were 721 ft (220 m) of pigs' intestine and 10 gal (40 l) of pigs' blood.

ton of chips Corkers Crisps, of Cambridgeshire, England, made a one-ton bag of sea salt-flavored potato chips. The chips were loaded on to a crane, then dropped into a bag that stood 18 ft (5.5 m) high—which is almost as tall as a house.

homemade shake Rob Rhinehart from San Francisco, California, only eats a homemade, nutrient-rich shake that he calls Soylent—and not only has the drink reduced his food bill, it has even cured his dandruff!

soy overdose University of Virginia student John Paul Boldrick suffered seizures, went into a coma and very nearly died from an excess of salt after drinking a quart of soy sauce (1 l) in 2011 on a dare. Consuming large amounts of salt was a traditional method for suicide in Ancient China.

asparagus surprise Ann and Jim McFarlane found a live tree frog nestled in a packet of Peruvian asparagus tips they had bought from a supermarket in Portsmouth, England. The frog, who was given the name Maurice, went on to live in a local aquarium, where the McFarlane's daughter was working.

caring robot Scientists at Cornell University, New York, have built a robot that knows when to pour its owner a beer. They have fitted the robot with a camera and a database of 3-D videos outlining basic human actions so that it can respond appropriately to each one. Powered by 16 laptop batteries, the robot can also make breakfast, put food in the refrigerator and tidy up.

insect diet David Gracer, an English teacher from Providence, Rhode Island, is so addicted to eating insects that in 11 years he has devoured 5,000 species—including cockroaches and scorpions. He has eaten insects sautéed, baked and roasted, and always keeps a ready supply of more than 12,000 bugs in his basement freezer.

ROBOT DANCERS

→ A restaurant in Tokyo, Japan, has its own troupe of dancing-girl robots. Each life-size, anime-style dancer at the Robot Restaurant consists of an upper torso and legs mounted on a metal, motor-driven base. With the help of human operators, the robots can move their arms, head, fingers, mouth and legs in time to the music as part of a colorful floorshow that also features flashing lights, giant LED screens and animatronic pterodactyl dinosaurs.

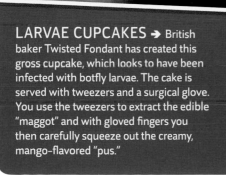

LARVAE CUPCAKES → British baker Twisted Fondant has created this gross cupcake, which looks to have been infected with botfly larvae. The cake is served with tweezers and a surgical glove. You use the tweezers to extract the edible "maggot" and with gloved fingers you then carefully squeeze out the creamy, mango-flavored "pus."

silver carrots German food company The Deli Garage has invented a tasteless edible spray-paint called Food Finish to give meals an exciting splash of color—it comes in shades of gold, silver, red and blue.

surprise stuffing When Linda Hebditch from Dorset, England, opened a packet of supermarket-bought dried sage leaves from Israel, a 3-in-long (7.6-cm) exotic praying mantis leapt out at her.

massive mushroom A huge fungus found in Yunnan Province, China, was made up of as many as 100 individual caps attached at the base of their stems. It weighed over 33 lb (15 kg) and measured 36 in (90 cm) in diameter.

fly burgers Villagers living near Lake Victoria in East Africa coat saucepans with honey to catch the trillions of flies that swarm around the area. Then they make the trapped insects into nutritious flyburgers, which they fry before eating.

milk vodka Farmer Jason Barber from Dorset, England, produces vodka from pure cows' milk. He ferments the whey using a specialist yeast that turns milk sugar into alcohol. It took him three years to perfect the recipe for his Black Cow vodka.

edible dress Donna Millington-Day, a baker from Staffordshire, England, created a cake in the shape of a stunning ivory wedding dress. The 6-ft (1.8-m) edible bridal gown weighed 55 lb (25 kg) and was made using 17 tiers of sponge cake. It was decorated with 48 lb (22 kg) of sugar-paste icing, 2 lb (0.9 kg) of royal icing, hundreds of sugar pearls and several hand-piped iced flowers. She filled the cake with 17 lb (7.7 kg) of vanilla butter cream and 7 lb (3 kg) of raspberry jam. It was big enough to feed up to 2,000 wedding guests.

pasta strand Lawson's Pasta Restaurant in Tokyo, Japan, created a single strand of pasta that measured 12,388 ft (3,776 m) in length—that's almost 2½ mi (4 km) long!

cobra eggs Snake-breeder Huang Kuo-nan from Tainan, Taiwan, sells boiled, fertilized cobra eggs as a health food.

monster pizza A team of chefs headed by Dovilio Nardi baked a pizza in Rome, Italy, that measured 131 ft (40 m) in diameter and had a circumference of more than the length of a football field. Covering nearly a third of an acre (a tenth of a hectare) and weighing more than 25 tons—four times the weight of an adult African elephant—the giant pizza was made using 10 tons of flour, 5 tons of tomato sauce, almost 4½ tons of mozzarella cheese, 1,488 lb (675 kg) of margarine, 551 lb (250 kg) of rock salt, 220 lb (100 kg) of lettuce and 298 gal (1,128 l) of yeast. It took 48 hours to bake.

lost in translation When restaurant owner Fred Bennett of Nelson, New Zealand, began serving Thai food, he added a sign printed in Thai and discovered only months later that it translated to "Go Away and Don't Come Back!"

fried cat At the controversial Gastronomical Festival of the Cat in La Quebrada, Peru, townsfolk feast on hundreds of specially bred domestic cats for two days. They believe that eating cat burgers, fried cat legs and fried cat tails can cure bronchial disease.

chili pie At the State Fair of Texas in Dallas, cooks made a 1,325-lb (601-kg) Fritos chili pie, containing 635 bags of Fritos corn chips, 660 cans of chili and 580 bags of shredded cheese.

7up In 2013, Joey "Jaws" Chestnut from San José, California, ate a record 69 dogs and buns in ten minutes to win the Nathan's July 4th Hot Dog Eating Contest at Coney Island, New York, for the seventh consecutive year.

SPIDER HUNTERS

→ This young Cambodian boy is fearlessly holding what is soon to be his lunch—a venomous (and still alive) tarantula spider. Children as young as five hunt tarantulas by using a stick to tickle the spider's web and lure it from its underground den. When the spider emerges—and a full-grown tarantula can be the size of an adult's palm—the children grab it just in front of its abdomen, taking care to avoid its toxic bite. They then put the spider in a water bottle, drown it and clean it before it is cooked in hot butter or oil. From catching the tarantula to eating it takes just ten minutes—the ultimate in fast food.

turtle burger A man in China tried to smuggle his pet turtle through airport security by stashing it in a KFC burger before boarding a flight from Guangzhou to Beijing. However, when X-rays detected "odd protrusions" sticking out of the burger inside his bag, the deception was uncovered and he was forced to leave his turtle behind with a friend.

fruit tree Fruit sculptor Shawn Feeney helped build a 10-ft-tall (3-m) fruit tree, made up of more than 1,200 pieces of pineapple, orange, strawberry, peach and mango, on a street corner in Calgary, Alberta, Canada.

global feast Carrie Hollis and Simon Day from Surrey, England, ate a 24-hour meal in 2013, during which they sampled 193 bite-sized courses from around the world, including grasshoppers from the Congo, meat gutab (stuffed flatbread) from Azerbaijan and birds' milk from Romania.

biting wine A woman from Shuangcheng in northern China was rushed to a hospital after she was bitten by a venomous snake that had been pickled in wine—a popular Chinese medicine—for three months. Liu had been given the snake wine to treat her rheumatism. She drank a glass of the wine every day, but when she went to refill the jar and used chopsticks to adjust the seemingly dead snake's position, the creature sprang to life and bit her. A snake expert suggested that the creature may have been able to survive in the jar for three months because it was hibernating.

dangerous shark Greenland shark meat—a popular dish in Iceland—is poisonous when fresh and is only safe to eat after it has undergone several months of fermentation and drying.

behemoth brownie Something Sweet Bake Shop in Daphne, Alabama, made a 234-lb (106-kg) brownie, which measured 11 x 6 ft (3.3 x 1.8 m). The giant brownie had to be cooked in a specially made, 262-lb (120-kg) pan and was big enough to cut into nearly 1,200 slices.

Snake Snack

➔ A dead snake is dried on a slab in the Chinese "Snake Village" of Zisiqiao, where **three million serpents are raised each year for food or medicine.**

The most common snakes reared there are sharp-nosed vipers and, after the venom has been extracted, the snakes are either chopped up and their meat put in soup or they are preserved in alcohol and sold for medicinal purposes. The village also breeds the notorious pit viper or "five-step killer," so called because its victims are said to die within five paces of being bitten.

BEYOND BELIEF

The star of the show was Billy, who was caught in 1906 in a swamp near New Orleans. Surprisingly docile, Billy would allow his handlers to put a saddle or reins on him to give children a ride. He would astonish tourists with his tricks, which included sliding down chutes and taking part in underwater battles with famous alligator wrestler George Link. Billy appeared in many films between the 1920s and 1960s, chosen for his reliable reaction to food—as soon as meat was dangled nearby he would open his mouth, ready for the perfect shot.

at the California Alligator Farm, Los Angeles, Cal.

→ The alligators were not only kept as a tourist attraction. The farm also produced alligator skin handbags, belts and purses—some decorated with genuine alligator heads and claws—which were all sold in the gift shop.

SOUVENIR from the CALIFORNIA ALLIGATOR FARM, LOS ANGELES, CAL.

"Drop In."

M_____

675:—"Chicken Dinner" at the Alligator Farm, Los Angeles, Calif.

The California Alligator Farm

The California Alligator Farm

SEE THE TRAINED ALLIGATORS

1000 ON EXHIBITION

OPEN EVERY DAY

Our Only SALESROOM is at the Farm

We make a specialty of Alligator Bags Ornamented with Genuine Alligator Heads and Claws

One of the most novel and interesting sights in the world. Most stupendous aggregation of Alligators ever exhibited.

OPPOSITE LINCOLN PARK LOS ANGELES, - CALIFORNIA
Lincoln Park Cars Stop at the Door CAPITOL 2460

Alligator Goods at Wholesale Prices

A snapshot of the past—a 1920s brochure for the California Alligator Farm, home to over 1,000 reptiles.

Ride that Gator!

→ **California was once home to a spectacular tourist attraction where visitors could stroke, feed and even sit on fully grown 300-lb (136-kg) alligators.**

The California Alligator Farm was opened in Los Angeles in 1907 by "Alligator Joe" Campbell and his partner Frances Earnest and, for just 25 cents, up to 130,000 people a year watched jaw-dropping reptile talent shows and live displays. The alligators even learned to climb ladders and dance the waltz.

The alligators ranged in size from just a few inches long to up to 13 ft (4m) and were kept apart, according to size, to stop the biggest of them from eating the smallest. Visitors to the farm, however, were encouraged to wander and even swim among them.

Despite their fearsome reputation, the alligators were very gentle, and the only recorded casualty on the farm was a guide who lost an arm while doing a demonstration with his head in an alligator's mouth. Luckily, visitors helped pull him free and he escaped with his head intact!

Campbell, a former ostrich rider, acquired his alligators by mimicking their calls in the wild. They would then rise to the surface of swamps and rivers, where they could be caught and taken to the farm.

Following a decline in visitor numbers, the farm closed in 1984, ending with a five-day cowboy-style rodeo to catch all the alligators, which were then flown to a private reserve.

→ **The farm advertised the largest alligator in captivity, "Okeechobee," who was claimed to be around 500 years old—something of an exaggeration given that the average lifespan for an American alligator is nearer 60 years. The farm also provided trained alligators and other reptiles for Hollywood films, including *Tarzan* and Walt Disney's *The Happiest Millionaire*.**

→ **From time to time, floods caused the water levels of the farm's lakes and swamps to rise alarmingly, allowing the alligators to escape. The reptiles would turn up in nearby public ponds, or in the gardens and swimming pools of neighboring houses!**

STATION CAT

➜ Passengers at Kishi station, Japan, are greeted by a four-legged stationmaster—a female calico cat named Tama. When the Wakayama Electric Railway had to get rid of staff at the stations on the Kishigawa Line, Tama, who lived near Kishi station with other strays, was named stationmaster. Tama's popularity has saved the station from closure. Kishi now has a Tama-themed café and souvenir shop, and the company runs a train named after her.

legally dead After disappearing from his Arcadia, Ohio, home in 1986 and being officially declared dead eight years later, Donald Miller Jr. turned up alive in 2005, but has been told he cannot have a driving license because he is still legally dead. A Hancock County judge rejected Miller's request to reverse the 1994 death ruling because he said there is a three-year limit for death notices to be repealed.

dig this! Retired JCB driver Billy Jones from South Wales was carried to his funeral in the bucket of the mechanical digger that he drove for 40 years.

rare penny A rare 1792 experimental penny that was never put into circulation and is one of only 14 still in existence sold for $1.15 million at an auction in Schaumburg, Illinois, in 2012.

private cells A jail in Fremont, California, allows prisoners to upgrade to better, private cells with cable TV at a cost of $155 a night—the same as a three-star hotel in the area.

zolps only Loyola University in Chicago offers a scholarship to pay toward the tuition of any Catholic student with the last name Zolp. Candidates must provide a birth, baptism or confirmation certificate to prove their eligibility.

happy mirror Students at the University of Tokyo in Japan have created a mirror that reflects happier versions of themselves. It uses a technique called incendiary reflection, where a camera secretly tracks facial expressions, lifting the corners of the mouth and crinkling the area around the eyes to make it look as if they are smiling.

slow drip The Pitch Drop Experiment has been conducted at the University of Queensland in Australia since 1927 to demonstrate the fluidity of the tarlike substance, and over the following 86 years a total of eight drops of pitch have dripped from the glass funnel at the rate of one every decade—but nobody has ever seen it happen. In August 2013, Professor John Mainstone, who had been custodian of the experiment for 52 years, during which time there were five unseen drips, died still waiting for the ninth drip to be captured on webcam.

hobbit hole For over 20 years Dan Price has lived in a tiny 8-ft-wide (2.4-m), circular, self-built, underground home dug under a horse pasture near Joseph, Oregon. The "Hobbit Hole," which has to be accessed on all fours, boasts underground electricity and a garage constructed from intertwined sticks in which he keeps his three-wheeled bike. He left his family and job to adopt his alternative lifestyle, paying $100 a year for the land and making money by doing odd jobs and writing about his experiences.

PALM PORTRAITS

➜ Spanish artist David Catá used a needle and different colored threads to sew more than 20 portraits of his friends and family into the palms of his hands. Using his body as a canvas, he pierces only the top layer of skin with a needle to avoid causing too much pain and then draws the thread through to make a stitch. Each picture takes him up to four hours to sew before he photographs it and then carefully picks out the thread to allow his skin to heal. The art project, which shows how people close to him are woven into his life, scars his palms for up to four weeks, after which he can start over with a new portrait.

→ As temperatures plunged to -34°F (-37°C) in January 2014, it was so cold that the U.S. side of the Niagara Falls froze before the water could reach the bottom, forming incredible 170-ft-long (52-m) icicles. The Polar vortex that created the big freeze affected 240 million people in the U.S.A. and southern Canada.

Frozen Falls

success story Founded in New York in 1853, the Otis Elevator Company estimates that its elevators transport the equivalent of the world's population every nine days.

nose painter Born with cerebral palsy, paraplegic French Canadian artist Gille Legacy paints with his nose. Although he has no movement in his arms and legs, he has full use of his brain and by dipping his nose in paint— a technique he has been using since the age of eight—he has had his paintings exhibited throughout the U.S.A., Canada and France.

goat acquitted Gary the goat was cleared of vandalism by an Australian court in 2013 after being accused of eating a floral display outside a Sydney museum. Police had fined Gary's owner Jim Dezarnaulds (also known as comedian Jimbo Bazoobi) $440, but when he appealed, man and goat had their day in court, Gary wearing a big colorful hat for the occasion.

bread lamp Yukiko Morita from Kyoto, Japan, makes beautiful lampshades from loaves of bread. To create her "pampshades" (*pan*—the Japanese word for bread, combined with "lampshades"), she hollows out baguettes, dries out the shells, applies a resin coating to prevent mildew and inserts LED bulbs.

airport intruder A kangaroo shocked passengers at Australia's Melbourne Airport by bouncing into a pharmacy store on the terminal's second level. The kangaroo, which was thought to have entered from nearby bushland, was captured in the skincare section after being tranquilized.

junk mail The Spanish town of Brunete dealt with a dog-poop problem by identifying the dogs' owners and sending the poop back to them in the mail. In one week, 147 boxes of poop were sent by special delivery to local dog owners in packages labeled "Lost and Found."

parallel lives Two British brothers, Ron and Fred Boyes, who had been separated for 80 years and were unaware of each other's existence, found when they finally met up that they had both reached the same rank in the Royal Air Force and played the same soccer position, and they both have a daughter named Wendy. The brothers were fostered separately in the 1930s and ended up in different parts of the U.K.— Ron in Derbyshire and Fred in Oxfordshire. They were reunited when a relative began researching their family tree.

bridge stolen Thieves in western Turkey stole an entire metal bridge, measuring 82 ft (25 m) long and weighing 22 tons.

cemetery bed Homeless Fábio Buraldo Rigol has slept in a cemetery in São Paulo, Brazil, for over 13 years. He sleeps in a six-chamber burial crypt next to the skeleton of his dead friend who is buried there.

flying dagger After leaping from a helicopter, daredevil wingsuiter Jeb Corliss of Malibu, California, flew at a speed of 100 mph (160 km/h) through a mountain gap that was just 25 ft (7.6 m) wide at its narrowest point. The spectacular jump, known as the "flying dagger," was made through a fissure in China's 900-ft-high (274-m) Langshan Mountain.

black turf West Salem High School, Oregon, plays its home football matches on black turf—the school saved nearly $150,000 because it did not have to have the synthetic turf dyed green.

formation jump In July 2013, 101 female skydivers jumped from airplanes to form a flower shape in midair over Kolomna, Russia.

ice marathon For Siberia's annual Lake Baikal Ice Marathon, runners wear balaclavas, fur hats, leggings and sunglasses, as well as running shoes, to race 26.2 mi (42 km) across 3.3-ft-thick (1-m) ice on a frozen lake in temperatures of just 10°F (–12°C). The air is so clean and the terrain is so flat on the world's deepest lake that runners can usually make out the distant finish line on the opposite shore almost as soon as they start racing.

dive day Despite vomiting and suffering bruises on his legs, 25-year-old Dennis Bettin, a student at the German Sport University in Cologne, made 714 dives from a 10-ft-high (3-m) board over the course of 24 hours in June 2013, equivalent to a dive every two minutes.

rally wigs A total of 32,682 Los Angeles Angels baseball fans wore red-and-white rally wigs during the fifth inning of the game against Houston Astros in Anaheim, California, which took place on June 1, 2013.

rocket boarder By duct-taping model rockets to his skateboard, 24-year-old Eddie McDonald reached a speed of over 38 mph (60 km/h) as he shot down the main street of Barcaldine in Queensland, Australia.

sporting guests The three-bedroom Penthouse Real World Suite at the Hard Rock Hotel & Casino, Las Vegas, Nevada, has its own bowling alley. At the nearby Palms Hotel, the Hardwood Suite has its own basketball court!

Muscle

➔ In India, where power supplies can be unreliable, fairgrounds can still run on clean energy, as this Ferris wheel powered by human muscle shows. Groups of men perform skillful and highly dangerous moves to keep the momentum going by swinging from seat to seat and hanging from the wheel as it rotates, which makes it function rather like a human hamster wheel.

SIDEWALL SURFING

➔ The new craze among car-mad youths in Saudi Arabia is driving their cars at speed on just two wheels, and if that's not crazy enough, their friends come along for the ride—on the outside of the vehicle! Sidewall surfing, as the stunt is known, is the latest extreme motorsport to catch on in the country, where drifting—sliding cars sideways at high speed—is also a popular underground activity.

tough guy At the 2013 World's Strongest Man competition in Sanya, China, Brian Shaw from Fort Lupton, Colorado, deadlifted over 975 lb (442.5 kg)—about the same weight as a horse. His biceps are nearly 2 ft (60 cm) in circumference, his neck is wider than most men's thighs and, when he used to play basketball as a teen, one opponent knocked himself out simply by running into Shaw's chest.

long club Golf professional Michael Furrh of Arlington, Texas, used a 14.2-ft-long (4.3-m) driver—almost four times the length of a normal club—to hit a ball 144 yd (131.7 m) through the air. He has previously hit a drive off a 6-ft-high (1.8-m) tee, while standing on a ladder.

Power

SURF SKIER ➔ Chuck Patterson is a pioneer in the extreme sport of "surf skiing," surfing down waves on water skis! The veteran mountain skier from California converted to surfing and experimented with custom skis designed to cut into the water. Chuck has even conquered 40-ft (12-m) waves at the "Jaws" surf break in Maui, Hawaii, one of the world's largest—so big that a jet ski had to tow him into position to catch the wave.

BOXING CORPSE → Mourners arriving at the wake of former boxer Christopher Rivera Amaro found his corpse posed standing in the corner of a simulated ring, dressed as if ready to fight. Wearing a yellow hood, sunglasses, and boxing gloves, 23-year-old Amaro, who had been shot dead the previous week, was propped up in the replica ring in San Juan, Puerto Rico, by the Marin Funeral Home in accordance with his family's wishes that his wake should have a boxing theme.

laundry blaze Nicola Boulton and her daughter Claire escaped a fire at their house in Leicester, England, after recently tumbled dry tea towels spontaneously combusted.

corpse companion Eighteen months after his death in December 2010, Charles Zigler of Jackson, Michigan, was still sitting in his favorite armchair, watching TV. His housemate, Linda Chase, kept his mummified body, washing it and dressing it every day, and talked to it while watching NASCAR races.

sweet breath Nicole Jones from New York City is addicted to eating deodorant. She eats half a stick a day and goes through 15 a month. She says, "It is really soft. It feels like it melts in my mouth. It has its own unique taste."

cremation prize Baseball fan Matt Kratoville, 54, from Novato, California, won a free cremation by taking first prize in a "Funeral Night" contest at a San Rafael Pacifics' game on August 23, 2013, in which he had to write his own obituary.

dressing down A 52-year-old woman from Paris, France, wrote a two-hour English exam posing as her 19-year-old daughter in an attempt to obtain a better grade for her. The mother wore thick makeup, low-cut jeans and Converse boots in an attempt to pass herself off as a teenager, but a supervisor spotted the deception.

dog tags Kelly Grace of Brisbane, Australia, found the dog tags of U.S. soldier John W. Sackett near a former army base and returned them to his family after tracking them down online 70 years after he had lost them during World War II.

life savers When 67-year-old Dorothy Fletcher, from Liverpool, England, suffered a heart attack on a flight to Florida, her life was saved because 15 of her fellow passengers happened to be cardiologists en route to a conference in Orlando. So when the stewardess asked for medical assistance, they all stood up, eager to help. They quickly fed drips into the patient's arms and used the in-flight medical kit to stabilize her condition. The plane was diverted to North Carolina, where Mrs. Fletcher received further treatment in intensive care before going on to make a full recovery. Her daughter Christine said, "My mum wouldn't be here today if it wasn't for those cardiologists on the plane, and we didn't even know their names."

woolen coffins Funeral directors John Fraser and Son from Inverness, Scotland, are offering new eco-friendly, woolen coffins. The caskets, which are supported by a strong recycled cardboard frame and are lined with cotton, can support a body weighing up to 588 lb (267 kg).

TWO NOSES

→ Snuffles, a five-month-old Belgian shepherd dog at an animal rescue center in Glasgow, Scotland, was born with a rare congenital defect that makes it look like he has two noses. Instead of his nostrils being fused together, they are split down the middle, allowing him to move both halves of his nose independently!

familiar face Sixty-four-year-old Henry Earl from Lexington, Kentucky, has been arrested more than 1,500 times over the course of his life—so often that his various police mug shots have been turned into an online video. Since his first arrest in 1970, he has spent nearly 6,000 days in jail—an average of more than one day in three behind bars.

TIGER WOMAN

➔ **Katzen Hobbes is a real-life Catwoman with 90 percent of her body tattooed with black tiger stripes.**

She used to have genuine tiger whiskers, which were sent to her by zoos around the world, implanted into her cheeks by means of specialist piercing rings. Now, her "whiskers" have been drawn on her face by scarification—scratches on the skin made deep enough to scar permanently.

It took over a decade for the mother-of-two from Austin, Texas (who is also known as Katzen Ink), to acquire all her tiger tattoos, during which time more than 160 tattoo artists have worked on her, including 23 at the same time! Having so many artists filling in the black lines on her back, legs and stomach caused her such pain that she fainted more than once.

Even so, she loves being half woman, half big cat. "I can't imagine not being a tiger. I am a living, breathing work of art."

sticky fingers Thieves in Bad Hersfeld, Germany, stole 5.5 tons of Nutella chocolate-hazelnut spread from a parked trailer.

beauty mask Women who are worried about their appearance can now simply glue on an expressionless face, thanks to the Uniface mask devised by Zhuoying Li, a graduate from New York City's Parsons School for Design. Li created the mask—with large eyes, long lashes, a high nose bridge and narrow chin and cheeks—as a comment on modern society's unrealistic standards of beauty.

study alert To prevent themselves from falling asleep while studying, some students in Fujian, China, tie their hair to the ceiling using clothes pins. Every time they doze off, the pins pull on their hair and jerk them awake.

head cage In a desperate attempt to quit his 26-year smoking habit, Turkey's Ibrahim Yücel started wearing a locked metal cage on his head every day. Every morning before leaving for work, he asked his wife or daughter to lock the cage, which he built from 130 ft (40 m) of copper wire, and to keep the keys. The cage allowed him to breathe, eat crackers or drink through a straw, but the mesh was too fine for him to be able to smoke a cigarette.

skin slice Torz Reynolds from London, England, spent 1½ hours using a sharp scalpel to slice the tattooed name of her ex-boyfriend, Stuart May, from her body. She then posted the severed piece of inked skin to him.

last request When football fan Scott Entsminger died at his Ohio home in 2013, he had one last request for his favorite team. His obituary read: "He respectfully requests six Cleveland Browns pallbearers so the Browns can let him down one last time." The Browns' last championship title came way back in 1964 and fans recently branded their stadium the "factory of sadness" after a series of disappointing results.

unsafe safe Two burglars were killed when they used an oxyacetylene cutting torch to open a safe full of fireworks at Hopkinton, New Hampshire. The torch ignited the fireworks, causing the safe to explode. It is thought the men had not known what was in the safe.

funeral singalong Robert Nogoy from Pampanga in the Philippines makes coffins equipped with karaoke machines to lighten up funerals.

hanging around Climbing enthusiasts Fang Jing and her husband Lu Zhao posed for their wedding pictures while dangling from ropes hundreds of yards above the ground on a cliff face in Liuzhou, China. After tying the knot, they were suspended in midair for more than three hours, as was their fearless photographer.

unusual trade A man was arrested by Florida wildlife officials after walking into a Miami convenience store and attempting to trade a live, 4-ft-long (1.2-m) alligator for a 12-pack of beer.

brush topper Sam Hunter Baxter from Tenby, Wales, won £10,000 ($16,500) in a weird inventions competition by devising a top hat that doubles as a toothbrush. He came up with the time-saving gadget after calculating that the average person spends 75 days of their life brushing their teeth.

wife's revenge A wife in Swansea, Wales, was so angry to learn that her husband was cheating on her that she changed the magnetic sign over his favorite pub, the Noah's Yard, to: "Paul, I am divorcing you." Still fuming, she later changed the sign to read: "Btw, I am keeping the dog."

cattle crush Malaysian police searching for stolen livestock were shocked to discover four live cows stuffed into the trunk of a car. After removing the back seat, the thieves had snatched the animals from a farm in Bukit Mertajam but were soon forced to flee on foot when their overloaded vehicle broke down.

church clock Every week for 30 years, Dr. John Farrer climbed a narrow, stone, spiral staircase to wind the church clock in the village of Clapham in Yorkshire, England. The clock suddenly stopped at 8.15 a.m. on January 1, 2014 —the exact moment that the 92-year-old doctor died.

OPEN WIDE

➜ In December 2012, a large carpet python was caught on camera in the gruesome process of swallowing its prey—a ringtail possum. The snake was hanging from a tree near the photographer's house in Byron Bay in New South Wales, Australia, and eventually disappeared into the forest with its catch. The carpet python squeezes the breath out of its victim before stretching its jaws in order to swallow prey that is much larger than its own head.

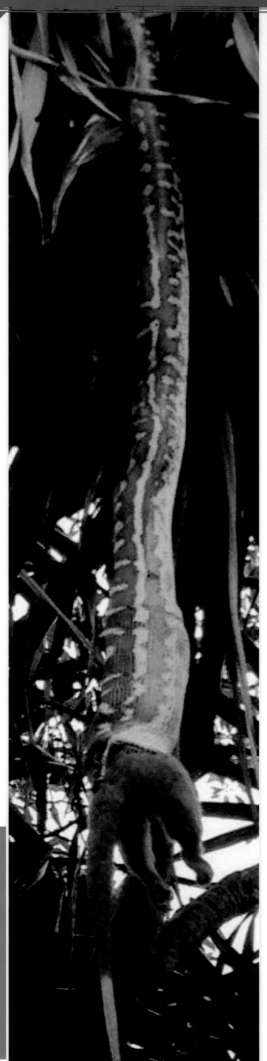

double raid On November 6, 2013, the same bookmaker's shop in Manchester, England, was robbed twice in five minutes by unconnected gangs.

klingon letter When politician David Waddell decided to quit the Indian Trail Town Council in North Carolina, he wrote his letter of resignation in Klingon, the language of the warrior race in Star Trek.

human toilets In 18th-century Scotland, some people worked as human toilets by walking the streets carrying chamber pots and wearing large privacy cloaks and charging money for their use.

naked prank A naked man had to be rescued from a washing machine while playing a game of hide-and-seek at his home in the town of Mooroopna in Victoria, Australia. He hid inside the top-loader so he could surprise his partner but became stuck— and it took police officers 20 minutes to free him using olive oil as a lubricant.

skydiving mice Around 2,000 dead mice were airdropped over a U.S. Air Force base on the Pacific island of Guam in 2013 to kill invasive brown tree snakes. The dead mice were pumped full of poison and dropped from low-flying helicopters, each rodent strung to a tiny parachute made of cardboard and tissue paper.

tree wedding Dressed in a white suit and carrying a bouquet of flowers, Peruvian activist Richard Torres "married" a tree at a park in Buenos Aires, Argentina, to draw attention to environmental issues. To make the ceremony feel more authentic, he even gave the tree a kiss.

buried cyclist A snowplow driver who was clearing heavy snow from a cycle path in Nøtterøy, Norway, found a cyclist completely buried underneath. The driver spotted the bike's handlebars sticking out of the snow and on closer inspection discovered its 26-year-old rider, who, although unconscious, soon recovered in the hospital.

sent home The mummified body of Australian Aborigine Tambo Tambo was sent home for burial in 1993 after lying in a funeral home in Cleveland, Ohio, for 109 years.

busy jails Although the U.S. has only five per cent of the world's total population, it has 25 percent of the world's prison population— some 2,200,000 people behind bars.

Ripley's Believe It or Not!® www.ripleybooks.com

Burning Man

➔ **This spectacular picture of a burning man was captured by Montreal-based photographer Benjamin Von Wong without using any special effects—but don't worry, it was all planned and nobody got hurt.**

Eager to capture the unique imagery of fire, he posted a message on Facebook asking: "Who wants to be lit on fire?" Fellow photographer Jo Gorsky volunteered to be the stuntman and was set ablaze wearing special flameproof clothing and fire retardant gelatine on his skin. The greatest danger to his safety was the strong winds that suddenly sprung up, making the fire more difficult to control.

flat-pack tenor Charles Vickery from San Francisco, California, offers a service where he will assemble flat-pack furniture for clients while singing opera. For an extra payment, he will wear a tuxedo with white gloves and a hat.

paper roses Software programmer Chen Li from Zhejiang Province, China, proposed to his girlfriend with a bouquet of 999 roses made from 200,000 yuan ($32,000) of banknotes. After withdrawing his life savings from the bank, he spent four days folding the notes into flowers.

junk prison After falling over a large pile of paper in the kitchen of his home in Essex, England, 85-year-old compulsive hoarder Noel Rainer was trapped for 30 hours amid a mountain of clutter that he had accumulated over a period of 20 years.

guilty conscience A thief who was consumed with guilt about stealing $800 from a store in Thornapple Township, Michigan, in the 1980s repaid the money anonymously three decades later— along with $400 interest.

victorian life Sarah Chrisman, 33, from Seattle, Washington State, has adopted a Victorian-era lifestyle, wearing custom-made Victorian clothes, cooking from recipes found in Victorian women's magazines and avoiding the use of any household appliances that did not exist in the 19th century. She also uses Victorian transport and has replaced her car with a 100-year-old bicycle.

METRO SURFING ➔ Definitely not to be recommended, "metro surfing" is a highly dangerous new craze among some Russian teenagers that involves them jumping on the back of stationary trains on the Moscow subway and clinging on for their lives as they hurtle through narrow tunnels just inches from death. Some thrill-seekers go a step further and climb on top of the train to ride it, but this can also prove deadly— tragically, two 19-year-old students were killed recently when they smashed into a low tunnel entrance while metro surfing.

- A parking enforcement officer slapped a ticket on a car in Seattle, Washington, in 2010, unaware that the person whom she thought was sleeping in the driver's seat was actually dead.

- Santa's sleigh was given a parking ticket in Cheshire, England, in 2011 while members of Poynton Round Table, dressed as elves, delivered presents to children.

- Desperate to avoid being fined for erratic driving, a bus driver in Zhongshan, China, hid under his parked bus for more than half an hour until police finally dragged him out.

- Disabled driver Peter Stapleton got a parking ticket in London, England, in 2007 while refitting his false leg that had fallen off.

- Nicky Clegg's flattened car was given a parking ticket in Worcester, England, in 2007 after it was crushed by a tree.

- A hearse was given a $35 parking ticket while parked outside a funeral in Milwaukee, Wisconsin, in 2010.

- A horse owned by retired Yorkshire blacksmith Robert McFarland received a parking ticket in 2001. Under the heading "vehicle description," the traffic warden had written "brown horse."

SNOW JOKE

➜ Pranksters in Aachen, Germany, built a full-sized snow sculpture of a Volkswagen Beetle and left it overnight in a no-parking zone. It was so realistic that traffic wardens, thinking there was a real car underneath the snow, left a parking ticket on it.

BANANA PIANO ➜ A new kit called MaKey MaKey turns everyday objects into touchpads so that you can use bananas as piano keys. The MaKey MaKey uses a USB cable to connect its circuit board to your computer. If you upload a piano on a computer webpage and attach the ends of bananas to MaKey MaKey via alligator clips, the bananas become piano keys allowing you to play a tune on them! The device works with any material that can conduct at least a tiny amount of electricity, including modeling clay, ketchup, pencils, coins and even people.

same clothes Teacher Dale Irby from Dallas, Texas, wore the same outfit for his school's photograph every year for 40 years. It started when he realized to his embarrassment that he had worn the same shirt and sweater in his second-year photo as he did for the first, and from then on it continued as a running joke right up until his retirement.

foolish feast A fire that gutted eight apartments in Holland Township, Michigan, leaving over 30 people homeless, was caused by a resident trying to cook a squirrel on his third-floor wooden balcony with a propane torch.

dodgy steering A 38-year-old Australian man was arrested for driving his car through the suburbs of Adelaide without a steering wheel. When police officers stopped the car, they found that the man was controlling it with a set of pliers that he had attached to the steering column.

walking plants July 27 is Take Your Houseplants for a Walk Day, when, according to the idea's American founders Thomas and Ruth Roy, walking your plants around the neighborhood can help them to thrive.

HIGH CHAIR

➔ This is the ultimate reclining chair for daredevil climbers — made of rope and fastened to a sheer rock face 350 ft (107 m) up a mountain in Rock Canyon, Utah.

It was created by local climber Dallin Smith, but after taking hours to haul it up the mountain, he left it there for only a week because other climbers angrily objected to the installation and threatened to throw it in the nearest lake.

Dallin's girlfriend Chelsea Katseanes reclines in the chair with one of the best views in the world. Just don't look down!

The chair took Dallin several weeks to make, using two surplus climbing ropes woven around a metal frame and securely fastened to the rock face by two strong hooks.

jungle life Father and son Ho Van Thanh and Ho Van Lang lived in the jungle for more than 40 years after fleeing their village in 1972 when it was bombed by the U.S. Army during the Vietnam War. They were eventually found in 2013, aged 82 and 41 respectively, having survived in the wild by living in a timber tree house, foraging for fruit and wearing loin cloths made from tree bark.

mystery blaze While the owners were away for a few days, a mysterious fire raged through a house in Fareham, England, without anyone noticing, until it was extinguished by burst water pipes. A neighbor who went to check on the house found it covered in soot and water gushing out from pipes.

grave home After being evicted from his home in Niš, Serbia, Bratislav Stojanovic has been living in a grave at an abandoned local cemetery for more than 15 years. He shares the burial plot with the remains of a family who died out over a century ago but has made the place more homely with a few candles, some blankets and a mattress.

dig that partner French choreographer Dominique Boivin dances with heavy construction vehicles. He matches his movements to those of his earthmover partner and also performs routines while perched on or hanging from its arm.

phone access According to the United Nations, more of the world's population has access to cell phones than proper toilets.

potty pottery A collection of ceramic, disk-shaped Roman artifacts that has been displayed at a museum in West Sussex, England, for 50 years in the belief that they were early gaming pieces have turned out to be a primitive form of toilet paper! The disks were deliberately flattened for use by the Romans who also used sponges mounted on sticks and dipped in vinegar as a means of wiping themselves clean.

truly alarming By combining a clock and a paper shredder, Rich Olson from Seattle, Washington State, has invented an alarm clock that will tear up a $1 bill if the user fails to get up and switch off the timer within a few seconds of it going off.

married bridge Australian artist Jodi Rose loves bridges so much that in a special ceremony on June 17, 2013, she married a 600-year-old French bridge, Le Pont du Diable in Céret. Although the union is not legally recognized in France, Jodi invited 14 guests to attend, wore a traditional bridal gown and veil, and commissioned rings for both herself and the bridge.

young scientist Jamie Edwards, a 13-year-old boy from Preston, England, successfully built a nuclear reactor in his school science class in March 2014.

HUMAN TRANSFORMER

➔ This guy's a real-life Transformer! Drew Beaumier from Fountain Valley, California, had always been a fan of the alien robots, so when he bought a used Power Wheels toy car for $300, he decided to take it apart and turn himself into a human Transformer. He pieced the car back together at the hinges and then glued it to a sports undergarment so that he could wear it like a suit. To make it look really authentic, he fixed wheels to his arms and legs so that when he curls down he can roll along the street like a car.

Emperor Norton

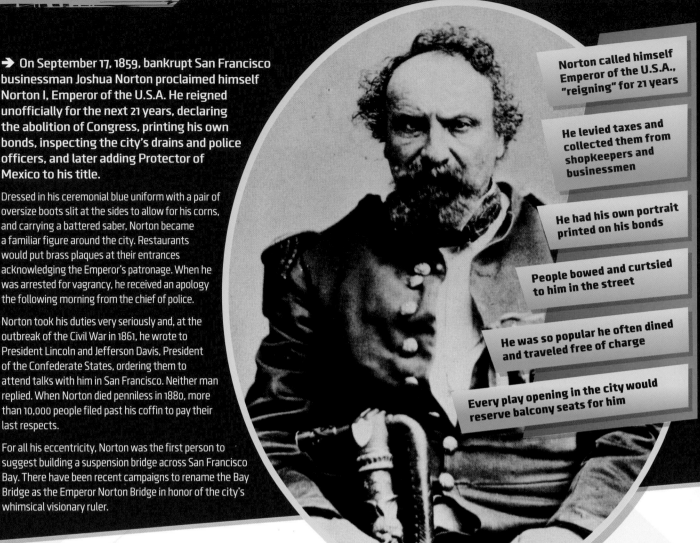

→ On September 17, 1859, bankrupt San Francisco businessman Joshua Norton proclaimed himself Norton I, Emperor of the U.S.A. He reigned unofficially for the next 21 years, declaring the abolition of Congress, printing his own bonds, inspecting the city's drains and police officers, and later adding Protector of Mexico to his title.

Dressed in his ceremonial blue uniform with a pair of oversize boots slit at the sides to allow for his corns, and carrying a battered saber, Norton became a familiar figure around the city. Restaurants would put brass plaques at their entrances acknowledging the Emperor's patronage. When he was arrested for vagrancy, he received an apology the following morning from the chief of police.

Norton took his duties very seriously and, at the outbreak of the Civil War in 1861, he wrote to President Lincoln and Jefferson Davis, President of the Confederate States, ordering them to attend talks with him in San Francisco. Neither man replied. When Norton died penniless in 1880, more than 10,000 people filed past his coffin to pay their last respects.

For all his eccentricity, Norton was the first person to suggest building a suspension bridge across San Francisco Bay. There have been recent campaigns to rename the Bay Bridge as the Emperor Norton Bridge in honor of the city's whimsical visionary ruler.

- Norton called himself Emperor of the U.S.A., "reigning" for 21 years
- He levied taxes and collected them from shopkeepers and businessmen
- He had his own portrait printed on his bonds
- People bowed and curtsied to him in the street
- He was so popular he often dined and traveled free of charge
- Every play opening in the city would reserve balcony seats for him

staged funeral Zeng Jia, 22, from Hubei, China, staged her own funeral so that she could see what people really thought of her. She hired a team of cosmetic artists to make her look dead and then lay in the coffin for an hour while mourners filed solemnly past paying their tributes. At the end of the wake, she surprised them by jumping up from the coffin and delivering a speech.

seeing double Married couple Nancy and Don Featherstone from Fitchburg, Massachusetts, have dressed in matching, his-and-hers clothes every day since 1978—even when they are apart. Dressmaker Nancy has made 600 identical outfits for herself and her devoted husband.

cow plunge A 45-year-old man in southeast Brazil was killed in his bed when a one-ton cow fell through the roof and landed on him. It was the third case of a cow falling through a house roof in the area in three years.

computer error New Zealand electrical company Meridian Energy mistakenly sent a letter to a lamppost in Oakura and threatened to cut off its power unless it supplied them with its customer details within seven days.

martian ambassador In anticipation of it one day being proven that there is life on Mars, the state of Delaware has appointed Dr. Noureddine Melikechi as its Ambassador to Mars with a mission to sell the virtues of Delaware to Martian tourists and investors.

taxi driver Prior to the 2013 general election, Norway's Prime Minister Jens Stoltenberg decided to find out what voters were really thinking by posing as an Oslo taxi driver for an afternoon. A hidden camera fitted in the cab recorded passengers' reactions, including several who recognized him.

men in skirts When railway bosses in Stockholm, Sweden, refused to allow male train drivers to wear shorts to work in the hot summer weather, the drivers got around the ban by wearing skirts instead!

mail madness Among items that British people tried to send by mail during 2012 and 2013 were a dead cat, a live hamster, a garden pond (including water and fish), a hot pie, 500 Barbie dolls, and a teenage girl, whom her mother tried to ship home from a school trip because she was homesick.

terminal boredom Rodrigo Ben-Azul spent more than two months stuck at Santiago Airport in Chile while waiting for relatives in Spain to send him money for his flight home. By day he wandered around with his luggage in tow and at night he slept in quiet corners.

fence message Johnny Mata Jr. proposed to Krystal Salazar by inserting plastic cups into a chain-link fence at Corpus Christi, Texas, to spell out the words 'KRYSTAL... MARRY ME?' He had used the same tactic to invite her to the school prom six years earlier. She said "yes" both times.

island recluse Australian businessman David Glasheen lost $10 million in a single day on the stock market crash of 1987—and after his Sydney home was repossessed he moved to remote Restoration Island, off the coast of Queensland, where he has been the sole inhabitant since 1993. His home is a boat shed and he makes his own beer, which he trades for fish on the mainland, 40 minutes away across crocodile-infested waters.

deer drama A woman who accidentally hit a fawn while driving near Colorado Springs, Colorado, was hit moments later by the fawn's mother. As the woman checked on the young deer's injuries, another car struck the mother deer, sending the animal flying into her.

vibrating tattoo To prevent users missing calls or text messages when their phone is on silent during a movie or music concert, cell-phone company Nokia filed a patent for ferromagnetic body tattoos that will vibrate when receiving alert signals from its phones.

death watch Fredrik Colting of Sweden has invented a watch that counts down every second to the wearer's death. The person's life expectancy is calculated based on medical history and lifestyle and when their current age is deducted, the countdown display starts on the Tikker, supposedly enabling them to make the most of the rest of their life.

live death Welsh actor Gareth Jones suffered a fatal heart attack in 1958 during a live broadcast of the U.K.'s TV drama series *Armchair Theatre*. The tragic event occured shortly before his character in the play was supposed to have a heart attack.

skeleton trip Susan Weese from Albuquerque, New Mexico, traveled around the world for a year with a life-sized, anatomically-correct, 42-lb (19-kg) plastic female human skeleton called Sam. She took pictures of her in cities including Paris, Rome, Berlin, New York and Chicago.

jet-powered coffin Inventor Robert Maddox from Medford, Oregon, has designed a jet-powered coffin inspired by The Munsters that does 0 to 60 mph (0 to 96 km/h) in just nine seconds. Based on Grandpa Munster's Dragula, the Maddoxjet Coffin Car has a cockpit for the driver to sit behind a wooden coffin with a steel tubing undercarriage. It took Robert a month to build at a cost of $1,300.

millionaire cleaner Yu Youzhen from Wuhan, China, is a property millionaire yet still works as a street cleaner for less than $10 a day. The 54-year-old mogul has been waking up at 3 a.m. six days a week since 1998 to sweep roads in order to set a good example to her children.

POOP GUARD

→ Larvae of the cereal leaf beetle crawl around with a pile of their own poop on their back to provide camouflage and prevent their body drying out. They deposit black specks of their feces and globules of mucus on their back to form a fecal shield—this envelops their body and makes it appear brown, shiny and wet, and therefore extremely unappetizing to predators.

floral theme When Nick Meadow married Tamsin Flower on the Isle of Wight, England, one of the bridesmaids was named Issy Bloom and guests included Richard Plant and Tom Gardener.

jesus tile Pilgrims flocked to Phoenix Sky Harbor International Airport, Arizona, in June 2013 after a smudge resembling Jesus was found on a floor tile in Terminal 3.

bad timing A burglar who broke into a house in Palm Beach County, Florida, made the mistake of leaving his phone behind—and his identity was revealed when his mother rang just as police officers arrived at the crime scene.

TRAIN RESCUE →
Forty Japanese passengers and rail workers joined forces to move a 35-ton train in order to rescue a woman who had fallen into an 8-in (20-cm) gap between it and the platform at a station outside Tokyo. They managed to tilt the carriage sufficiently to allow her to be pulled free, and after just an eight-minute delay the train continued its journey.

adult tag Every February for nearly 25 years, ten former high school friends from Spokane, Washington State, have played a nationwide game of Tag. As their careers and locations have diversified, the men—now all in their forties—often travel the length and breadth of the U.S.A. planning elaborate ruses to tag each other and remove the stigma of being "It" for another 11 months. One of them, lawyer Patrick Schultheis, sometimes escapes to Hawaii in February to reduce his tag risk.

While Scott Janssen was participating in Alaska's 2012 Iditarod Dog Sled Race, one of his dogs collapsed and stopped breathing, but he was able to revive the dog with mouth-to-snout CPR.

un-bee-lievable! A baseball game between the Los Angeles Angels and the Seattle Mariners on September 22, 2013, was delayed when the Angels' Stadium was twice invaded by a swarm of bees. Fans fled the stands and others pulled blankets over their heads until a beekeeper lured the insects away with a bucket of honey.

By using a nontoxic, fart-smelling formula sealed in a clear envelope, Fart By Mail, a California-based mail order service started by Zach Friedberg, allows people to send greetings that smell like real farts.

living merman Eric Ducharme from Crystal River, Florida, has been fascinated by mermaids since he was a child and he now lives his life as a merman, often swimming underwater wearing a fake tail. He even runs his own business that designs custom-made mermaid tails from silicone and latex rubber. He says, "When I put on a tail I feel transformed."

For more than five years, Liu Lingchao from Liuzhou, China, has carried his house on his back, like a human snail. His portable home is 5 ft (1.5 m) wide, 7 ft (2.2 m) tall and consists of plastic sheets attached to a bamboo frame—and because it weighs just 132 lb (60 kg), it is easy for him to carry it around with him while he travels the country earning a living by collecting discarded bottles.

zip line Instead of walking down the aisle at their wedding, Lauren Bushar and Ben Youngkin from Asheville, North Carolina, chose to fly into the ceremony on a zip line.

Danish ultra-marathon runner Jesper Olsen has run around the world twice. Three years after completing his first run, he set off in July 2008 from Norway and, via South Africa and Argentina, arrived in Newfoundland in July 2012 at the end of his 23,000-mi (37,000-km) journey.

strange deaths Just after sunset on days between September and November each year, hundreds of birds from over 40 different species die after crashing into buildings and trees at Jatinga, a village in Assam, India. Disoriented by the monsoon fog, the birds are attracted to the village lights and fly blindly toward them, hitting walls and trees en route. To promote tourism, the local authorities have created an annual Jatinga Festival around the mysterious "bird suicides."

U.S. artist Joe Sola created six oil paintings that were so tiny that his exhibition was held inside the gallery owner's ear! As even a single paintbrush bristle was too large, he used a 0.12-mm acupuncture needle along with a microscope to see what he was painting. Each painting was composed of tiny granules of pigment, mounted on small white backgrounds and placed in the ear canal of Los Angeles gallery owner Tif Sigfrids for public viewing.

ancient debt A court in Glarus, Switzerland, finally wiped out a 655-year-old debt so that a farmer and his family no longer have to pay $70 a year to the Catholic Church to keep a sanctuary lamp burning. The debt dated back to 1357 when Konrad Mueller killed Heinrich Stucki and, to save his soul, he gave a lamp to the local church and vowed to fuel it with oil from his walnut trees for eternity—a promise that was kept by all subsequent owners of Mueller's land until the new ruling.

Sandra Nabucco was left with 272 spines painfully stuck in her scalp after a porcupine fell from a lamppost and landed on her head while she was walking her dog in Rio de Janeiro, Brazil. Surgeons used tweezers to remove the quills and gave her antibiotics to prevent the wounds from becoming infected. She said: "It was a huge shock. I felt a thud on my head and then felt spines with my hands. The pain was enormous." The porcupine survived because Sandra had broken its fall.

math test Canadians who win lotteries and prize draws must solve a simple math problem to collect their prizes because games of pure chance are illegal in Canada.

BLOOD POPSICLE

➔ As temperatures in Australia hit 115°F (46°C) in January 2014, it became so hot that zookeepers gave Harari, a lion in Melbourne Zoo, a popsicle made from 8 gal (30 l) of frozen blood to help him keep cool. They also made frozen meat, fish and fruit into popsicles for Honey, a Syrian brown bear.

SUMO MARATHON

→ **Around 150 competitors donned inflatable suits and ballooned into sumo wrestlers to wobble around Battersea Park in London, England, for the annual 3-mi (5-km) Sumo Run.**

Billed by organizers as an event designed to put the fun back into fun runs, the runners jogged around the park trying not to fall over and pop themselves.

heavy price Robert McKevitt was fired for inappropriate use of company property after using an 8,000 lb (3,628 kg) forklift to free a chocolate bar that had got stuck in a vending machine at Milford, Iowa.

early toothache Scientists studying a fossilized jawbone of *Sinosaurus*, a carnivorous dinosaur that lived around 190 million years ago, concluded that it was the earliest known animal to have had a toothache. The specimen, discovered in Yunnan Province, China, had a completely filled tooth socket, indicating that the loss of the tooth was the result of dental problems rather than external force.

elevator ordeal Swedish-born hotel owner Thomas Fleetwood survived after being trapped for four days without food or water in a broken-down elevator at his deserted hotel in Bad Gastein, Austria. He broke a glass panel in the elevator door to get some air and was rescued only when a friend noticed mail piling up outside the hotel.

darth challenge Since founding the Darth Valley Challenge in 2010, every summer Jonathan Rice from Longmont, Colorado, dons an all-black *Star Wars* Darth Vader costume and sprints 1 mi (1.6 km) across the Death Valley National Park near the California—Nevada border in sweltering 129°F (54°C) heat. He completed the 2013 run in 6 minutes 36 seconds and says the biggest problem is the mask, which hardly lets in any air.

still ticking The Beverly Clock, located in a foyer at the University of Otago in Dunedin, New Zealand, keeps ticking despite the fact that it has not been wound since 1864.

bridge terror Fifty-five-year-old Wanda Keating McGowan from Florida clung on for her life as she dangled 22 ft (6.7 m) in the air above Fort Lauderdale's New River after the railway bridge she was walking across opened before she could get off it. She was hanging there for 20 minutes until firefighters could raise a ladder to rescue her.

mistaken identity The Indian army recently spent six months keeping track of what it thought were Chinese spy drones, only to eventually realize that the distant specks in the sky were actually the planets Jupiter and Venus.

[YOUR / UPLOADS]

FOLDING EAR

Jordan Anderson from Oklahoma City, Oklahoma, sent Ripley's this picture demonstrating his incredible ability to fold his ear almost in half!

REMOTEST TOILET

→ Perched on a cliff 8,500 ft (2,600 m) above sea level in the Altai Mountains, Siberia, this has got to be a contender for the world's most isolated toilet. It serves five workers at a weather station at Karaturek—a spot so remote that food and water are delivered annually by helicopter and their only other visitor is the postman who drops by once a month to collect the weather data.

police intelligence A police officer in Stoke-on-Trent, England, was convinced he had caught four men using duplicate passports after thinking all the suspects were named Abu Dhabi. He had confused the names on the passports with the country from which the men had flown.

solitary existence For five years until his death in 2012, Englishman Brendon Grimshaw lived alone on a tropical island in the Seychelles. He had only his dogs and 120 giant tortoises for company.

prison imposter A former inmate at New York's Rikers Island prison sneaked back into the jail disguised as a guard. Matthew Matagrano used a badge and I.D. card to gain entry and was spotted only when he moved inmates between cells.

body shock Three men stole a van in Germany, not knowing it contained 12 corpses. The thieves pounced while the van driver stopped to wash his hands on his way to a crematorium in Meissen. They dumped the bodies, in their coffins, in a forest in Poland.

MAN KILLS HIMSELF WITH PLAYING CARDS

■ Believe it or not, on October 20, 1930, William Kogut, a convicted murderer awaiting execution on San Quentin's death row in California, committed suicide using ordinary playing cards. In those days, the ink in red playing cards contained nitrocellulose, which is dangerously volatile when wet. So, after removing a hollow steel leg from the bed in his cell, he tore up a number of red cards and rammed the small pieces into the metal pipe before plugging the other end with a broom handle. He then poured water into the open end, soaking the cards to create an explosive mixture, and put his homemade pipe bomb on top of the kerosene heater next to his bed. Finally, he lay down and placed his head up against the open end of the pipe. As the heater turned the water to steam, the pressure inside the pipe built up until a blast shot the shards of playing cards out with sufficient force that they penetrated his skull, killing him.

COMIC STRIP → Combining his love of tattoos and comics, artist Patrick Yurick from San Diego, California, has had four blank panels tattooed on his forearm that he fills in daily to create an ever-changing comic strip. He had the tattoo inked on his left arm so that he could draw with his right hand. It takes him about 15 minutes to draw each strip onto his flesh.

gps detour Sixty-seven-year-old Sabine Moreau meant to drive only 38 mi (60 km) to meet a friend at her local railway station in Brussels, Belgium—but when her GPS told her to keep going, she ended up 900 mi (1,450 km) away in Croatia. In the course of her two-day detour, she crossed five international borders, but was so distracted that it was only when she arrived in Zagreb that she realized she was actually no longer in Belgium.

back from dead Just as she was being put into her coffin by an undertaker, 101-year-old Peng Xiuhua from Lianjiang, China, suddenly sat up and demanded to know why so many people were in her house. She had been declared dead after her daughters could not detect a heartbeat and her body had gone stiff.

road theft A 40-year-old man was arrested for stealing an entire stretch of road in Komi, northern Russia. He dismantled 82 reinforced concrete slabs—worth a total of about $6,000—and loaded the pieces onto three trucks, which were later intercepted by police.

wrong door Jiang Wu got so drunk following a night out in Qingdao, China, that he mistook a shipping container for his budget hotel and woke up to find himself sealed in for a two-week boat trip due to leave for the U.S.A. Luckily, he had his phone with him, but although he rang the police, there were thousands of containers and they had no idea which one he was in. Eventually, by hammering on the metal side, he was tracked down to a box stacked 60 ft (18 m) in the air.

UNDERCOVER CROC

→ To get up close and personal with deadly Nile crocodiles and hippos, American TV naturalist Dr. Brady Barr decided to dress up as them.

Wearing a crocodile suit consisting of a prosthetic head attached to the front of a protective, canvas-draped metal cage, he was able to crawl on his hands and knees and get within touching distance of 13-ft-long (4-m) crocs in Tanzania without his cover being blown. Dressed in a heavy, armored hippo suit smeared with hippo dung to hide the human scent of the occupant, he slowly approached a 10,000-strong herd of hippos in Zambia's South Luangwa National Park, only to get stuck in the mud and be forced to radio for help.

INDEX

Page numbers in *italic* refer to the illustrations

ACKNOWLEDGMENTS

Cover doglikehorse/Shutterstock, Mikhall Bakunovich/Shutterstock; 4 Isaiah Webb; 9 (t/r) Photos by James P. Judge, (c/r) Ocean Park Hong Kong, (c/l) Ripley's Museum London; 10 (c/l, b/l) Christopher Z. Collier-Sudduth, (t, c, c/r) Kelly Mill Elementary; 14 (c) Tim Marsden/Newspix/ Rex Features, (b/c) CBP/ Rex Features; 15 (t) Tim Marsden/Newspix/ Rex Features, (b) SIPSE/AP/Press Association Images; 16 (t/c) NASA/ Charlie Duke, (l) Rex/James D. Morgan, (b/r) Keng Lye; 17 Keng Lye; 20 (t) Bob and Linda Carey - The Carey Foundation, (b) Caters News; 21 Reuters/Stringer; 22 (b/r, sp) AA/ABACA/Press Association Images, (t/l) AA / TT/TT News Agency/Press Association Images; 23 (b) Dennis Elliot, (c) Rui Vieira/PA Archive/Press Association Images; 24 Animal Clinic of Regina; 25 (b) Matt York/AP/Press Association Images; 26 (b) © Viviane Moos/Corbis; 27 www.toutsgallery.com; 28 (t) Newsflare / Caters News, (b) Supplied by WENN.com; 29 (t/l) Imagine China, (c/l) Gavin Maxwell/naturepl.com, (b/r) © EuroPics[CEN]; 31 Reuters/Stringer; 32–33 (bg) Andy Bardon/ National Geographic Creative; 32 (t) © Palenque - Fotolia.com, (c/r) Getty Images; 33 (b/r) Zuma/ Rex, (t/r) Utmost Adventure Trekking, (c/r) Dave Watson/AP/Press Association Images; 34 (c/l) Karli Luik/ Caters News, (b/l) Caters News; 35 Boaz Rottem; 36–37 (bkg) © Thomas Bethge - Fotolia.com; 36 (t/l) Reuters/Beawiharta, (t/r) Rex/Amos Chapple, (b) Rex/KeystoneUSA-Zuma; 37 (r) Rex/HAP/Quirky China News, (l) © EuroPics[CEN]; 38 (t) Rex/Marc Henauer/Solent News, (b) Mona and Chris Dienhart; 39 Eduardo Blanco Mendizabal; 40 (t) © CEN Europics, (b) Craig Ferguson / Demotix/Demotix/Press Association Images; 41 Reuters/Stringer; 42–43 Rex/Paul Koudounaris/ Heavenly Bodies : Cult Treasures and Spectacular Saints/BNPS; 44 (b/r) Reuters/Tore Meek/NTB Scanpix, (b/c) Terje Bendiksby/AP/Press Association Images, (t) © Tony Waltham/ Robert Harding World Imagery/Corbis; 45 (c/l) Charles Rex Arbogast/AP/Press Association Images, (t, b) Reuters/John Gress; 46 (b) © Thierry Tronnel/Corbis, (t) Imaginechina/Rex; 47 Eric Lafforgue; 48 (t/l, t, r) Rex/Warren Krupsaw/Solent News, (b) Reuters/Stringer; 49 Mark Thiessen / National Geographic; 50–51 (dp) Getty Images; 51 (t/r) © Bettmann/Corbis, (b/l) Roger Viollet/Getty Images; 52 (c) Bill Dixon, (t) Simon Beck; 53 (t) Simon Beck, (b) ChinaFotoPress via Getty Images; 54–55 Graham Hughes, Rocco Fasano, Grethe Børsum, (bg) © i3alda - Fotolia.com; 54 (t/l) © mrtimmi - Fotolia.com, © Al - Fotolia.com; 56 © EuroPics[CEN]; 57 (t) Justin Lee / Caters News, (b/l, b/c) Rex/Sipa Press; 58–59 (bg) © Sergey Kamshylin - Fotolia.com; 58 (t/l) © Pictorial Press Ltd / Alamy, (b) © Royal Geographical Society / Alamy; 59 (t/l, t/r, b/l) © Royal Geographical Society / Alamy, (b/r) © Pictorial Press Ltd / Alamy; 60 (t/c) Dusan Vranic/AP/Press Association Images, (b/l) Matthias Wietz; 61 Yuri Ovchinnikov / Caters News; 63 Cindy Chambers; 64–65 Michael Rougier/Time & Life Pictures/Getty Images; 66 (b) Steven Downer / John Downer P / naturepl.com; 67 Phil Lautner; 68 EFE; 69 (l) © Picture Alliance/Photoshot, (t, r) Rex/Hans Christoph Kappel / Nature Picture Library; 70–71 (t) Reuters/Lisi Niesner; 70 (b/l) Patrick Castleberry / Caters News; 71 (b/r) Rex/Steve Shinn, (t/r) Reuters/Lisi Niesner; 72 Sell Your Photo; 73 (t) Sell Your Photo, (b) © Stephen Dalton/ naturepl.com; 74 (t) AA /TT News Agency/Press Association Images, (c) © Luiz Claudio Marigo; 75 © EuroPics[CEN]; 76 (t) Rex/Timothy Clapin/Newspix, (b) Susheel Shurestha; 77 Nicky Bay; 78 (t/l, b/l) J.M. Storey, Carleton University, (t/r) Elsie Mason of Ship to Shore Lobster Company, Owls Head Maine; 79 Isak Pretorius - theafricanphotographer.com; 80 Gil Wizen; 81 Catalina Island Marine Institute; 82 (t) Robert McLeod, (c) Rex Features, (b) Efrem Lukatsky/AP/Press Association Images; 83 Ian Salisbury / Caters News; 84 www.skullsunlimited.com; 85 (t) Sakchai Lalit/AP/Press Association Images, (b) Trond Larsen; 86 (l) WENN, (t/r) Myles S. Bratter; 87 Cindy Chambers; 88 (t) Mauricio Handler / Nat Geo Creative, (b) Jeff Cremer; 89 (bg) Anna Jurkovska - Shutterstock..com, (sp) Roger-Viollet / Topfoto; 90 (t) Getty Images, (b) © John Cancalosi / Alamy; 91 Francois Savigny/ naturepl.com; 93 Ryan Taylor/Red Bull Content Pool; 94–95 All Photos courtesy of Eastwind One Corp., Ed Spielman. Pres. All Materials in and to 'The Mighty Atom' - Copyright – Eastwind One Corp., Ed Spielman. Pres. *Content from the 'The Spirital Journey of Joseph L. Greenstein', 'The Mighty Atom', World's Strongest Man by Ed Spielman, (c, b/r) Photos supplied by www.oldtimestrongman.com; 96 Tim Sorenson / Red Bull Content Pool; 97 Barbara L. Thomas; 98 (t) Reuters/Darrin Zammit Lupi, (c) AFP/Getty Images, (b) Reuters/China Daily; 99 Daniel Reinhardt/DPA/Press Association Images; 100 (b/l, c/l) Thomas Senf/Red Bull Content Pool, (c/r) Rex/Zuma; 101 (b) Ryan Taylor/Red Bull Content Pool, (t) Seth Wenig/AP/Press Association Images; 104 (bkg) © W.Scott - Fotolia.com, (t/l, t/r, b) Laurentiu Garofeanu / Barcroft USA; 105 Laurentiu Garofeanu / Barcroft USA; 106 Reuters/Stringer; 107 (t/r) © leisuretime70 - Fotolia.com, (t) Richard Gibson, (b/r) Sruli Recht; 108 (l) Rex/ Steve Meddle, (t/r) Windsor Star / Caters, (c/r) QMI / Caters; 109 AFP/Getty Images; 110 Amit Agrawal/ Pavan Agrawal; 111 John Robertson / Barcroft Media; 112 Mirrorpix; 113 (t/l) Mary Evans Picture Library, (b/l) Getty Images, (r) ©ullsteinbild / TopFoto; 114 Reuters/Faisal Al Nasser; 115 (t) Imagine China, (b) SWNS; 118 (t) SWNS, (b) Rex/HAP/Quirky China News; 119 Alessandra Tarantino/AP/Press Association Images; 121 (t/l, c/l) Library of Congress, (b/l) Getty Images, (c) SSPL via Getty Images; 122 BNPS; 123 Laurentiu Garofeanu / Barcroft USA; 124 (b/l) Ayanna Williams; 126 Kha Hoa/AP/Press Association Images; 127 VTC News; 128 (l) Solent News, (r) Reuters/Marko Djurica; 129 Isaiah Webb; 130 (t/c) Phillip Romano, (t/r) Keith Walters Photography, (b) University of Syracuse; 131 Jean Jabril Joesph; 133 Nicole Wilder/Syfy/NBCU Photo Bank via Getty Images; 134 (t/l) Library of Congress, (b/l, b/r) James G. Mundie, (c/r) Bob Blackmar; 135 (b/l) Bob Blackmar; 136 (t/l) AFP/Getty Images, (b/l) Rex/Startraks Photo; 137 EatonNott / Barcroft Media; 138 (t) Juhana Nyrhinen and www.masauniverse.tumblr.com, (b) Actual; 139 (t/r) Kate Melton Photography, (l) Steven Lawton/FilmMagic; 140 Rex/Jonathan Pow; 141 (t) Laurentiu Garofeanu / Barcroft USA, (b) Rex/Adam Duckworth/Geoffrey Robinson; 142 (t) Bill Mudron / Caters News, (b/r) Caters News, (b/l) Mikey Jones / Caters News; 143 (b/l) Tolga Akman/ Rex, (b/r) Kayleigh O'Conner/Solent News/ Rex, (c) Getty Images; 144 (t/l) © Eye Ubiquitous/Photoshot, (t/r) © Andrea Izzotti - Fotolia.com, (b) WENN; 145 Double Vision Media; 146 (t/l) Gabriel Chapman, (b/l/c) Izzy Parnell and Ned, (b/r/c) Eden Parnell and Ned, (b/l) David Gaylord; 148 (t) Rex/Quirky China News, (b) Rex/Imaginechina; 149 (t) AP/Press Association Images, (b) Zak Hussein/PA Archive/Press Association Images; 150 Nicole Wilder/Syfy/NBCU Photo Bank via Getty Images; 151 (t) Studio Banana Things, (b) Francois Guillot/AFP/Getty Images; 152 (t) Randy Hoff, (b) Noah Kalina; 153 Courtesy of the Artist, Chrissy Conant © 2005; 155 Vrbanus Workshop; 156 (t/r) Reuters/Jon Woo, (t/l) Lt. Matthew Hertzfeld/Toledo Fire & Rescue Department, (b) Richard Eaton / Demotix/Demotix/Press Association Images; 157 (t) Rex/East News, (c) © Imaginechina/Corbis, (b) © EuroPics[CEN]; 158 (t) Jason Shron, (b) Seabreacher; 159 See-ming Lee; 160 (t) François Gissy/ Régis Rabineau, (b) Getty Images; 161 (t) Daniel Glover, (b) Reuters/Stringer; 163 (sp) © Visions of America, LLC / Alamy; 162 (b) Richard Pardon Photography; 164 (t) SWNS, (b) Raccoon Vehicle Branding; 165 Vrbanus Workshop; 167 Mustang Wanted; 168 (t) Courtesy of the Library of Congress, (c/r) © Pictorial Press Ltd / Alamy, (b) Niagara Falls Public Library; 169 (t/l, l) Getty Images, (t/r) Niagara Falls Public Library; 170 Simon de Trey White / Barcroft India; 171 Mustang Wanted; 172 (l) AFP/Getty Images, (r) SWNS; 173 Rex/Naomi Jellicoe/Newspix; 174 (b) Axel Heimken/DPA/Press Association Images, (t) SWNS; 175 Hotspot Media; 177 (t) © Bettmann/Corbis, (b) © Underwood & Underwood/Corbis; 178 (t) Apic/ Getty Images, (c, b) San Diego Aerospace Museum; 179 (b) © Bettmann/Corbis, (t/r, c/l) San Diego Aerospace Museum; 180 (t) WENN.com, (b) Patrick Post/AP/Press Association Images; 181 AFP/Getty Images; 182 Seattle Public Library; 183 Steve Doman Nighteagle; 185 WENN.com; 186 (sp) Rex/London News Pictures, (t/r) Rex/ISA HARSIN/SIPA; 187 (t/c, t/r, c/r, b/r) Rex/ISA HARSIN/SIPA, (c/l) Rex/AGF s.r.l., (b/l) Rex/London News Pictures; 188 Rex/ Jody Steel; 189 (t/l) AFP/Getty Images, (t/c, t/r) Mariane Borgomani, (b/r) Charlie Layton; 190 Getty Images; 191 (b) Anastassia Elias / Caters News, (t/l) Edouard Martinet; 192 Ariana Page Russell; 194 Imagine China; 195 (t) Reuters/Ilya Naymushin, (b) Janos Meszaros/AP/Press Association Images; 196 (t) Maskull Lasserre, (b) Rex/HAP/ Quirky China News; 197 Johannes Stoetter; 198 Laura Benjamin; 199 (t/r, t, c/r, c/l) Irby Pace, (b/r) Caters; 200 (t) Chris Maynard, (c/r, b/r) Rex/ Rob Prideaux; 201 Ulf Lundin; 202 (t) Supplied by WENN.com, (b) Caters / Museum of Bad Art; 203 WENN.com; 204 Jelly Belly Candy Company; 205 (t/c, t/r) Andrew Myers, (b) Isaac Salazar - isaacesalazar.com; 207 Ocean Park Hong Kong; 208–209 Ocean Park Hong Kong; 210 (b, c) Sideserf Cake Studio, (t) Chocolate By Mueller; 211 (b) Domenico Crolla / Demotix/Press Association Images, (t) Reuters/Michael Kooren; 212 (t) Wynkoop Brewing Company, (b) Alton Thompson/ Alton Images; 213 Rex/HAP/Quirky China News; 214 (t) Rex/Kyle Bean, (b) © byjeng - Fotolia.com; 215 Elizabeth Marek/ Artisan Cake Company; 216 (t) Reuters/Michael Dalder, (b) Reuters/Edgar Su; 217 Xinhua/Photoshot; 218–219 Julie Green/ Toni Acock; 220 Reuters/ Mohamed Al Hwaity; 221 (t) The Frontier Chicago, (b) Boy Eats Bug/ Chris Verraes/ Rex Features; 222 (c) Imagine China, (t) © Kirsty Pargeter - Fotolia.com; 223 (r) Reuters/Yuriko Nakao, (l) Fantasy Fondant; 224 (b/l) George Nickels / Caters News; 225 Rex/Sinopix Photo Agency Ltd; 227 Julian Makey/ Rex; 228–229 Lake County (IL) Discovery Museum, Curt Teich Postcard Archives, (bg) © leremy - Fotolia.com; 230 (t) AP/Press Association Images, (b) David Catá; 231 Reuters/Aaron Harris; 232–233 (b) Reuters/Reinhard Krause; 232 (b/c) Kevin Frayer/AP/Press Association Images; 233 (t) Reuters/Mohamed Al Hwaity, (b/r) Greg Huglin/ Solent News/ Rex Features; 234 (t) Ricardo Arduengo/AP/Press Association Images, (b) Ross Parry Agency; 236 REX/Austral Int.; 237 (b) Caters News, (t) WENN; 238 (t) © EuroPics[CEN], (b/l, c/l) JoyLabz; 239 Caters News; 241 (sp) Maria Justamond, (b/l) Norihiro Shigeta/AP/Press Association Images; 242 James D. Morgan/ Rex; 243 (t, t/r) Julian Makey/ Rex; 244 (t) Caters News, (l) © nickolae - Fotolia.com, (b/r) David Difuntorum Photography/ Rex, (c/r) Patrick Yurick/ Rex; 245 (sp) National Geographic, (b) Brady Barr

Key: t = top, b = bottom, c = center, l = left, r = right, sp = single page, dp = double page, bg = background

All other photos are from Ripley Entertainment Inc. Every attempt has been made to acknowledge correctly and contact copyright holders and we apologize in advance for any unintentional errors or omissions, which will be corrected in future editions.

Ripley's ODDITORIUMS

31 CRAZY ODDITORIUMS!

There are 31 Ripley's Believe It or Not! Odditoriums spread across the globe for you to visit, each packed full with weird and wonderful exhibits from the Ripley collection.

Atlantic City NEW JERSEY
Baltimore MARYLAND
Blackpool ENGLAND
Branson MISSOURI
Cavendish CANADA
Copenhagen DENMARK
Gatlinburg TENNESSEE
Genting Highlands MALAYSIA
Grand Prairie TEXAS
Guadalajara MEXICO
Hollywood CALIFORNIA
Jackson Hole WYOMING
Jeju Island SOUTH KOREA
Key West FLORIDA
London ENGLAND
Mexico City MEXICO
Myrtle Beach SOUTH CAROLINA
New York City NEW YORK
Newport OREGON
Niagara Falls CANADA
Ocean City MARYLAND
Orlando FLORIDA
Panama City Beach FLORIDA
Pattaya THAILAND
San Antonio TEXAS
San Francisco CALIFORNIA
St. Augustine FLORIDA
Surfers Paradise AUSTRALIA
Veracruz MEXICO
Williamsburg VIRGINIA
Wisconsin Dells WISCONSIN

ANNUALS

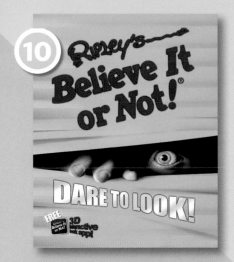
(10) Ripley's Believe It or Not! DARE TO LOOK!
FREE 3D interactive app!

(9) Ripley's Believe It or Not! DOWNLOAD THE WEIRD

(8) Ripley's Believe It or Not! STRIKINGLY TRUE

(7) Ripley's Believe It or Not! ENTER IF YOU DARE!

(6) Ripley's Believe It or Not! ALL NEW SEEING IS BELIEVING

(5) Ripley's Believe It or Not! Prepare to be Shocked! TAKE A LOOK AT THE WORLD'S WEIRDEST FACTS

(4) Believe It or Not! The Remarkable... Revealed TAKE A LOOK AT THE WORLD'S WEIRDEST FACTS

(3) Believe It or Not! ALL NEW Expect... The Unexpected TAKE A LOOK AT THE WORLD'S WEIRDEST FACTS

With ALL-NEW stories and pictures in every edition of this bestselling series, our books entertain, shock and amaze!

(2) Ripley's Believe It or Not! Planet Eccentric! TAKE A LOOK AT THE WORLD'S WEIRDEST FACTS

(1) Ripley's Believe It or Not! TAKE A LOOK AT THE WORLD'S WEIRDEST FACTS

To order copies go to www.ripleybooks.com

collect them all ←

TWISTS

Fascinating facts and heaps of fun—don't miss Ripley's award-winning **TWISTS**!

ROBERT RIPLEY BIOGRAPHY

The definitive biography of Robert Ripley, A CURIOUS MAN, written by acclaimed biographer Neal Thompson, tells of the strange and brilliant life of the extraordinary founder of Ripley's Believe It or Not!

FUN FACTS & SILLY STORIES

Our third FUN FACTS & SILLY STORIES book will entertain younger Ripley fans for hours with incredible pictures and crazy facts on every page.

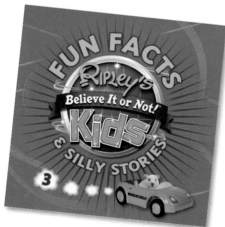

NEW CHILDREN'S ANNUAL!!

FUN FACTS & SILLY STORIES – THE BIG ONE!

Get ready for a laugh a minute with Ripley's new children's annual, FUN FACTS & SILLY STORIES, THE BIG ONE! A bumper edition from our Fun Facts range, it's packed with ALL-NEW funny stories, extraordinary facts, and amazing pictures.